Author's Introduction to Sixth Printing

This sixth printing of *The Art of Executive Protection* comes in 2006, five years after the September 11, 2001, terror attacks that shook the United States. Those terrible events brought security into the spotlight like never before. Interest in executive protection—even among people who had never previously considered it—rose to new heights.

People sometimes refer to the "post-9/11 era" as if it were a different world, detached from all that we knew before. Some threats have changed, but in reality the world has always presented dangers. The right response is to build today's security program, tailored to current conditions, on a foundation of the time-tested fundamentals.

This book presents the basics—the concepts and vocabulary that every executive protection effort must master. Threat assessment, advance work, security driving, home and office security, smart travel practices, workplace violence…these building blocks of an excellent executive protection program are all covered in this volume.

In addition, this book's companion volume has just been published. *Executive Protection: New Solutions for a New Era* (2006) addresses fresh challenges that executives face today, describes the latest resources available to executive protection specialists, and examines trends in executive protection methods.

Together, the two books present the full spectrum of executive protection knowledge: the timeless fundamentals and up-to-the-minute solutions.

Robert L. Oatman, CPP
R. L. Oatman & Associates, Inc.
2006

The Art of Executive Protection

Robert L. Oatman

Noble House

Arnold, Maryland

The Art of Executive Protection

Library of Congress
Cataloging in Publication Data
ISBN 1-56167-384-6

Library of Congress Card Catalog Number:
97-068324

Published by

Noble House

1290 Bay Dale Drive, Suite 297
Arnold, Maryland 21012

Manufactured in the United States of America

"I have known Mr. Oatman for a number of years and can attest that in the field of security he represents the highest degree of professionalism. His years of experience and dedication to his work make him uniquely suited to writing a book which can serve as a guide for those who would follow in his footsteps. The book is not only highly readable, but insightful, methodical, and thorough in its exploration of a field which, unfortunately, is growing in its necessity rather than diminishing."

Shimon Peres
Former Prime Minister of Israel

"After having had Bob Oatman provide protection for me and my family during three Olympic Games, I can think of no one more qualified to introduce a wide audience to the challenging profession of executive protection. I cannot begin to express the peace of mind that comes with knowing your family's security is being insured by someone with Bob's skill and experience. This is a comprehensive guide for anyone whose work or travel puts him or her at risk."

Robert C. Wright
President and Chief Executive Officer
National Broadcasting Company, Inc.

"Anybody who reads the newspapers knows that in recent years the world has become increasingly dangerous—to nations and to individuals. Bob Oatman has written a timely and comprehensive book describing how an effective executive protection program can mitigate those risks. Anybody who is a potential target—a businessman, soldier, or even a traveler—can enhance his personal security by a careful reading of this excellent book."

Ambassador L. Paul Bremer, III
Former U.S. Ambassador-at-Large
for Counter-Terrorism

"Bob Oatman has taken a very complex and difficult task—the art of executive protection—and dissected the essential elements. His explanation of the various facets is discussed in common language. The use of case histories and anecdotes brings the protective concepts to life and allows them to be readily understood. This text is an important contribution to the executive protection profession. It should be beneficial to both the EP operative developing a career in this field and the principals who are served."

John R. Smith
Deputy Assistant Director
Protective Operations (retired)
U.S. Secret Service

"This book is an extraordinary read. I found it interesting as well as informative. It's a must read for any security director charged with responsibility for executive protection."

Mark J. Cheviron
Vice President
Corporate Security and Administrative Services
Archer Daniels Midland Company

"I read this book with immense enjoyment. It takes the reader step by step through the minefield of protection duties. It should be read by anyone involved in the field, both established and would-be protection officers. I forecast it will become the standard textbook for executive protection."

Allen Evershed
Chief Superintendent (Ret'd)
Diplomatic Protection Group
New Scotland Yard

Dedication

This book is respectfully and affectionately dedicated to LHW and ASW—principals who represent the ideal by confidently supporting the protective effort through empowerment and acceptance. This work is also dedicated to my wife Janice, without whose support none of this would have been possible, and to my daughter Andrea and son Rob.

Acknowledgements

The essence of this book grew from my association with one of the most challenging of all the world's professions—American law enforcement. The Baltimore County Police Department was the springboard for my career in executive protection and taught me the fundamentals so essential to success. I am indebted to the men and women of that fine organization, with whom I served in a variety of line and staff assignments for 20 years.

The United States Secret Service, through its generous expenditure of time and resources, supported the training of state and local law enforcement officers in the conduct of protective operations. I was one of the many beneficiaries of the USSS Protective Operations and Dignitary Protection programs and am grateful for having been given that opportunity.

The FBI National Academy in Quantico, Virginia, taught me advanced principles of police management. The academy experience also provided an invaluable, international networking resource. For years the network supported the operational needs of my police career, and it continues to support my private sector protective assignments.

Theodore Shackley has been a supportive advisor and guide. As a former CIA associate deputy director for operations, he sees and understands the big picture of worldwide risk.

Dr. Richard W. Kobetz, a longtime friend and mentor, is director of the Executive Protection Institute and a pioneer in this field. Many years ago, he gave me my first opportunity to train students who were interested in learning executive protection skills.

I am grateful to Jerry Glazebrook, Dr. James McGee, Tom Morrow, Allen Minnick, Thomas Levering, and Tony Scotti for the expertise, professionalism, and friendship they provided throughout the strenuous but exciting project of putting this book together.

Terry Lee Hunt, Jr., is a young man whom I admire for his contagious enthusiasm, courage, and spirit. His success in overcoming the challenges he faces is an inspiration to everyone whose life he has touched.

I gave my trust on this life's project to two principal collaborators. Peter Ohlhausen, a security and criminal justice writer, provided invaluable assistance in the research, writing, and editing of the book, and helped to capture and clearly convey the reality of executive protection as I practice it. Throughout the length of this project, his patience, resilience, perseverance, and grace have amazed me, and I am grateful beyond expression.

Bill Archer, a longtime colleague, is also a gifted writer and "no holds barred" critic. He was intensely analytical of every page and lent constructive, original thought to the project. Bill is central to my professional life and is a trusted friend.

The murderous Red Brigade terrorist organization triggered the largest manhunt in Italian history with the kidnapping of Brigadier General James Dozier from his Verona, Italy, home on the evening of December 17, 1981. At the time of his abduction, General Dozier was the highest-ranking officer in NATO's Southern European Command's LANDSOUTH headquarters. His rescue 42 days later signaled the beginning of the end of the terrorist movement in Italy. It is a fascinating and inspiring story of determination, endurance, and courage on the part of General Dozier and of rare international cooperation and intrigue on the part of law enforcement, intelligence, and military authorities. I am honored to have General Dozier's comments grace this work and am grateful for his kind participation and insightful, personal perspective.
—*Robert L. Oatman*

Foreword

James L. Dozier
MGEN, USA Retired

Since the dawn of human evolution, we have instinctively struggled to protect ourselves from, among other things, the threat from each other. No doubt, our ancestors' urgency for survival led them to organize to protect themselves and their families.

The fear of harm and our instinctive desire to live safely is as powerful today as it was then. Threatening members of our society are still among us. What is different is the magnitude and effectiveness of personal self-defense, which has developed in parallel with modern human technology. We don't throw stones now to defend ourselves (unless no other means are available). Instead, our societies rely on highly evolved institutions like the military, law enforcement, and private security forces for protection. As individuals, we depend on common sense, strong locks, alarm systems, and, occasionally, firearms. Some of us, however, need and have the means to acquire a more sophisticated and comprehensive approach to personal protection. This book is a road map to that end.

I am a born-again believer in the value of a first-class personal security program. Before being kidnapped by the Italian Red Brigade, I was one of the skeptics who paid little heed to the necessity of personal protection. Six weeks later, after my rescue, I was an ardent advocate. My rescue was the result of some fine police work by the Italian authorities. From that moment on, my views on personal protection underwent a radical about-face. Good fortune, strong faith, and smart police work allowed me to escape a fate that others did not. At home and abroad, personal security for key individuals became a routine part of our military operational planning.

Bob Oatman has crafted a book that should be read by everyone who has the potential to be exposed to the kind of risk that took me from my family for six long weeks—and that nearly cost me my life. You don't need to be a NATO commander to be threatened by such people. You just need to have something they want badly enough, or represent something they hate enough, to make them take a chance. The world is full of people like that.

This book is a study of the art of protection (a phrase I found intriguing), and it will profit the practitioner as much as the principal. My hope and expectation is that its solid and practical advice will help prevent, for someone, the kind of ordeal that I personally experienced.

Contents

Introduction

In a flawed, dangerous world, risks abound. Everyone knows that, and we all take steps daily to reduce the risks we face. We buy insurance; we look both ways before crossing the street; we avoid dangerous parts of the city. We protect ourselves instinctively.

That level of protection, however, is not the end; it is only the beginning. Personal protection can be elevated significantly. And for some people—executives, celebrities, persons of high net worth—personal protection *should* be taken to a much higher level. Those persons typically face a higher level of threat than do others and have the means to hire someone who can help them counter that threat.

The crux of personal protection is shaping one's own destiny. The prevalence of risk is no reason to lie down and accept it, just as the prevalence of disease is no reason to avoid vaccination. On the contrary: a heightened awareness of risk is the very reason to increase one's level of protection. Doing so is man's way of exerting a measure of control over a mostly uncontrollable universe.

At root, executive protection means improving your odds, taking matters into your own hands.

With proper study and discipline, a person can expand the range of risks he or she[1] deliberately avoids. That, however, is a complicated, challenging endeavor. Just as an executive understands tax laws in general but still hires an accountant to master the details, so an executive should consider it efficient to engage a protection specialist instead of trying to become an expert in yet another field.

Mastery of executive protection demands much. Adversaries, whether armed criminals, protesters bent on causing embarrassment, former employees burning for revenge, or merely the hand of fate, hold nearly all the cards: they choose the time, the place, and the method of attack. To counter that advantage, the executive protection (EP) specialist must use his intellect, diplomacy, and cunning to balance secrecy against exposure, safety against freedom of movement, boldness against caution. Doing so constitutes the art of protection—executive protection.

EP specialists devote their energies, training, and talent to anticipating threats against their principals[2] and then helping their principals avoid them. Note the word "avoid." That is a key part of the strategy of executive protection. It is all but impossible to prevent threats. Theoretically, a highly aggressive posture could scare away almost all potential attackers, but that approach relies on greatly restricting the principal's movements and risks offending business associates, friends, and family. Such an approach might even backfire and draw more attention from adversaries.

Much more effective is to follow the ancient guidance of Sun Tzu. This Chinese strategist, who wrote in the sixth century

---

[1] Both women and men are active in the field of executive protection, and of course both women and men are among those who require such protection. However, over the next several hundred pages, to avoid a thousand iterations of the cumbersome constructions "he or she," "his or her," and "him or her," the author respectfully asks the reader to interpret "he," "his," and "him" as applying to both sexes, as is traditional, where it is logical to do so.

[2] The person an EP specialist is charged with protecting is typically called a principal, executive, client, or protectee. The EP specialist himself may be called an agent, protection specialist, or other term. When an EP specialist works as part of a team, that team is often called a detail.

B.C., offers time-honored truths in his military classic, *The Art of War*. His advice applies as much to executive protection as it does to conventional warfare. Make no mistake: to an executive under attack, or a corporation whose chief executive is at risk, executive protection is warfare. Sun Tzu's insights show that blustering and blundering against an enemy is an ignorant approach. What is called for, fundamentally, is cleverness. The point of war, and the point of executive protection, is to win—not to show the world how tough one is or to expend lives in valiant but stupid campaigns. If the point is to win, how much better a victory it is to win without battle, to win before a battle ever begins. Sun Tzu writes,[3]

> True excellence is to plan secretly, to move surreptitiously, to foil the enemy's intentions and balk his schemes, so that at last the day may be won without shedding a drop of blood.

What a perfect description of executive protection. Adversaries always hold the upper hand unless the EP specialist outwits them. And that, precisely, is the EP specialist's job: to defeat the adversary with intelligence, planning, unpredictability, and avoidance of danger.

This book is carefully designed to address both the EP specialist and the executive. Through this book the user and the provider of executive protection can develop a common understanding of what the undertaking involves, what underlies it philosophically, and how it should proceed. When the user and the provider understand executive protection in the same way, the tensions that result from the unknown are reduced, and together the EP specialist and the executive can deploy their resources in the most effective manner.

The type of EP specialist this book addresses is the private sector specialist, the person who must protect a principal without the vast resources that government EP specialists have at their disposal. The book's guidance serves experienced EP

---

[3] Sun Tzu, *The Art of War*, ed. James Clavell (New York: Delacorte Press, 1983), p. 20. All other Sun Tzu quotes in this book come from the same work.

specialists, novices, and those who contemplate entering the field.

As for the users of executive protection, this book serves all those who may need special protection. For that audience, the book raises and answers important questions that an executive should examine. For example, what does executive protection involve? How will it help me? How much will executive protection affect my life? What should I look for in a provider? Sad to say, the field of EP is full of phonies; this book will help executives spot and avoid them.

Note that the field has almost nothing to do with the popular perception of a "bodyguard." The author hesitates to mention the word "bodyguard" because of the associations it carries. Anyone who has ever seen a Hollywood film's depiction of one (the slick-haired, wheel-spinning, gun-blasting hot dog) should push that image aside while reading this book.

Why? Because executive protection is a highly evolved skill. Its serious practitioners study and train extensively to improve their craft. EP specialists rely on intelligence and alertness, not wild shoot-outs. Firearms are a rarely used and absolute last resort. (In fact, although protection specialists often carry weapons, it is axiomatic among us that if you have time to draw your firearm, you have time to shield or remove the principal instead.) EP is more about threat assessment, protective intelligence, transportation, choreography, advance work, 10-minute medicine, resources, technology, and support.

This introduction began by stating that risks abound. Just what types of risks are we talking about? Obviously, not everyone—in fact, hardly anyone—is a likely target of terrorist attack or assassination. An executive faces a much higher risk of injury (intentional or unintentional), victimization by ordinary criminals, being caught in the wrong place at the wrong time (crossfire on the street, hotel fires, etc.), deliberate embarrassment, a medical emergency, even kidnapping (which does happen—quite often in some parts of the world). The risks to be protected against aren't dreamed up out of thin air. They are deduced from careful risk analysis. Fortunately, for any individual, risks—whether high or low—can always be reduced.

In the business world, executive protection has little to do with cloak and dagger and much to do with corporate profit and loss. Threats to an executive constitute a business risk. Therefore, EP—by protecting the executive, a valuable corporate asset—fulfills a legitimate part of the corporate risk management mission. And not only does it protect that asset, but it maximizes the utility of that asset. How? By being, in large part, a facilitation resource. Executive protection permits the chief executive to live safely in, and move efficiently through, this dangerous world. Under proper protection, the executive need not worry about personal safety and can concentrate fully on the business at hand. Clearly, underlying the mission of transporting the executive safely from point A to point B is the basic mission of transporting the executive from point A to point B at all. Therefore, in performing the task of executive protection, the EP specialist frees the executive to do whatever he does best. The best protection agents are not tough guys from the security fraternity but effective, well-informed, and articulate components of corporate risk management.

Since executive protection safeguards principals against a range of threats and facilitates many of their important activities, it is rational to give serious consideration to engaging an EP specialist. Nevertheless, there may be readers who, after examining the case for EP, still question its value.

Such readers may wish to recall "Pascal's wager." Blaise Pascal, the great 17th century mathematician and philosopher, exhorted his readers to examine the probabilities of life in this manner: If God does not exist, one stands to lose nothing by believing in him anyway, whereas if He does exist, one stands to lose everything by not believing. Along those lines, even if an executive cannot easily foresee the risks he faces, the executive stands to lose little by taking some precautions against them anyway. And if those risks are real and no precautions have been taken, the executive stands to lose everything.

To some, the idea of engaging a protection specialist may be unappealing—it can be unpleasant to contemplate the world's risks. But neglecting to address those risks does not make them go away, any more than neglecting to buy life insurance grants one immortality. As Sun Tzu wrote:

> The art of war is of vital importance to the state. It is a matter of life and death, a road either to safety or to ruin. Hence under no circumstances can it be neglected.

*The general who wins a battle makes many
calculations in his temple before the battle is
fought. The general who loses a battle
makes but few calculations beforehand.
Thus do many calculations lead to victory,
and few calculations to defeat.*
Sun Tzu

Chapter 1
Threat Assessment

Why do some highly placed businesspeople, wealthy persons, celebrities, and others need executive protection? What are they so worried about? What do they hope to be protected against?

The cold truth is that they face the same types of threats to their safety and well-being that most other people face, and often to a higher degree. They might live in safer neighborhoods than some other people, but they are more attractive targets for criminals. They might travel more comfortably, but their busier travel schedules expose them to more potential accidents and attacks. They might work in safe offices, but to anyone seeking revenge against an employer they symbolize the company more than other workers do.

Premise

The EP specialist has a finite sum of protective resources. Those resources, which include money, staff, influence, knowledge, and contacts, must be spent wisely. It would be foolish and inefficient to divide the resources evenly among the universe of conceivable threats. It makes much more sense to allocate those resources toward preventing the threats that present the greatest possibility of harm.[4]

Therefore, before any protection plan can be developed, the principal and the EP specialist must identify the threats that are to be avoided. Although it is impossible to know just when and how a particular threat will arise, the general categories of threats that are applicable to the principal must be ascertained before any meaningful defenses can be erected.

Range of Threats

The range of threats to a person's safety and well-being is vast. The following list is not meant to frighten anyone, but it represents real threats faced by many high-profile, high-net-worth persons. Even though the list is not exhaustive, it is formidable:

- assassination
- kidnapping
- street violence
- attacks by insane persons or zealots
- workplace violence
- embarrassment (deliberate or accidental)
- injury (unintentional)
- illness or medical emergency
- that which is least expected

Obviously, not all of these threats apply to a particular principal, and the ones that do don't apply all the time. To determine which

---

[4] The possibility of harm is defined here as the likelihood of the threat's occurrence times the potential damage the realized threat would inflict. This calculation is similar to standard risk management formulae.

threats apply and when, the EP specialist should analyze them systematically through a process called risk analysis.

In executive protection, information is the name of the game. Much of the success of an executive protection effort depends on how well—and how cleverly—the EP specialist gathers, processes, conceals, and reveals information. By comprehensively *gathering* information, he ensures that no threats are overlooked. By intelligently *processing* information, he determines which threats present the highest risk, or likelihood, of occurring and thereby lays the groundwork for the most effective allocation of security resources and the smartest decisions regarding all parts of the protection plan. By judiciously *concealing* information, the EP specialist preserves a low profile for the protectee and keeps adversaries in the dark, thereby reducing their opportunities for attack. And by selectively *revealing* information, he either presents the protectee as a hard target that an adversary should not attempt to attack or misleads the adversary in whatever false direction is desired.

The two major forms of information gathering and processing that the EP specialist needs to undertake are risk analysis and protective intelligence. The two operations are complementary, but risk analysis, which defines the nature and scope of any protective program, comes first. It is the foundation of the protective effort.

Comparing the two undertakings, risk analysis is more general, looking at sources of threats to the protectee because of who the protectee is, works for, represents, or does. Risk analysis asks and answers such questions as these:

- Who would want to harm my principal?
- How are adversaries gaining information about my principal?
- What is the current likelihood of the various threats I have identified?
- What institutions or causes might my principal represent to an adversary?
- Does the principal desire, require, and accept protection during the work day? Only when traveling? Twenty-four hours a day?

3

Protective intelligence is more specific, describing the details of a particular trip or activity planned for the principal. Protective intelligence asks and answers such questions as these:

- What's going on today, tomorrow, and next week in the city to which my principal is traveling?
- To whom can we turn for help in that city if help is needed?
- What airports, roads, hotels, and vehicles will we be using there?
- Who, specifically, lives in or frequents the travel destination and represents a threat to my principal?

Risk analysis is described more fully below; protective intelligence is expanded on in Chapter 4, The Advance.

Risk Analysis

Where does one begin in the all-important examination of threats against the principal? Once the EP specialist starts gathering information, he will find no shortage of data to process. The challenge is to make sure no key points are overlooked, to update data continually, and to analyze the information in an organized way.

What makes risk analysis possible is the use of a methodical approach. Risk analysis requires the EP specialist to expend a substantial amount of time and effort, but the task is absolutely essential. Without a high-quality risk analysis, the EP specialist and the principal will be operating in the dark. With a high-quality risk analysis, they will be able to see much of what may lie in wait for them. It is not too much to say that one cannot have executive protection without risk analysis—and that one cannot even know whether executive protection is needed without a risk analysis. Risk analysis is, simply, the essential framework of any protective effort.

To perform a risk analysis, the EP specialist can start by asking *who, what, when, where,* and *why,* reserving *how* for the protective intelligence phase. The particular questions under each heading may vary according to the situation, but in general they are these:

- Who am I protecting? (corporate president, celebrity, wealthy person, controversial activist)

- What, therefore, must I protect him from? (mugging, embarrassment, kidnapping, harassment, stalking)
- When must I protect him? (eight hours a day, 24 hours a day)
- Where must I protect him? (at work, at home, while commuting, while traveling)
- Why must I protect him? (preserve protectee's privacy or life, protect corporation's leading human asset, facilitate protectee's safe movement through the community and world)

The most important of these questions is "Who am I protecting?" It is vital for the EP specialist to know as much as possible about the principal so that intelligent, informed decisions can be made in the event of a question, problem, or crisis. Detailed biographical information must be known by and be available to the agent to help resolve crises and even to help determine whether a crisis exists. For example, on determining that the principal is missing from his vacation home, the agent can help the police much better if he knows how many cars the principal keeps there and which one is missing. Alternatively, while accompanying the principal to the hospital in an ambulance after a car crash or heart attack, the agent can help the paramedics much better if he knows the principal's blood type and medical history.

Detailed knowledge about the principal and his family can even help determine whether a supposed incident in progress is real or fraudulent. For example, if a self-proclaimed kidnapper calls to say he is holding the principal's daughter hostage, an agent who knows how to contact the daughter's school quickly and determine whether she is still there may be able to foil the phony kidnapper and save the principal much grief and expense.

Among the types of information that an agent should gather about the principal and his family are these: physical description; pseudonyms; tape recording of voice; fingerprints; personal telephone number; extensive handwriting sample; medical requirements and history (including allergies and dietary requirements); banks and bank officers (who can release funds for ransoms);

5

credit card numbers and issuers' phone numbers; phone numbers of doctors who serve the principal and his family; children's schools' names, emergency contact arrangements, and routes the children take to and from school; notable civic and other outside activities of both principal and spouse; names and phone numbers of close relatives; recreational and hobby vehicles owned; firearms and other weapons owned by the principal and his family (to reduce surprises inside the house); floor plans and utility maps of residences, along with video footage of interiors; and reports of any past threats against the principal and his family.

The answers to the "who, what, when, where, and why" questions set the parameters for the rest of the risk analysis. The EP specialist can continue by considering each of the threats mentioned earlier, gathering information about the threat, and reaching a conclusion as to how great a risk it poses to the protectee. The threat list presented earlier serves as a starting point; the risk analysis process will suggest other threats that the EP specialist can add to the list. This chapter explains the method of determining risk levels; the means of reducing those risks are addressed in later chapters.

The general process of gathering information relevant to the various threats requires some organized sleuthing. The following are some of the steps the EP specialist can take to obtain information about threats to the protectee's safety and security:

- Interview the protectee about past incidents and any areas of concern.

- Examine the protectee's (or his organization's) threat file—the record of threatening letters, phone calls, and incidents—if one exists.

- Obtain information on crime levels from local police contacts or state crime analysis experts. Learn, for example, what areas to avoid and what types of crimes are most prevalent at which hours of the day. Also, discover the level of various crimes around the protectee's office and home, and find out about seasonal fluctuations in crime.

- Read newspaper accounts of crimes against people similar to the protectee. Search for news reports of past incidents by using a proprietary on-line service, the Internet, or the library.
- Examine any public relations materials or other information about the protectee or his organization that is available to inquisitive members of the public. Sources include annual reports, company promotional materials, newspaper and magazine articles, industry directories, and even waste paper sent to unsecured trash bins. A major and growing information source is the Internet. The EP specialist or an adversary can use various "search engines" to hunt for references to keywords in thousands if not millions of data sources. Though the depth of information is not always great, the breadth is. By finding out what a potential adversary could learn about the protectee, the EP specialist can stay a step ahead in planning a defensive strategy.

Risk assessment is so important that if the agent cannot perform it adequately, he should consider hiring the assignment out. Various firms provide risk assessment and threat analysis professionally.[5] In some cases, contracting the assessment out may be the only way to obtain good information and hence would be the best course of action. However, there is much for the agent to gain from conducting the assessment personally—skill in recognizing risks, better internalization and understanding of the results of the analysis, and a somewhat more personalized analysis, based on his greater familiarity with the principal.

Assassination

What would an application of the preceding information-gathering method tell the EP specialist about, for example, the risk of assas-

---

[5] A company to consider for international risk assessment is Control Risks Group, 8200 Greensboro Drive, Suite 1010, McLean, VA 22102. Phone (703) 893-0083. The company provides an on-line risk assessment service that covers more than 130 countries.

sination? A search of news stories and communications with police would inform the EP specialist that few protectees are likely targets of assassination attempts. The most common targets of that crime are political leaders, not celebrities or corporate executives. The EP specialist would likely conclude that the protectee is in little danger of assassination and that few, if any, assassination-specific defenses should be raised. In executive protection in general, and in risk analysis in particular, it is important not to exaggerate the threat.

However, that is not to say the risk of assassination is now and forever zero. Several factors could raise the risk to a level of concern. Does the protectee associate with political leaders? Has he been appointed to a quasi-governmental status, such as leader of a government task force or go-between in a peace negotiation? Has his corporation become involved in a controversial practice? Has he made a film or written a book that gravely offends a religious or ethnic group? Such questions show that the risk of a particular threat can rise and fall over time. That is why the EP specialist must keep up to date on the various types of threats to the safety of the protectee, even if those threats do not currently seem applicable.

As mentioned before, most assassination attempts target politicians—but not all. The classic example of an assassination of a businessperson is the attack on Alfred Herrhausen. Much has been written about the Herrhausen incident; the tale makes fascinating reading, and every EP specialist should study the details. The brief version is this: In 1989, Herrhausen, a major figure in German business and chairman of Deutsche Bank, was riding to work in his chauffeur-driven armored car. The car was the middle vehicle in a three-car convoy. Two security personnel were in the lead car, two in the follow-up car. When Herrhausen was about 500 yards from his home, his car was destroyed by a bomb concealed in a knapsack on a bicycle parked along the road. The triggering mechanism was a photoelectric cell. Responsibility was claimed by the *Rote Armee Fraktion*,[6] a German terrorist group that violently opposed the "military-industrial complex."

---

[6] Translated variously as Red Army Fraction or Red Army Faction.

Several lessons can be drawn from the Herrhausen story. First, businesspeople, not just political leaders, are sometimes the target of assassins. Second, EP specialists and their adversaries are in a neck-and-neck race to outwit each other. Able adversaries can beat lax EP specialists; they can even beat security schemes that are excellent but have just one chink in their armor. Third, EP specialists can't depend on others to observe and report potential dangers. A month before the assassination, a neighbor of Herrhausen's had actually handled the bomb's arming cable, yet he had no idea what it was and forgot about it. The days of close neighborhoods—where it was obvious who belonged there and who did not, and where neighbors would tell each other if something suspicious happened—are long gone. The responsibility for close observation lies with the agent, not the neighbors. Fourth, as one observer has noted, "if security is raised to the level afforded Herrhausen, the possibility of an attempted kidnapping is virtually ruled out. Thus, if a vehicle ambush takes place, it is more likely to be an assassination attempt."[7]

In general, the risk of death due to international terrorism is small. The U.S. State Department's figures for 1996 show that international terrorist attacks killed 311 people worldwide. Nearly 200 of those deaths were the work of the Tamil Tigers, a separatist group in Sri Lanka. The number of American victims of international terrorism in 1996 was 24. Nineteen were killed in the June 25 truck bombing of an American military base near Dhahran, Saudia Arabia, and five more died in bombings and shootings in Israel.

Of course, not all assassinations of businesspeople are conducted by internationally known, highly sophisticated terrorist groups. In the course of a news search, the EP specialist would certainly come across accounts of recent business-related killings in the countries of the former Soviet Union. For example, in October 1995 during a soccer game at a stadium in Kiev, Ukraine, a bomb exploded in a stand for honored guests. The blast killed Al-

---

[7] Anthony J. Scotti, "A Calculated Assassination," *Security Management*, November 1990, p. 31.

exander Bragin, the president of one of the soccer teams and chairman of Luxe, one of the city's largest commercial firms. Five other persons in the VIP stand were also killed.[8] Similarly, on April 30, 1997, an attacker tossed a grenade at Emomali Rakhmonov, president of Tajikistan. Rakhmonov and 57 others were wounded, and two more died. The attack occurred as the president shook hands with supporters outside a theater.[9]

Even if a particular principal is not, most of the time, a likely target of assassination, is it so implausible to think that he might sometime travel abroad and be invited to a public event by someone who is a more likely assassination target? Not being the target isn't good enough—the principal should not even be standing next to the target. That doesn't mean he must avoid all contact with other important persons. It simply means that, to some extent, the principal takes on the threat level of whoever he is with. And that gives the EP specialist one more factor to weigh when performing risk assessments.

It is important to note, also, that politicians and successful businesspeople are not the only objects of lethal attacks. Professors, researchers, even salespeople associated with universities, other research institutions, or high-technology corporations are sometimes targeted. The Unabomber, for example, killed three persons and injured 23 with 16 package bombs in the anti-technology crusade he conducted from 1978 to 1996. His goal: to ruin industrial civilization. The shifting risks that a principal faces are the reason no threat can be dismissed completely and forever. That, consequently, is why risk analysis must be updated continuously.

Kidnapping

What about kidnapping? It might sound exotic and far away, but is it? A careful analysis would show that, for most protectees, the risk of kidnapping is not great. On average, how many people are

---

[8] "Bomb at Stadium Kills Kiev Magnate," *Washington Times*, October 17, 1995, p. A10.

[9] Umed Babakhanov, "Tajikistan President Narrowly Escapes Assassination in Attack with Grenade," *Washington Times*, May 1, 1997.

kidnapped each year? Not many, of course, but business executives, wealthy persons, and other VIPs are not average people. The risk of kidnapping begins to rise as certain factors emerge: personal wealth (to a degree that seems high to the attacker, regardless of whether the principal feels wealthy compared to colleagues), entanglement with criminals or criminal organizations, a high profile in support of a controversial cause, intervention in political hot spots, travel to countries in which kidnapping is common, and vulnerability of family members.

Once an EP specialist begins to look into the subject, kidnapping may not seem such a remote possibility after all. Even a cursory search of government and news sources turns up many warnings and reports of kidnapping. Although the crime is more common outside the United States, it is not unknown here. Each year the FBI investigates hundreds of kidnappings—some years almost a thousand. Of those, typically 50 to 100 involve ransom. Given the demands for secrecy that often accompany kidnapping, there is reason to believe that official reports may understate the threat.

Accounts of kidnappings make fascinating, frightening reading. Brief summaries of a few incidents will suffice here, but EP specialists should familiarize themselves with all available details of such cases when planning their defenses.

- May 26, 1992, Mountain View, California: Charles Geschke, the 52-year-old president and chief executive officer of computer software firm Adobe Systems Inc., was kidnapped at gunpoint by two men as he arrived at work. FBI agents arrested a suspect after he picked up the $650,000 ransom left by Geschke's family at a drop-off point. The suspect led agents to a house where his accomplice was holding Geschke, who was freed unharmed.[10]

- July 26, 1993, Las Vegas, Nevada: Kevin Wynn, the 26-year-old daughter of casino tycoon Steve Wynn, was kidnapped from her townhouse in a gated, guarded

[10] "Kidnapping Victim Freed; 2 Arrested," *Chicago Tribune*, May 31, 1992.

luxury community. The kidnappers demanded a large ransom from her father, who was able to gather it quickly from the casino of his Mirage Hotel. After an employee delivered $1.45 million in cash to a drop site, the kidnappers revealed the daughter's location. She was found bound and gagged but otherwise unharmed on the back floor of her car at the airport parking lot. The whole event took less than three hours. Three men were eventually convicted of the kidnapping.[11]

- August 4, 1993, New York City: Harvey Weinstein, 68-year-old chief executive of Lord West Formalwear, one of the country's largest tuxedo manufacturers, was kidnapped as he left the Queens diner where he ate breakfast every morning before heading to work. He was shackled and then forced into a small, muddy hole covered by wooden boards, cinder blocks, and six inches of dirt. Fed irregularly by his captors, he spent 13 days there before being rescued by police—after his kidnappers took delivery of the ransom money but failed to release him. Charged with his kidnapping were a collar maker employed by the tuxedo company and the collar maker's brother and girlfriend.[12]

It is worth noting that the victims in those cases were not politicians, and the kidnappers were not terrorists. Moreover, the settings of the crimes were not exotic or unusual. Clearly, kidnapping in the United States is a threat that poses at least some risk. As history shows, too, the victims are not always the executives but sometimes their family members, who typically receive less protection. In addition to Kevin Wynn, the infamous cases of Patty Hearst and Samuel Bronfman attest to the vulnerability of family members.

What about overseas? Basically, in many countries kidnapping runs rampant. For protectees who travel, concern for kidnapping may jump from the back burner to the front. In November 1995,

---

[11] "Daughter's Abduction Jolts Tycoon," *Chicago Tribune*, August 1, 1993.
[12] "Manhattan Hell Hole," *Time*, September 12, 1993.

police in Phnom Penh arrested the suspected leader of a kidnapping ring who allegedly masterminded a series of abductions of high-profile businessmen there, including the chief operating officer of the country's largest foreign investor.[13] The same month, in the midst of a strike involving 13 French universities, students in Metz kidnapped an envoy of Education Minister François Bayrou and only released her after Bayrou pledged to reopen negotiations on increasing state funds.[14] In Mexico, the criminal economy, which is built around narcotics trafficking, arms smuggling, kidnapping, and other forms of illegal activity, has become by far the largest part of the economy, dominating the entire landscape.[15] Kidnapping of businesspeople in the Philippines has become so common, it is said, that to facilitate the transactions, kidnappers are beginning to accept checks for ransom payments.[16] Finally, in Brazil, criminals have begun charging "pre-ransom" when they threaten wealthy people with kidnapping. One recent pre-ransom consisted of seven installment payments totaling $1 million, which the victim paid in exchange for not being kidnapped.[17]

Street violence

Street violence—holdups, carjackings, robberies, and crossfire—is a highly localized phenomenon. The EP specialist should gather crime data for each area in which the principal must be guarded: office, commuting route, home, and other areas to be traveled to and through. Such information can be obtained from local police, newspaper articles, and commercial services that provide risk data for specific geographic locations.

In addition to being a local phenomenon, street violence possesses another important characteristic: it is not likely to be directed at a principal because of who he is personally; rather, the

---

[13] "Kidnappers Arrested," *Cambodia Times*, November 15, 1995.

[14] "French Students in Mounting Strikes, Kidnapping," Reuter, November 16, 1995.

[15] "Mexico: What's Next?" remarks by Christopher Whalen, Council on Foreign Relations, New York, N.Y., March 6, 1995.

[16] "What's Next, Credit Cards?" *The Detroit News*, November 30, 1995.

[17] "Rio Kidnappers Charge Pre-Ransom," *Washington Times*, December 6, 1995.

principal will be selected because of his appearance as a good (that is, affluent) target. One of the challenges of defending against stalkers, bombers, terrorists, crazies, or other adversaries is that they choose freely from a wide range of times, locations, and methods of attack. By contrast, street criminals are mostly limited to certain predictable times, locations, and methods, making the EP specialist's job a little easier. However, the world is home to many, many more street criminals than trained terrorists, so the risk of attack by a street criminal is actually much greater.

Data on the rate of criminal attacks specifically against business executives, celebrities, and wealthy persons is not available. It is hard to say whether their exposure to street crime is greater or less than that of other persons. On one hand, such principals often live and work in safer than average neighborhoods and frequent establishments that provide some level of security. On the other hand, they may stand out as attractive targets and travel more than others, increasing their exposure to street crime.[18]

To place street crime in perspective, the rate of criminal victimization in the United States is relatively high: the FBI's Uniform Crime Reports show a rate of 5,278 serious crimes per 100,000 population in 1995.[19] Those crimes are in such categories as murder, rape, robbery, aggravated assault, burglary, and arson, and together they are used to derive what the FBI calls its Crime Index. Not surprisingly, the Crime Index rate is higher in the nation's

---

[18] A recent example: On April 17, 1997, just a block from where the author was protecting a principal in London, three men in a BMW tailed a man driving in his Rolls-Royce with his wife. When the wealthy couple parked their car in a garage near their home, the muggers stopped their own car, hopped out, pulled masks over their faces, and attacked. They slashed the man's face and head with a 12-inch knife, threw him to the ground, stole cash and credit cards, and ripped a £1,000 necklace from his wife's neck. In seconds, the muggers were gone. According to the London *Times* (April 18, 1997), "The muggers are believed to watch for possible victims as they leave restaurants, hotels and shops in areas such as Park Lane, Belgravia and St. John's Wood. They follow them home and then strike in car parks or on the street. Up to a dozen muggers operating in small and interconnected gangs could be involved." Police said the thieves had probably chosen the couple because their car showed they were rich.

[19] The FBI released its 1995 Uniform Crime Report data on October 13, 1996.

metropolitan areas (9 percent higher than the national average) and small cities (0.7 percent above the national average) and much lower in rural areas (60 percent below the national average).

Getting more specific, the rate of violent crimes (murder, forcible rape, robbery, and aggravated assault) in 1995 was 685 per 100,000 inhabitants. The total number of such crimes was 21 percent above the 1986 level. The murder rate was 8 per 100,000 inhabitants, and the rate of property crimes was 4,593 per 100,000 population.

A careful risk analysis clearly shows that street violence is, statistically, a higher risk than many of the more exotic concerns, such as kidnapping and assassination. Protection against street violence is a constant, daily service required of the EP specialist and is well within his powers and skill to provide.

Attacks by insane persons or zealots

This category is driven by motives that may be inexplicable and irrational, and hence not susceptible to anticipation by rational EP specialists. Attacks by insane or overzealous persons take much the same form as attacks by other adversaries, except that these particular opponents usually do not worry about eluding detection; they may not even care whether they survive their attack. Like the kamikaze pilots of the Second World War, such attackers necessitate a high degree of defense and allow for no errors by security staff.

If it can be based on anything, the risk analysis for this threat must be based on the following:

- records of past threats against the principal or the organization
- interviews with the principal about any concerns he might have, based on odd sightings, phone calls, letters, etc.
- conversations with police, who may have information on unusual activities around the principal's home or office

Beyond that, the EP specialist cannot easily predict that an attack will come from insane or overzealous persons and must instead guard the principal against the particular *types* of attacks those persons might make, such as assassination, kidnapping, bombing, and other assaults. Every prominent principal will receive regular attention from a certain number of locals who are, to some degree, mentally unbalanced. Most of them are harmless, pathetic souls who engage in inappropriate hero-worship or telephonic harassment. The trick is to know who is among the harmless and who is not.

Workplace violence

This is a new and escalating threat to executives. In some instances, after a firing or major loss of some sort, an attacker seeks out an organization's top executive because the executive represents the business. The executive personally may or may not feel responsible for the incident that upset the attacker. It is important to know that that does not matter to the aggrieved person. Other attacks are unrelated to business and have to do with personal problems spilling over into the workplace. Such incidents include assaults by an employee's spouse or lover against the employee. In such cases, the violence can spread beyond the primary target. Therefore, the EP specialist should seek reports of any current or developing situations or relationships that could lead to violence, so he can maintain an up-to-date, valid threat assessment.

When assessing the risk of workplace violence, the EP specialist may be able to learn only a little from the usual data sources. News reports and police data are unlikely to offer any insight into whether violence should be expected at the protectee's office. However, two sources close to home may help. First, the EP specialist should speak with the principal to see whether threats have been made in the past and should ask to be notified about any future actions that might spark violence, such as firings, plant closings, or personal relationships that are becoming dangerously sour. Second, the EP specialist should look into the policies and procedures at the protectee's workplace that might affect his vulnerability to workplace violence. For example, how are firings handled? Are persons who are fired escorted from the building? Are they allowed to return to the building later? Are all security employees adequately briefed or informed about terminations? Who may enter the executive's area of the building? May visitors bring in packages? Are those packages, along with mail, screened for weapons and explosives?

Regardless of who the EP specialist reports to, the corporate executive protection program needs to be coordinated with several other key departments: security, loss prevention, maintenance, public relations, and human resources. Ideally, members of those departments should clearly understand the types of incidents and conditions (firings, lurkers spotted, threats received, etc.) that they should automatically report to the executive protection program.

Much workplace violence takes place between or against line-level workers. But executives are certainly not immune. One of the most chilling examples of recent workplace violence is the following incident, in which the assailant attacked everyone from lower-level employees to executives.

On July 1, 1993, Gian Luigi Ferri walked into the 34th-floor offices of the San Francisco law firm Pettit & Martin, hauling a black canvas bag stuffed with guns and ammunition. He walked into a conference room and began shooting, then walked throughout the firm's offices on two floors of the building, continuing to shoot people. Ferri, who felt he had a grievance against the firm, killed eight people and wounded six; then he shot himself. A note he left behind showed him to be a resentful man frustrated for years by what he saw as conspiracies to thwart his business deals. A little less than two years later, the firm's partners voted to dissolve the firm, which at its height in the 1980s had employed 240 lawyers.[20]

When weighing the cost of executive protection, EP specialists and executives should take note of the Pettit & Martin incident. Aside from the immense human cost and the possibility of legal liability that can arise from workplace violence incidents, those in-

[20] "San Francisco Carnage: Gunman Kills 8, Self," *Chicago Tribune*, July 2, 1993; "San Francisco Gunman's Rage Is Revealed in Four-Page Letter," *Chicago Tribune*, July 4, 1993; "Law Firm Dissolving After Mass Murder," *Chicago Tribune*, March 7, 1995.

cidents can be so demoralizing that the organization completely folds afterwards. How much is it worth in security expenses to keep a corporation from shutting its doors permanently?

Workplace violence is not rare. Aside from the anecdotal evidence, found in news accounts of workplace attacks, that such violence is growing, government research shows that workplace violence has become a major cause for concern. According to the National Institute for Occupational Safety and Health (NIOSH), during the decade of 1980 to 1989, 7,603 workplace homicides occurred in U.S. workplaces, for a rate of 0.7 per 100,000 workers. Homicide was the leading cause of occupational death for women and the third leading cause of death for all workers during that period.[21] Although business executives were not among those at greatest risk, workplace violence appears to be a growing trend spreading to more and more types of settings. Moreover, it is worth noting that guns, which often harm persons other than the intended target, were the weapons of choice in 75 percent of the homicides.

Embarrassment

A very different type of threat to an executive is embarrassment—in other words, being made to look bad. That threat can be intentional or unintentional. The threat assessment process regarding embarrassment is not highly technical or research-based. Rather, it is based on awareness and anticipation. Once the sources of embarrassment are discovered, a careful agent can protect the principal from them through forethought and careful choreography.

Intentional forms of embarrassment come from protesters or hecklers, among others. By taking the trouble to find out in advance what sort of crowd awaits a principal who is going to make a speech, the agent may be able to tell him that hecklers are present. The principal can then mentally prepare to deal with them. Similarly, by radioing ahead to staff at a stockholders' meeting, the agent might learn that protesters have massed by the main en-

---

[21] "NIOSH Urges Immediate Action to Prevent Workplace Homicide," *NIOSH Update*, October 25, 1993.

trance to the room. If there is reason to believe that protesters might attempt to throw, for example, fake blood on the principal to protest animal testing, advance warning helps. If the EP specialist thinks ahead and steers the executive around to a different entrance, it will be harder for the protesters to approach closely and cause a scene.

Another threat that would turn up in the EP specialist's risk analysis is unintentional embarrassment. One main source is people who are physically near the principal or in some way associated with him. For example, the agent might notice over time that, even in fine restaurants, tables that seat six or more tend to harbor louder, more raucous groups than small tables. That knowledge gives the agent, when booking a table for the principal, one more factor to work into the protective equation. Some seating locations make sense from a physical security standpoint, some from a comfort and lack-of-embarrassment standpoint. Why not select the spot that is both safest and least likely to be next to a disturbance that could become awkward or embarrassing? The disturbance could even come from the principal's own party (perhaps from an intoxicated guest). The astute agent could then discreetly suggest that it is time for the protectee to leave.

Another source of unintentional embarrassment comes from little physical mishaps in public places. During the 1996 U.S. presidential campaign, Bob Dole fell off a stage in Chico, California, when a retaining wall gave way. His fall was broken by a railing and a few surprised news photographers standing in front of the stage. Although he was not seriously injured—and in fact immediately returned to his feet, resumed shaking hands, and retook the stage—the accident gave the media an opportunity to remind everyone of the large age difference between Dole (73) and President Clinton (50).[22] Anything a protection specialist can do to check for loose electrical cords that could be tripped over, shaky chairs that could collapse, or other accidents waiting to happen is a great service to the principal.

---

[22] Thomas Hardy, "Dole Makes Strong Rebound After Fall," *Chicago Tribune*, September 20, 1996.

Accidental coincidences in public places, particularly hotels, are another potential source of embarrassment. The careful EP specialist, before booking a hotel room for the principal, would find out what groups are staying there at the same time. With that information, the EP specialist and the principal can then decide whether to stay on a floor far from a potentially troublesome group or use a different hotel altogether. For example, would a female executive really want to stay on the same floor as an entire college football team? Would the CEO of General Motors wish to be photographed walking through a hotel lobby bedecked with signs trumpeting a Ford dealers' convention?

A final source of potential embarrassment to the executive is the executive himself. The EP specialist needs to be able to speak up, politely but plainly, if, for example, the executive decides to drive after drinking too much. In such a case, the agent isn't trying to be the executive's conscience; he is merely bringing to the executive's attention a matter that could become embarrassing (and deadly).

Injury (unintentional)

If the EP specialist's job is to keep the executive alive, well, and functioning at peak performance, providing protection against the more dramatic threats—assassination, kidnapping, and violence on the street and in the workplace—only goes so far. A look at official vital statistics shows that it makes a lot of sense to protect the executive against the more mundane but also more probable threats, too. Death from car crashes, fire, drowning, falls, poisoning, and choking represents a greater risk than death from the aforementioned dramatic threats. While most protectees are sensible achievers who already know safety precautions for reducing everyday risks, the EP specialist can raise the effectiveness of his protective efforts by reminding, encouraging, and actually helping the protectee to play it safe. Protective measures are discussed later, but statistics clearly show that injury is a significant source of danger to most people.

The annual death rate for all unintentional injuries together is 35.4 deaths per 100,000 population.[23] That stands in high contrast

---

[23] *Accident Facts* (Itaska, Illinois: National Safety Council, 1995), p. 2.

to the murder rate, which is 8 per 100,000. The rate of death from selected injuries is as follows: motor vehicle accidents, 16.5; falls, 5.1; fire, 1.6; and drowning, 1.5. Those figures are for the population as a whole; for persons in the age ranges mostly likely to receive personal protection, the rates differ. Also, the rates for men are in almost all instances higher than those for women. See the table in the next section, on illness and medical emergencies, for comparisons of some of the rates.

If an EP specialist is to assess a particular protectee's risk injury, the two best indicators are official vital statistics, analyzed for a group that most closely resembles the protectee (for example, statistics for white females aged 55 to 64 years), and a close look at the protectee's style of living and personal exposure to injuries. Injuries may seem like random accidents, but by modifying behavior and avoiding certain situations, the EP specialist and the protectee obviously have some control over the likelihood of injuries. In addition, by learning and practicing basic emergency medical techniques, the EP specialist can reduce the protectee's likelihood of death from injuries that are not prevented.

Illness or medical emergency

This category of threat resembles the preceding one, unintentional injury. It is not dramatic in the way a kidnapping is, nor is it the sort of exotic threat that would by itself merit executive protection measures. However, the EP specialist with an eye on the bottom line—keeping the executive alive and well—needs to analyze the risk of illness or medical emergency, for it is a very great risk indeed. In analyzing it, he can look at both epidemiological statistics and the protectee's life style. Like injuries, illnesses and medical emergencies are not completely preventable, but they are not completely random, either. In addition, the EP specialist's knowledge of basic emergency medical techniques can reduce the harm that comes from illnesses and medical emergencies that are not prevented.

The following is a small sample of statistics from the National Safety Council.[24] Additional data presented by sex, race, age, and

---

[24] *Accident Facts*, p. 12.

more specific type of accident and illness is available in the *Statistical Abstract of the United States*, published by the U.S. Department of Commerce (available at most libraries).

Cause and Age	Death Rates		
	Total	Male	Female
45 to 54 Years			
Cancer	150.3	153.8	147.0
Heart disease	114.6	173.7	58.1
Unintentional injuries	27.3	41.0	14.2
Motor vehicle	13.6	19.0	8.4
Poison	2.9	4.3	1.5
Falls	2.2	3.5	1.0
Fires and burns	1.3	1.9	0.6
Drowning	1.2	2.2	0.3
Other	6.1	10.0	2.4
HIV	20.3	38.1	3.4
Stroke	17.5	19.3	15.7
Chronic liver disease	16.7	24.8	8.9
Suicide	14.7	22.4	7.3
Diabetes mellitus	11.7	13.5	10.0
Chronic obstructive pulmonary disease	18.3	8.7	7.9
Homicide	7.5	11.8	3.3
55 to 64 Years			
Cancer	437.8	513.4	369.7
Heart disease	346.5	503.9	204.9
Chronic obstructive pulmonary disease	48.3	56.3	41.0
Stroke	46.4	53.2	40.3
Diabetes mellitus	34.0	35.9	32.3
Unintentional injuries	30.6	44.8	17.8
Motor vehicle	13.7	18.8	9.2
Falls	3.9	5.8	2.1
Fires, burns	1.9	2.7	1.2
Surgical, medical complications	1.5	1.7	1.2
Poison	1.2	1.7	0.8
Other	8.4	14.0	3.3
Chronic liver disease	27.6	40.2	16.3
Pneumonia	16.5	21.2	12.2
Suicide	14.8	24.1	6.5
HIV	8.5	15.9	1.9

A few of those statistics are particularly worth noticing. The threats against which an EP specialist traditionally protects an executive (such as homicide) barely make it onto the list of top causes of death. Also, nearly every cause of death presents a much greater risk to males than to females. Further, in the male, 45- to 54-year-old group, suicide is twice the threat that homicide is—a situation that meshes well with the concerns of the next section, threats from unexpected sources.

After analyzing these and similar statistics and observing the protectee's life style, the EP specialist can determine whether and how forcefully to recommend risk-reducing changes in the protectee's behavior. It is important to keep in mind that these statistics are based on very broad population groups; the risk level may be very different for a particular protectee.

In general, an EP specialist should not inhibit the principal's life style, so any advice regarding personal activities that may lead to injury or illness should be given sparingly, if at all. Whatever instinct the EP specialist must employ, it is not to be confused with the maternal instinct. In some cases, it may be more advisable for the EP specialist to steer the principal away from certain risky settings and activities subtly, without the protectee even realizing it.

That which is least expected

How can an EP specialist prepare for the unexpected? Basically, by reducing as much as possible the number of eventualities that have not been considered. Those unexpected eventualities may involve the source of the threat (a trusted insider), the type of threat (an unanticipated style of attack), or another aspect of a threat (an unusual time or place). As the principal becomes a harder and harder target, most adversaries will be turned off—they will look for easier targets somewhere else. However, an adversary who is dedicated to attacking a particular principal will look hard for a gap in the principal's protection. That gap, naturally, will be the one mistake in the defensive plan.

One especially painful tale of the least expected threat—the kind that comes from an insider or former insider—is the story of Sidney Reso, the New Jersey Exxon executive who was kidnapped as he left his home April 29, 1992. He was shot in the arm when he was seized, and he died five days later, bound and gagged in a sweltering storage locker. The kidnappers were Arthur Seale, a former Exxon security official, and Seale's wife. Seale, who had left Exxon five years earlier, reportedly was angry at the company and resentful because former FBI agents were promoted over him at the Exxon security division.[25] As the Roman satirist Juvenal wrote, "Who is to guard the guards themselves?"

The threat from current or former security personnel, or other people deemed insiders, is for almost all protectees smaller than the threat from outsiders, yet insiders are especially difficult to protect against. They may know the EP specialist's defenses and be able to find gaps in them, or their insider status may enable them to pass through normal security barriers without being scrutinized. An Arabic proverb rightly states, "Better a thousand enemies outside the house than one inside."

The death of Israel's Prime Minister Yitzhak Rabin illustrates the truth of that proverb. Rabin, assassinated November 4, 1995, was killed not by a militant Palestinian or Islamic extremist but by a fellow Jew. Yigal Amir, the 27-year-old assassin, passed easily through security, approaching close enough to Rabin to shoot him with a handgun. How did he manage it? Apparently, few Israelis thought an Israeli would kill an Israeli. Gideon Ezrach, former deputy head of the Shin Bet, Israel's secret service, was quoted as saying that when Rabin was in the West Bank town of Nablus, his EP specialists were "more psychologically alert" than they were in Tel Aviv, where Rabin was killed.[26]

Being on supposedly friendly grounds can create a false sense of security. On February 25, 1997, police found a bomb planted in a Jacksonville, Florida, synagogue just before a speech was to be made there by former Israeli Prime Minister Shimon Peres. Police charged a 31-year-old kosher butcher with planting the bomb and making a bomb threat that blamed the act on an Islamic group.

---

[25] "Revenge Motive Seen in Exxon Kidnapping," *Chicago Tribune*, July 12, 1992.

[26] "What Went Wrong? Baffled Israelis Ask," *Washington Times*, November 6, 1995.

Again, being on home turf may statistically be safer, yet adversaries, knowing that, may seize the opportunity to attack when security staff are less vigilant.

Protecting against the least expected threat requires filling all possible gaps in the protective plan. As Sun Tzu wrote, "He wins his battle by making no mistakes. Making no mistakes is what establishes the certainty of victory, for it means conquering an enemy that is already defeated." That, of course, is a tall order.

The task of executive protection resembles the many other endeavors in life that require triage or allocation of limited resources. Before administering treatment, the battlefield medic first ascertains who needs help most (or who has the best chance of surviving). Police dispatchers send officers to confirmed bank robberies in progress before unconfirmed alarms at warehouses. Admirals learn where the enemy's ships are before sending their own ships into battle. An EP specialist's resources can only be allocated correctly if he thoroughly understands what is to be protected against. To use another analogy, the twin activities of threat assessment and risk analysis lay the foundation on which the entire protective edifice is built.

The preparatory steps are time-consuming, and they require hard thinking. Nevertheless, any serious agent will take the trouble to perform those steps well. The prudent EP specialist does not rush into a protection plan, disregarding the specific dangers that threaten the principal. Addressing the House of Commons in 1792, the great British statesman Edmund Burke said, "Dangers by being despised grow great." His declaration rightly points out that ignoring threats never causes them to disappear—it only allows them to increase in severity.

The consummate leader cultivates the Moral Law
and strictly adheres to method and discipline; thus
it is in his power to control success.
Sun Tzu

Chapter 2
The Philosophy of Protection

The preceding chapter discussed threat assessment, a process that helps in painting the big picture. This chapter continues the book's progress from the general to the specific by presenting another part of the big picture—the philosophy of protection. In other words, after determining the range and degree of threats to the client's well-being, it is time to consider how best to minimize those threats.

The task of protecting another human being is so complex, and so much is at stake, and so clever are the adversaries that the only way to make the task manageable is to apply some guiding principles. Such principles are like different lenses on a camera: some view a large sweep of information, while others help to focus the details. Some of the principles apply mainly to the EP specialist and others to the executive. The guiding principles do not constitute the only ways of looking at the challenge of executive protection, but they represent some of the clearest lenses through which the protector and protectee can view the task. Moreover, they serve as rules of thumb that agents can memorize for use in making decisions.

The following principles are key tenets in the philosophy of protection. They are not the practical steps (those will be presented later); rather, they are mindsets or ways to approach the practical steps.

1. Shape destiny.
2. Anybody can protect anybody.
3. If you have to stop and think about it, it's too late.
4. EP specialists get their clients out of trouble and keep them out of trouble.
5. For the executive, security and convenience are usually at opposite ends of a continuum.
6. The greatest tool in executive protection is the EP specialist's mind; technology is of limited use.

Principle 1

Shape destiny.

Much about life and executive protection is beyond one's control. However, much is within one's control. The client and the EP specialist should make a conscious decision to seize the problem—dangers threatening the executive—firmly, and wrestle it to the ground. Perhaps executives and EP specialists do not need to be reminded to take active measures to accomplish their goals; after all, both parties presumably got where they are by being energetic achievers. Nevertheless, along the way, the client was probably not concentrating on his personal safety—it may not have been an issue until the person became CEO or attained substantial wealth or fame. Similarly, those who are interested in becoming EP specialists often come from backgrounds where the governing instincts are contrary to those required in executive protection; for example, they often come from law enforcement, where a mindset of aggression, rather than retreat, prevails.

Therefore, it is important to make a deliberate, firm commitment to shaping one's destiny. This is an exciting, positive way to look at executive protection. It reminds the agent that good results—and good fortune—follow from thinking hard and working hard to stay at least a step ahead of trouble. As many sages have observed, "I find the harder I work, the more good luck I have." Another way to look at this comes from Friedrich Nietzsche, who wrote, "Life is short, but the hour is long." We do not live forever, but we live long enough to accomplish much.

This principle—shaping your destiny—stands taller than all the rest. It leads to many of the practical steps that will be discussed in later chapters. In most of executive protection's practical endeavors, such as vehicle security, workplace security, and countersurveillance, it is necessary not to sit back and receive what comes but instead to shape destiny:

- to reach out mentally to anticipate threats
- to catalog the protection program's strengths and the agent's resources—in order to use them when needed
- to identify the protection program's vulnerabilities (undoubtedly, the adversary is doing so)
- to reckon the adversary's probable approach and thereby outwit him

The EP specialist should take charge of the client's protective needs, quietly dominating the risks he faces. Many examples of the use of this principle appear in the following chapters; here is one to illustrate the principle now. When protecting an executive during travel, the agent should remember that hotel inspectors don't die if a poorly inspected hotel burns; the guests do. Therefore, he can—and should—shape destiny by preparing an escape from burning hotels and carrying smoke masks.

Principle 2

Anybody can protect anybody.

This principle is almost literally true, and the EP specialist should bear it in mind to bolster his confidence. True, protecting another human being—a complicated, unpredictable, mobile person—is a daunting task. But must the agent stand seven feet tall? Have a 180 IQ? Possess complete knowledge of all tasks required in the protection of the principal? Of course not. To protect a client, the EP specialist uses his own strengths—whatever they may be—and fills in the gaps by delegating tasks to others with

29

different abilities. Perhaps a particular agent is brave, intelligent, and strong but has little experience in defensive driving. That lack does not disqualify him for the field of executive protection. Rather, applying the principle that anybody can protect anybody, the agent can decide to lobby for the hiring of a professional driver or can become one himself through training and practice. Although much of the action resides in the purely physical realm—driving cars, watching for attackers, moving quickly to avoid threats—executive protection is primarily a brain game. Therefore, anyone—that is, anyone who is intelligent—can protect anyone.

Principle 3

If you have to stop and think about it, it's too late.

This guiding principle reminds the EP specialist that a thoughtful, deliberate reaction to a dangerous situation will almost always *fail*. Why fail? Isn't this a thinking person's business, an endeavor based on careful planning and making the right decisions? Yes, but when the threat, or attack, or danger actually arises, it typically explodes onto the scene—leaving no time for that "thoughtful, deliberate reaction." By remembering this principle, the EP specialist can keep in mind the necessity of constantly practicing reactions to different scenarios. Such practice may be physical, whereby he rehearses protective movements and quick escapes or practices driving or shooting. Or it may consist of little *gedankenexperimente*, the name Einstein used for the mental experiments he conducted when physical experiments were infeasible. For an EP specialist, that might mean constantly asking "what if?" during the course of protection. If both physical practice and mental or "what if?" practice are maintained, then he has a better chance of being able to react to an emergency or potential emergency appropriately and immediately, without thinking—because the thinking has already been done.

Assaults and assassination attempts start and end with astonishing rapidity. A good example is the speed with which George Wallace and President Reagan were attacked and how quickly those incidents were over. In order for the protectee to have an even chance of survival, the agent needs to use every possible advantage. Being mentally prepared to respond far outweighs the value of any other precaution.

Principle 4

EP specialists get their clients out of trouble and keep them out of trouble.

This principle points out that EP specialists are not fighters, bodyguards, or soldiers. It's not the agent's primary job to knock down, arrest, or kill the bad guys. It is his primary job to avoid the bad guys—and any other danger, such as fire, street crime, or embarrassment. This principle reminds the EP specialist that in an encounter with a would-be assassin, it is appropriate to push the client out of harm's way, shield him, and remove him from the area as quickly as possible. It is not appropriate, when it can be avoided, to stand and fight. An example of *getting* the client out of trouble is the scenario in which, upon spotting an armed aggressor, agents push their protectee into a car and speed the protectee away to safety. An example of *keeping* the client out of trouble would be an arrangement whereby the EP specialist and the client can communicate subtly, by a nondescript phrase or visual signal, that it is time to leave certain company or a certain place before an embarrassing or dangerous condition arises.

Principle 5

For the executive, security and convenience are usually at opposite ends of a continuum.

This principle reminds the agent and the client that total security is not only impossible but also undesirable. Why is that?

Executive protection specialists often state that security and convenience inhabit opposite ends of a continuum. At one end of the continuum is total security, or the absence of all risk. At the other end is total convenience, or the absence of inhibiting factors on one's life style. Movement toward one end results in an equal movement away from the other end. In practice, that is an exalted way of saying that the more security an executive demands, the less convenience he will have, and that, likewise, the more freedom he demands, the less security he will have.

Basically, this principle helps the agent and the client keep their security measures in perspective. Obviously, neither extreme— total convenience or total security—is suitable. The client and the agent must discuss this concept and decide where on the continuum—that is, closer to which end—the client wants to be. Even if the extremes are avoided, it helps to be aware of the tradeoffs that any locations on the continuum impose. Each time an EP specialist thinks up a new way to protect the executive, this principle can serve as a reminder that increasing security beyond a certain point may needlessly hobble the executive, making him less effective and hence a victim of protection instead of a victim of attack.

Moreover, this is not a static analysis. The protectee's place on the continuum shifts, as does the risk picture, moving closer to security for a time and then back toward convenience again.

Principle 6

The greatest tool in executive protection is the EP specialist's mind; technology is of limited use.

This principle serves as a reminder that protective equipment, while necessary, is not sufficient. Firearms, alarm systems, armored cars, two-way radios—all these are useful tools in the EP specialist's collection, but not one of them—not even all of them working together—can be wholly relied on to protect an executive. The reason is twofold; its first part relates to the person protected, the second part to the threat against him.

First, unlike a brick of gold, a valuable executive moves around. He can't be locked up in a vault or perpetually sequestered. If that happened, he'd be no longer an executive but a prisoner, and the protection would devalue him as thoroughly as any adversary could. One can't protect a living flower by locking it in a dark vault; the same holds true for human beings. Executives aren't buildings that can be surrounded with fences, motion detectors, and steel doors. Rather, they are constantly on the move. An overreliance on security technology tends to place the protectee in a vault.

Second, adversaries are more intelligent than equipment. A dedicated adversary can defeat or circumvent alarms, disable armored cars, eavesdrop on two-way radios, etc. A protective agent can hope to buy defensive time with equipment, but when the adversary strikes, salvation lies in the agent's brain power—his ability to make conditioned decisions on how to remove the principal from harm's way. Certainly, in gun battles that have taken place in the executive protection field, almost none have lasted more than a few seconds; likewise, in every U.S. presidential assassination attempt to date, there's been no chance to return fire. Again, equipment is necessary but not sufficient.

The preceding six principles are worth remembering. For some readers they might serve as mindsets or philosophies; for others they might serve as decision tools. For all readers they can serve as quiet encouragements—reasons to see the task of executive protection, though challenging, as doable.

This is the last of the preparatory chapters. Now it is time to put threat analysis and the philosophy of protection into action.

Without harmony in the state, no military expedition can be undertaken; without harmony in the army, no battle array can be formed.

Sun Tzu

Chapter 3
Working the Principal

The defining relationship in the field of executive protection is the relationship between the EP specialist and the principal. In some ways, it is an odd relationship. The principal clearly plays the role of the employer, the boss, yet the EP specialist must be able to give orders to the principal in times of danger and advice at most other times. Sun Tzu observed that a proper relationship must exist between the general (analogous here to the EP specialist) and the sovereign (the principal), in which the two remain in their proper spheres. The general follows the wishes of the sovereign, but the sovereign does not interfere in the duties of the general by issuing impossible, unwise, or too numerous commands.

In executive protection, a professional, not too personal relationship enables both protector and protectee to perform their jobs freely. However, the relationship is not like other business relationships: The agent may have to lay down his life for the principal, and that is not something one does strictly for money. Meanwhile, the executive places his life and reputation in the hands of the agent.

When the agent and the executive know what constitutes the right relationship between them, and they work to develop and maintain that relationship, the protective effort has the greatest chance of success. That's why this chapter discusses so many aspects of the protector-protectee relationship, including the necessary characteristics of an EP specialist, the ways he should conduct himself, the ways he should interact with the principal (including physical, verbal, and attitudinal aspects), and a very important bottom-line question.

The descriptions given are geared specifically to close, inner-perimeter protection of the principal. Although it is impossible to describe exactly what should happen in every conceivable contingency, the following discussion should serve as the foundation of proximity protection.

Characteristics of a Good EP Specialist

As mentioned earlier, the popular conception of executive protection has little to do with reality. The gap between fiction and fact is particularly wide in the matter of what makes a good EP specialist. Movies, television programs, and novels often portray "bodyguards" either as musclebound, ill-tempered, and dimwitted or as dissolute, shady, and dishonest. In the real world, the attributes that make a successful agent are far different.

The ideal protection specialist bears some resemblance to a particularly upstanding Boy Scout—with a dash of worldly sophistication thrown in. Key attributes are similar to those an employer would look for in any employee, except that the standard is set higher, since the person will likely be responsible for protecting the principal's life (and possibly the lives of family members). A good EP specialist has a large measure of common sense, loyalty, and integrity. He is honest, discreet, alert, mentally fit, and physically fit (and refrains from smoking). Further, a good EP specialist is quiet, dignified, and, above all, effective. These characteristics are desirable in themselves, of course, but in an EP specialist they are also genuinely useful.

Protective work is likely to bring the specialist into contact with unfamiliar places, settings, activities, and people. *Common sense* guides him through any alien territory. An agent's *loyalty* and *discre-*

tion give the principal enough comfort to allow him protective access to important, sensitive, or personal settings—without any fear that the agent will intentionally harm or embarrass the principal. *Integrity* and *honesty* give the agent the courage to speak up about a threat to the principal's interests, even when the principal may not wish to hear what must be said. *Alertness* and *mental fitness* enable the agent to spot and recognize dangers and opportunities, even after long hours and in the face of distractions. Although an agent does not need prodigious physical abilities, basic *physical fitness* (plus a little extra) helps him act effectively when physical intervention is needed. For example, the agent might have to use the "fireman's carry" to remove the principal from a dangerous situation, and he should be able to subdue an attacker, to box, and to use martial arts. Physical fitness also builds the physical and mental endurance needed during long shifts and far-flung travels. Being a *nonsmoker* is, in a sense, a small point, but it illustrates the agent's desire to put duty ahead of self. Refraining from smoking frees the agent's hands for sudden activity, reduces distractions, and keeps him from inadvertently attracting attention through the sight or smell of smoke or the need for matches and ashtrays. Chewing gum also sends the wrong signals. Behaving in a *quiet* and *dignified* manner makes it feasible for the agent to accompany the principal into important, formal settings (such as business meetings, black-tie dinners, weddings, and political events), where a less serious demeanor would not be allowed. The agent's presence in such places makes him more *effective*.

Of utmost importance, among all the requirements of character and intellect, is the need for a selflessness that enables the agent to subordinate his well-being, and even life, to that of the principal. That important bottom-line consideration is examined in this chapter's last section, "The big question."

The Agent's Command of Self

The EP specialist is his own best implement in the effort to protect the principal. The most important resources at the agent's disposal reside inside. The way he dresses and carries himself sends a message to the protectee, those with whom the protectee does business, and any potential attackers. The basic equipment the agent carries makes a big difference in what he can do on the spot, at the moment of need. His practice of scanning the surroundings and thinking constantly about potential threats and escape measures makes quick response to trouble a more real possibility. Finally, his dedication to professional behavior supports all of the preceding.

Appearance and equipment

Body language, expressed through both the clothes the agent wears and the way he stands and moves, serves several purposes in executive protection. The agent usually wants to blend into the settings in which he protects the principal, whether they are business meetings, formal parties, or recreational activities. Most principals prefer that the agent not attract attention; doing so may unnecessarily affect the setting. For example, in the business environment, if the EP specialist has too strong a presence, others may be distracted and may not be able to conduct their business comfortably. Therefore, in such a setting the agent would want to be dressed in a civilian, businesslike manner. If the agent comes from a military or police background, where uniforms are the norm, that may be a challenge.

Fortunately, anyone who wants to dress properly for business can readily consult books or magazines for practical tips on selecting suitable clothes. Other sources of help in dressing appropriately include displays at upscale clothing stores, experienced tailors, and observation of the principal's style of dress. (Note: it is important for the agent not to dress better than the principal; doing so may draw unwanted attention to the agent and unfavorable comparisons with the principal.) A few tips specific to dressing for protective work include these:

- If the agent plans to carry a firearm under his jacket, he should wear the weapon when having the suit tailored. That way, the tailor can reduce any potential bulging from the weapon.

- The agent may well need to wear the proverbial "belt and suspenders"—the belt to hold equipment and the suspenders to hold up the pants.
- The agent should avoid the tough guy or too-cool look that comes from wearing overly stylish sunglasses. Sunglasses are especially to be avoided indoors—the agent doesn't want to look like a television bodyguard. Of course, it's fine to wear sunglasses in bright sunlight.

The correct look depends not just on what the agent wears but also on how he wears it. Clothes must be pressed, cleaned, professionally laundered—whatever is appropriate. The agent's personal cleanliness is also extremely important. It might seem like a too-basic observation, but clean hands, a clean-shaven face, and other marks of personal cleanliness project a more professional image. They also make it easier for him and the client to spend long periods around each other.

The flip side of appearance considerations (and this applies not just to clothing but to the agent's total appearance) is that, while still blending in as far as ordinary observers are concerned, the agent may wish to be noticed by potential assailants. An EP specialist looks more effective if he refrains from holding a drink, if he keeps his hands out of his pockets, and if he stands erect, not leaning against walls or doorways.

Appearing to be fit and alert is not a minor consideration; it is part of presenting a hard target. The hard target concept will be illustrated throughout the book in various protective settings, but in general it means that certain adversaries can be deterred by the impression that a particular target will be difficult to attack. They then move along and select another target. Not all adversaries are affected that way; some may have a grudge against a particular executive and want to harm only him. However, many potential attackers, be they as humble as street criminals or as sophisticated as international terrorists, look at a particular protectee as a type—a representative of something the attackers hate or a source of economic gain. In such cases, if one protectee seems hard to reach, the adversaries may move on and choose an easier target.

For example, Arthur Bremer stalked President Nixon for months, trying to find a suitable opportunity to shoot him. Finally, frustrated over and over by the protection around the President and the speed at which the President's motorcade always passed by, Bremer changed targets and successfully attacked presidential candidate George Wallace. Bremer's muddled diary shows that he wanted to shoot someone famous and become famous himself, and that he held vague, confused grudges against anyone he saw as connected with U.S. power in general and with U.S. involvement in Vietnam. Thus, his intended victims were somewhat interchangeable "types."

Note that the President's protective measures did not counter or repel Bremer's attack; they prevented it from ever occurring. Preventing an attack from occurring is always better than attempting to halt an attack that has already started. The main reason is that certain types of attacks are nearly impossible to defend against once they are initiated. Bremer's diary shows he had no particular interest in escaping after he shot his target; he wrote, "Still don't know whether it's trial and prison for me or—bye bye brains. I'll just have to decide that at the last few seconds. Must succeed. Gota."[27] To use another example, it is better to discourage the kamikaze pilot from taking off in the first place than to defend against him once he is flying straight at your ship.

Therefore, by appearing to be a professional, alert, organized EP specialist, and by performing his job correctly, the agent protects the principal by discouraging adversaries from even attempting an attack. As Sun Tzu describes it, "To fight and conquer in all your battles is not supreme excellence. Supreme excellence consists in breaking the enemy's will without fighting." This observation is part of Sun Tzu's strategy of winning by use of the "sheathed sword."

In addition to presentation and an effective image, the EP specialist is responsible for carrying the right equipment and understanding its uses and limitations. Later chapters will discuss the

---

[27] Arthur H. Bremer, *An Assassin's Diary* (New York: Harper's Magazine Press, 1972), p. 106.

equipment appropriate for particular settings, but certain items are needed in almost all assignments. The item that first springs to most people's minds when they think about executive protection is a firearm. Without a doubt, there is a place for firearms in most executive protection assignments; in the most extreme situations, the agent might absolutely need to use a gun. However, the utility of firearms is much more limited than one might expect.

Firearms as protective instruments are overrated, and for the untrained they can be counterproductive. If shooting starts, the correct response is to remove the principal from the situation, not to stop and attempt to shoot the assailant. A classic example is the March 1981 assassination attempt against President Reagan in Washington, D.C. Dozens of firearms were drawn by police and Secret Service agents in response to John Hinkley's gunfire, yet not a single shot was fired in return.

There are several reasons for that approach. An agent's return shots could miss, with the result that time that could have been used to move or shield the principal is wasted in shooting; the agent's shots could injure bystanders; or the agent's shots could hit the assailant, leaving him a good ten seconds to fire off six or eight shots before expiring. None of those scenarios is very desirable.

An agent might consider himself well trained in marksmanship and tactical shooting, yet real-life conditions are starkly different from range conditions. On the range, the shooter is primed and ready to react, he fires on command, and no obstacles stand between him and the target. By contrast, in real life the agent does not know when or from which direction the attack will come and is constantly exposed to false stimuli—the man with one hand in a pocket may just be reaching for a handkerchief.

Further, mental reliance on being armed may leave the agent mentally disarmed when it is time to travel to a destination where he may not bring a gun—whether that is another state or another country. Before carrying a firearm, he must research the local laws on that subject; before traveling with one, he must research the laws at the destination and the laws of each jurisdiction through which he will pass. *An EP specialist must not under any circumstances carry a firearm contrary to law.*

If an agent is going to carry a firearm, it is his responsibility to learn to become proficient, to practice firing it often, and to deploy it in the most effective manner. Applicable practice means firing the weapon in cold weather, in hot weather, during the daytime, at night, in rain and snow, and from a moving car—not just in a controlled firing range environment. It is also important to get away from the idea that only the largest, most powerful handgun will do. That type of gun is actually more of a hindrance than a help. The trained EP specialist knows gun types and, more importantly, ballistics. That way he can select the right weapon and ammunition for the job. In addition, it is useful for everyone on the protection team to carry the same type of firearm, so that in an emergency one agent can use another agent's gun without any difficulty.

The bottom line on firearms is this: an EP specialist must depend much more on his brain power, his powers of observation, and his physical conditioning and reaction times than on any firearm.

Other tools with which the agent may need to equip himself include a pager (which should be set to vibrate, not beep); a small notebook, an electronic organizer, or 3x5 index cards for jotting down important details; a miniature flashlight; a first-aid kit and smoke mask; a multi-tool, such as a Gerber multi-pliers or a well-equipped Swiss army knife; and, if trained and certified to carry one, an ASP (a type of expandable baton).

While it is necessary for the agent to carry a certain amount of equipment around, he should never inadvertently display any gear, such as a weapon or radio, that identifies him as a protection specialist. (A recent trend is the dramatic reduction in the size of 9mm handguns. Both Glock and Sig Sauer produce fully functional, small, semiautomatic pistols that help reduce the bulge under the coat.) The agent should select suit coats whose cut hides the equipment, yet he must keep coats unbuttoned to facilitate access to the equipment. Even in hot weather, if removing the coat would reveal a gun or radio, the coat should stay on.

Scanning and calculating

When working a principal, an agent will find that conditions change. The agent may safely bring the principal to a particular destination, such as a conference at which he is making a speech, but the job does not stop there. Once inside a meeting hall, for example, the agent should start scanning and calculating—that is, scanning the surroundings for items, people, or arrangements that appear potentially threatening or seem somehow out of place, and calculating possible reactions should trouble arise.

Even during a long speech, as in this example, the agent needs to stay alert, constantly scanning the hall. What about that fidgety, inappropriately dressed man in the front row? Who are those people in the back with signs, pushing their way through the crowd? What if a fire broke out in the catering area? Where are the exits in relation to the principal? This is the time for the agent to notice things—especially people's hands, objects they may be carrying, and visible signs of nervousness—and constantly to ask himself, "What if?" That is the operating premise that drives the professional.

As Chapter 2 pointed out, when trouble arises, if the agent has to stop and think about what to do, it's too late. Fortunately, the act of scanning and calculating keeps him ready for split-second reaction. It's as if he were a computer placing all available data temporarily into RAM. Such a computer could process data and execute programs immediately, without pausing to load data stored on the hard drive.

The act of scanning and calculating also provides data to use in an important post-event activity—that is, asking the question, "Have I been visited?" In other words, the EP specialist asks himself whether anything that occurred during a particular protection assignment was a clue to a future threat. Was the man who lurked by the principal's car scoping it out for a future bombing? Was the fellow who brushed against the agent checking whether he was armed? Was the odd man in the front row, who seemed to disapprove so strongly of the principal's speech, stockpiling anger to fuel a future attack?

The "what if?" exercise helps the agent bring to mind and thereby prepare for incidents for which there are no visual clues.

If the principal has enemies in a particular country or region, those enemies might well choose to attack when the principal is in a different region altogether, calculating that the protective services will not be looking for them there. For example, a protectee from the Middle East who faces a high level of threat at home is not immune to attack when traveling in the United States. A careful threat analysis might show the risk of attack to be lower in the United States, but the risk doesn't drop to zero. In fact, the EP specialist's rational expectation that the risk is substantially lower may be enough to raise the likelihood of such an attack—conducted by adversaries from the Middle East who travel to the United States for a better attack opportunity. Alternatively, a protectee whose main threat comes from foreigners when he is visiting their countries might unexpectedly be attacked at home by a fellow countryman, as in the Rabin assassination. Accordingly, the EP specialist needs to keep his guard up at all times.

Professional behavior

When an agent is working a principal, professional behavior is not just the icing on the cake; rather, it is the cake itself. In other words, the hallmarks of professionalism—such as punctuality, dependability, responsibility, discretion, and high-quality performance—are highly practical attributes in executive protection.

Regarding punctuality, "being there" on protective assignments constitutes a large part of the challenge and accomplishes much of the agent's goal. In most cases, providing executive protection requires getting up early (certainly earlier than the principal), arriving on time (at least) or ahead of schedule (better), and staying up late. An agent who stands by the principal's side cannot prevent every threat, but an agent who has not yet arrived at the principal's side cannot prevent any threat. The agent's presence also adds to the principal's image as a hard target.

Dependability and responsibility help the agent maintain an effective safety shield for the principal—no gaps, no cracks, no holes. Being dependable, responsible, and alert keeps the concentric rings of protection in place. Implementation of concentric protection is discussed in the next major section, but the theory is this: To protect the principal, who is a moving, living, and somewhat unpredictable target, the agent creates a multi-layer safety zone around him. That way, threats must pierce several defenses before harming the executive. The concentric rings are real, of course, consisting of different protective measures spaced at varying distances from the principal. However, the rings are also a theoretical construct that helps the agent remember to protect the principal against attacks originating from any direction. EP specialists refer to 360-degree protection when they discuss the need to scan constantly in all directions.

Rather than creating a shield to keep hazards from getting in, discretion—that is, quietness about what the agent and principal do, where they go, and what the agent sees—creates a security net around the principal, keeping vulnerabilities from getting out and being exploited. It's the old "loose lips sink ships" story. When Arthur Bremer was stalking President Nixon, he watched television to learn motorcade routes. At one point, he asked a police officer along the route, "Where's a good place to watch the President?" The officer pointed out an advantageous corner.[28] Another time, Bremer followed signs from a hotel lobby to a place called the "White House Press Room." He walked in and saw notices on a bulletin board giving a detailed schedule of Nixon's movements for the next day. "I wrote it all down," he observed in his diary. "The papers and T.V. had not given this out so detailed."[29] There's simply no point in handing potential adversaries information that makes their job easier. A discreet agent does his part by keeping mum.

Finally, high-quality performance, achieved 100 percent of the time, is the most practical of a professional's attributes. It may seem like an uncomfortably demanding standard, but few attacks against protectees succeed when the EP specialist does everything right. Almost always, an attack succeeds only if some small mistake allows it. As Chapter 1 pointed out, Sun Tzu believed firmly in this high standard: "He wins his battles by making no mistakes.

---

[28] Bremer, p. 70.
[29] Bremer, p. 84.

Making no mistakes is what establishes the certainty of victory, for it means conquering an enemy that is already defeated." A more recent formulation of much the same idea comes from the Irish Republican Army. After exploding a bomb at the Grand Hotel in Brighton in 1984, in an unsuccessful attempt to kill Prime Minister Thatcher and other ministers, an anonymous IRA caller was quoted by newspapers as telling the government, "Today we were unlucky. But remember, we have only to be lucky once. You will have to be lucky always." However, what is needed always is not luck but skill and professionalism.

The Agent's Dealings with the Principal

Once the agent has gained sufficient self-mastery, bringing his skills and thought processes to a high degree of proficiency, it is time to apply that self-mastery directly to the task of protecting the principal. The agent's interaction with the principal takes many forms—physical and social, in calm and in crisis.

Relationship and communication

In general, the relationship between an EP specialist and a principal should be friendly but not familiar. The EP specialist needs to know the executive in order to protect him successfully, yet some emotional distance is needed so the agent can make rational, detached decisions. A careful EP specialist stays one step removed from the executive's innermost circle, does not get involved in company politics, and doesn't become overly friendly with the executive's family members. Since the EP specialist and the executive have to be able to get along with each other, it behooves the agent to learn about the executive's likes and dislikes, personal goals, and political sentiments—and then to avoid making a faux pas when speaking about any of those subjects.

Some protectees wish to be treated with deference; others may be of a more egalitarian bent. Like the doctor-patient relationship, this relationship requires that the agent know as much about the executive as possible in order to treat him properly. And also as in the doctor-patient relationship, keeping professionally distant enables the agent to operate objectively. But the comparison with the doctor-patient relationship isn't perfect. The executive is clearly the boss, so when it comes to developing a relationship, the agent has to take his cue from the executive.

Adding to the complexity of the relationship is that the principal may wish to keep confidential the role of the protection specialist. Doing so may also help the protector disguise his job function. One way for an executive to minimize the number of people who know he employs a protection specialist is to assign the agent a job title that obscures, or at least does not trumpet, what he actually does. "Chief of operations" and "executive assistant" are titles that might serve well.

Keeping quiet about protection is not a matter of trying to avoid embarrassment. Rather, the point is that some potential adversaries might become inflamed or emboldened if they knew that someone they dislike has protection. And while presenting a hard target is certainly appropriate sometimes, at other times the presence of an obvious protection specialist only serves as a signal to evildoers that here is someone who can afford protection, someone who therefore might be worth attacking.

One other form of communication that the executive and the agent should work out together is the subtle signal that one person gives the other that means, "Let's go." An example could be the scenario mentioned earlier, where the agent who is busily scanning the auditorium for possible danger signs notices an agitated, sign-carrying throng pushing through the audience. The agent cannot approach and speak to the principal without being obvious to the protesters, but the agent wants to spirit the principal out a side door before the potential adversaries get too close. In such a case, the EP specialist uses a physical, visible signal—known only to the client and employed only in emergencies—that alerts the principal to leave the area. Open communication makes the development of such signals possible.

Another example would be a business lunch at a restaurant. The person meeting with the executive is upset about a business maneuver. Having drunk too many martinis, and being a hot-headed sort, he begins to speak too loudly and then to shout. The agent, a polite distance away, cannot tell whether the person's behavior is becoming threatening, but the executive feels it is at least embarrassing and possibly threatening. This time, the executive sends the signal, the EP specialist steps up to announce that the principal has a phone call, and the two depart before real trouble develops.

Choreography

The physical positioning and the interaction between an agent and a principal are crucial. The agent's main mission is not to open doors for the principal, or to help the principal wriggle out of awkward social situations, or to fill the principal's ears with deferential comments. Those activities may be desirable or otherwise useful at times, but the agent's main mission is to keep the principal physically safe. That means being there, standing in the right place, and moving the right way. It is a question of choreography.

Different protective settings require different approaches, and the actual movements and placements needed in such situations as travel, residential security, and workplace protection are discussed in later chapters. However, some general comments can be offered here.

In many protective scenarios, only one agent is available to provide security to the principal. The natural question is how the agent should position himself, in terms of distance and bearing, from the person he is trying to protect. An interesting rule of thumb, from the perspective of the principal, comes from a former high-ranking U.S. government official who is now receiving private protection. He tells his protective detail: "Stand close enough to protect me, but not so close that I have to introduce you."

When the principal is walking, typically the protective agent walks behind and to one side of him. That arrangement enables the agent to look carefully in all directions without attracting undue attention. However, walking behind the principal is not always the best arrangement. For example, before the principal enters a room, hallway, elevator, or stairwell, the agent should precede him to make sure the area is safe. Politeness has its place, but holding the door so that the principal may enter a room first is unchivalrous if the effect is to send him unprotected into an attack. If necessary, the agent should push ahead of the principal, saying "Excuse me" perhaps, but nevertheless making sure to be the first one into the room in order to bear the brunt of any assault that may be lurking there.

It takes time for a principal and an agent to become comfortable with the space question. Most principals do not want EP specialists breathing down their necks or getting underfoot. However, serious physical threats usually occur at close range, so it is counterproductive to keep the agent at too great a distance. If the level of threat is high enough, for whatever reason, the agent may even have to accompany the principal into public rest rooms. Why? The relative privacy of a public restroom facilitates several sorts of crimes. For example, an unplanned mugging could easily take place, or a well-planned child-molestation setup could be staged there. If the agent and executive can overcome their reticence and make it standard for the agent to accompany the executive into isolated places, the mugger will likely wait for another victim and the con artist or blackmailer will be foiled by the presence of a witness.

As mentioned earlier, physical protection requires making the executive a hard target. In some cases the EP specialist should make it obvious that the executive is well protected, whereas in other cases it is better to be noticed as little as possible. But regardless of whether he *appears* to be a hard target, he should *actually be* one. The target analogy works on several levels, especially if one thinks of "hard" as both "strong or physically unyielding" and "difficult." Comparing the executive to a paper bull's-eye and the adversary to an archer, it is certainly harder to hit such a target if it is (a) far away, (b) moving, or (c) encased in a steel box. The analogous situations for a client are (a) staying out of the public eye or keeping a significant physical distance away from crowds, dangerous parts of a city, etc., (b) driving as fast as is practical when traveling by car and not stopping when an adversary tries to force a stop, and (c) being protected by a security perimeter, whether that perimeter consists of a protection team, physical barriers, or a combination thereof. Situations (a), (b), and (c) will be covered in more detail in chapters on motorcade security, residential and office security, and protection during travel.

General observations about point (c), however, are that the protective perimeter often consists of the principal's protective team. Proper positioning for a one-person protective effort was discussed above; when the team consists of three, four, or more EP specialists, the challenge for the team leader is to use the several agents to best advantage. In executive protection, the phrase "use your resources" is used frequently to remind agents that they must make use of any advantage they can. In this setting, where the advantage is having several EP specialists, that might mean putting one agent in front of the principal, one behind the principal, and one across the street (for a better vantage point). The agents must be able to move in a coordinated, natural flow, so as not to trip each other up or make the principal feel surrounded. This is true choreography.

The ideal is to maintain balanced, 360-degree coverage around the principal. Two agents can do so by stationing themselves at the protectee's left and right, or front and back, or any two positions that are separated from each other by 180 degrees. They may need to shift positions constantly to remain opposite one another. They should try to avoid standing too close to each other, facing the same direction, and leaving most of the area to their backs unobserved. One of the agents should stand closer to the principal in order to maintain verbal contact with him and be able to respond quickly should an assault or other emergency occur. If a third agent is available, he should stand at a greater distance and provide general, overall surveillance.

Other formations, such as wedges, diamonds, and lines, may be employed to deal with crowds, various building layouts, escalator and elevator use, receiving lines, and other situations:

- *Crowds.* Moving the principal through a crowd, especially a hostile or exuberant crowd, is best done by three agents in a wedge formation. In that arrangement, one agent walks in front of the principal, one to the principal's left, and one to his right. The EP specialists can make the wedge even more effective by linking their arms around the principal to keep others from pressing in too close.

- *Receiving lines.* The key to securing a principal who is shaking hands with guests in a long receiving line is to maintain surveillance of the line at some point before guests reach the principal and to watch carefully both behind and on the opposite side of the protectee. The agent should remember to watch individuals' hands, rather than their eyes, especially in very crowded conditions. If a person is approaching the principal with his hands in his pockets, the agent should feel free to ask him, politely but firmly, to take his hands out. Most people will not take offense at such a request.

- *Elevators.* If two agents are available, their arrangement in a hallway or lobby while waiting with the principal for an elevator to arrive is as follows: the first agent stands facing the closed elevator doors, while the principal and the second agent wait off to one side, out of direct view from within the elevator car. As the doors open, the first agent, who is in a position to block the view from within the car, enters first, turning around to hold the doors back as the principal and second agent enter. The second agent moves to the rear of the car, behind the principal, and the first agent stands in front, facing the doors. That way, when the doors open again, all three are in a good position for forward movement. If only one agent is working the principal, he should make the movements suggested for the first agent.

- *Escalators.* If two agents are available, one should stand in front of the principal, looking forward and to both sides, and the other should stand behind the principal, looking behind and to both sides. If a staircase parallels the escalator, one agent should walk on the stairs alongside the principal (who is on the escalator) and the other should ride close behind the principal.

The ring or concentric rings of protection may consist of four agents standing around the principal in a diamond formation, or it may consist of one agent standing next to the principal while others hold positions somewhat farther away. If the concentric rings consist of both personnel and equipment, and a high level of security is in order, the levels of defense would theoretically be devised as follows. At the illustrated level of security, it is likely that law enforcement assistance would be required.

- *Outer perimeter.* This is composed of surveillance or counter-sniper agents or teams (on the ground and possibly in the air), response cars, and uniformed law enforcement officers on static post assignments. The idea is that an attacker must first pass through this line of defense.

- *Middle perimeter.* This consists of EP specialists and possibly police officers. Some agents would be assigned to checkpoints at corridors, doors, and elevators; would operate magnetometers at those checkpoints; and would conduct bomb sweeps. Other agents would guard the specific rooms and hallways the principal is expected to use.

- *Inner perimeter.* This is the last layer of defense protecting the principal from the outside. It consists exclusively of the principal's protective staffers, who arrange themselves around the principal in the ways discussed earlier.

Another aspect of the physical interaction between the principal and the protection specialist involves courtesy and thoughtfulness that go beyond ordinary good manners. An agent charged with protecting a principal who will be making a speech should see that all electrical wires are safely taped down on the path the principal will take to the dais. Tripping off a stage is no better for an executive than being knocked over by a mugger. The agent should constantly scan for little hazards and take a few extra steps to prevent them. The agent might feel it beneath his level of sophistication to spend time looking for such everyday sources of injury, but loose rugs, slippery steps, ice patches, inhaled smoke, and car crashes injure more people than muggers do. It is not a mark of success to protect an executive from agitated shareholders only to have him crack his head when he trips over a loose wire right at the EP specialist's feet.

Of course, this does not mean to suggest that the boss is clumsy. On the contrary, many protectees practice activities that require great agility and training—and their agents had better be able to keep up. If the principal likes to sail, the agent should know how to swim (of course, every agent should know how to swim), and maybe even how to sail. Likewise, an agent protecting an equestrian principal had better be able to ride a horse. It isn't necessary for an agent to master all the activities the principal participates in, but the agent has to be able to keep up.

Action vs. reaction

This is the time when all of the agent's instincts, training, and condition come together. When an attacker pulls a knife, fires a shot, rams the principal's car with his own, lunges at the principal, or makes some other clearly dangerous, aggressive move, there's no time for the agent to stop and ponder. In fact, it's amazing how quickly such an incident can arise and be played out. The whole sequence, from the agent's first sighting of the threat to evacuation of the principal, might take as little as four seconds. What makes the agent's task even more difficult is that he must react correctly the first time.

A good example of how fast an attack can happen and how fast the correct response must take place is the March 30, 1981, assassination attempt against President Reagan outside the Washington Hilton. John Hinckley fired six rounds in less than three seconds. On hearing the shots, Secret Service agent Jerry Parr reacted instinctively and pushed the President into a waiting limousine, which rushed to George Washington University Hospital. Many responses happened at once. In a matter of seconds, with no time to stop and think, some members of the protective detail shielded the President with their own bodies, others pushed him into the car, and others surrounded and piled on top of the assailant; and the "wheel man" knew where to take the wounded President. These quick reactions come from a degree of mental and physical rehearsal that had created the possibility of a conditioned (that is, automatic) response. This episode was a classic example of "cover and evacuate."

When an attack occurs, what should happen is that the agent reacts immediately. He can do so because he has been scanning and calculating, is in the proper physical position with respect to the principal (standing nearby or driving the car), and has mentally rehearsed the several actions that he must take in the next few seconds. The alternative is to stand there confused, after the incident, wondering what all the commotion was about.

Note that having to take these emergency actions—even if the agent performs them successfully—indicates a partial failure already: the principal should be kept out of harm's way as much as possible. Allowing a close-range incident to occur is riding much too close to the edge of disaster. The lifeguard who rescues a drowning child is only a partial hero if it was his job to keep swimmers from going out too deep in the first place.

One accepted action chain consists of four main parts. The short, memorizable names for those parts are *arm's reach*, *sound off*, *cover*, and *evacuate*. How would that action chain work in an incident where a man draws a handgun and points it at the principal? *Arm's reach* defines the agent's first reaction. It is the point at which he decides whether to go after the attacker or shield the principal from harm. Basically, if the attacker is within an arm's reach of the agent, the agent should move to immobilize him. If the attacker is beyond an arm's reach of the agent, the agent should move to cover the principal.

If the agent decides to go after the shooter, he should push the shooter's gun down and away and then use hand-to-hand techniques to subdue him. There are several reasons to push the gun down instead of up: it is easier to hold something down than to hold it up, and pushing the gun down aims it at less-lethal targets, such as the floor or someone's legs or feet, while raising it may end up pointing it at someone's head. The best approach is to neutralize the weapon first, then the attacker.

Another factor that influences the decision about whether to reach for the principal or subdue the attacker is the totality of other physical circumstances. For example, if several agents are guarding a principal, one would grab the principal and others would disarm the attacker. If there was only one EP specialist but the incident took place in the middle of a crowd of people, then the second step in this four-part action chain, *sound off*, might bring assistance from bystanders, who could grab the attacker while the agent shielded and evacuated the principal.

The second step, *sound off*, means shouting out "Gun!" or "Gun to the right!" or something similar. The message should state the type of weapon displayed and the direction, in relation to the protectee, from which it is coming. Sounding off tells other agents to spring into action and attempts to involve other people in the situation. This is something to shout, not whisper; if there are only a few seconds in which to evade the problem, there's no time for other agents or the public to respond, "Pardon me?"

Cover means something quite serious here. It isn't limited to finding cover, meaning a safe place for the agent and the principal to flee to. It primarily means that the agent has to cover the principal's body with his own—to be, as the English monarch's protective staffers phrase it, a "bullet-catcher."

If the decision is made not to disarm the attacker (because of distance or other factors) but instead to shield the principal, the agent moves immediately to cover him, with the agent's own body, from the impending attack. The object is not only to shield the principal but also to make him a smaller target. Shielding can be performed in several different ways and must be done immediately, without apology or explanation. One method is to grab the principal by the belt against his back and, pulling hard, simultaneously push down on his shoulders from the back—essentially, folding the protectee in half. Another method is to grab the lapel of the principal's suit, from the front, and pull him down to the floor. A third method, called the "cave-in," can be used when several EP specialists are working together to shield the principal— they simply cave in around the principal, falling on top of him and pulling him to the ground. However, bringing the principal to the ground presents some risk of injury. Therefore, it should be done only in situations where immediate evacuation is not possible.

Evacuate refers to the overriding need to get the principal out of danger. The difference between police or military personnel and executive protection specialists—that the former are supposed to pursue their opponents, while the latter are supposed to avoid their opponents—cannot be overemphasized. It's not a question of bravery; rather, it's a question of effectiveness in attaining one's goals. Stopping to fight an adversary when it would be quicker to dash out a side door is simply ineffective; it raises, not lowers, the odds that the principal will be injured.

In most cases, the protective detail should concentrate on shielding and removing the principal, leaving apprehension of the attacker to the police. There's a tactical reason, too, for not surrounding the attacker. Sun Tzu writes, "When you surround an army, leave an outlet free. This does not mean that the enemy is to be allowed to escape. The object is to make him believe that there is a road to safety, and thus prevent his fighting with the courage of despair."

Although much of the mental preparation, risk assessment, intelligence gathering, and projection of being a hard target may be considered part of the team's offense, on the physical level, executive protection is absolutely, solely defensive. From a legal standpoint, too, it is better to err on the side of restraint. The defensive approach—removing the principal as quickly as possible from danger—is much less risky legally than standing and fighting. If shooting is involved, the last thing a principal wants is for his protective staff to injure or kill an innocent bystander. Even if shooting is not involved, there's always the possibility of a misunderstanding. The presumed attacker may not be attacking but may simply be pushing through the crowd for an autograph. Wouldn't it better to have needlessly fled from the autograph-seeker than to have needlessly wrestled him to the ground in front of dozens of witnesses?

Assuming the threat is real, however, the key is to remove the principal immediately from the "kill zone," which is the area defined by a nine- to 12-foot radius around the principal. Most attacks are waged from within that small zone. Long guns or other stand-off weapons are rarely used in attacks against VIPs. Even political leaders, against whom the assassination threat level is typically high, are almost never attacked from a long distance. The assassination of President Kennedy is truly atypical. It is true that bombs may be controlled from a distance or even detonated at some distance from their target, outside the small kill zone; nevertheless, in practice most attacks are waged in close quarters.

The good news about that is that the protective agent doesn't need to move the principal miles from the scene of the attack; hustling the principal into another room or into a waiting car may be enough to escape the kill zone. The smoothest, most effective way to move the principal is to grab him by the belt (at the back) or by the back of the collar, shove his head downward (to shield it), and push him quickly out of danger. If the exit involves rushing into a waiting car, the agent will typically push the principal into the back seat and then lie on top of him to prevent injury and to force him to stay down low.

When an evacuation is necessary, the importance of advance surveys becomes obvious. It is essential that the agent know the layout of the facility. Inadequate preparation can result in tragic or embarrassing conclusions. The last thing the protective staff needs, when an incident arises, is confusion about where to go. No one wants to be in the position of having evacuated a protectee to a locked exit door or other dead end.

In all cases, but especially where a male EP specialist is protecting a female client, the two should discuss in advance the fact that the agent may have to grab the client bodily and even, as described, get uncomfortably close for a minute or two. In addition, no matter how formally or deferentially the executive normally likes to be treated by the EP specialist, there are times when the agent has to bark out a command. In those instances (active or imminent crises), the executive—and his family—should understand that following terse, forceful commands may be necessary for survival. When the agent shouts "Get down!", "Run to the car!", or "Slam on the brakes!", the principal should do so immediately and not take time to feel ill-treated.

The examples listed in this discussion of the *arm's reach-sound off-cover-evacuate* action chain involved a close-range shooting attempt.

For most protectees the risk of assassination is low, but many other rather common threats—mugging, attacks by disgruntled employee, etc.—require the same protective measures.

Protection and service

Another quirky aspect of working the principal is this: protection service is both protection and service. That means the agent, although performing a professional service, must also perform other tasks that come along. Some of those tasks have a practical significance to the protective effort. For example, when the principal and the agent are traveling, the agent can reduce the principal's exposure to possible danger or undesired encounters by taking care of hotel check-in and making arrangements for luggage handling in advance. That way, the principal can walk briskly through the lobby, board an elevator, and arrive quickly at the safety of his room.

Other tasks, however, may seem a little humble, probably beneath the agent's real dignity, but nevertheless part of the job because the agent, more than anyone else, is there. Such tasks might include taking care of the principal's pets—even cleaning up after them—so the principal won't have to take them out for a walk in an unsecured area, or even just because the principal doesn't want to do it and the agent is the only other person around. The job of executive protection clearly contains an element of facilitation, and some of that involves freeing the executive from undesired tasks that consume his valuable time.

What the Principal and Agent Would Like to Tell Each Other But Usually Don't

Communication between the principal and the agent was discussed earlier, yet there are certain comments that often go unsaid in the relationship and that become awkward points. Agents typically show deference to their protectees and hesitate to make comments that might be taken as offensive. Nevertheless, some of those comments are important to the protective effort. One is, "Let me drive." In most cases, it is best for the agent to drive and the principal to sit in the right rear seat. The agent can watch for dangers, is usually trained in evasive driving, and can relieve the principal of responsibility for traffic tickets and other such problems. Meanwhile, the principal can make good use of the travel time to work or rest and can more readily duck down low in case of an attack.

Another comment many agents would like to make is, "Don't draw me into long conversations." On most public buses, signs warn passengers not to talk to the drivers; the drivers have a lot on their minds and need to concentrate. EP specialists have much more on their minds than just driving and can do their jobs more effectively if they are not engaged in long, complicated conversations. An EP specialist makes an expensive chatting buddy—a distracting conversation with the agent could cost the client his physical safety.

Of course, clients of EP specialists have a few matters they would like to point out, too. One is, "Be there when I need you; don't be there when I don't." That's a tall order, of course, a little like Sun Tzu's admonition to make no mistakes. Still, it's a standard to reach for, like the seemingly invisible butler who refills your glass before you knew it was empty and who then disappears, or the parent who lets the child play and climb freely, materializing only when the child falls and needs to be caught.

Another message from clients to EP specialists is, "Don't embarrass me." The ways in which an agent should conduct himself in business settings were discussed earlier; the point here is that some clients really do worry about being embarrassed. A good EP specialist gives the client confidence that nothing untoward will happen. An attentive agent notices whether he is often asked to stay some distance from the principal or remain in the car and then asks himself, "Is it me?" If so, he upgrades his appearance and behavior as required.

The Big Question

The big question for a prospective EP specialist is this: "Are you willing to risk your life to save the principal, even if that requires deliberately putting yourself in the way of a bullet?" That's an important question, and the answer has to be "yes." However, the question—in isolation—doesn't paint the whole picture. No EP specialist wants to get killed; after all, while executive protection is for many agents a calling, it is also a job, and no salary is a good deal if it requires getting killed.

What helps all of this make sense is the context and degree of risk. No one walks in off the street, unskilled and inexperienced, and becomes an EP specialist. Undertaking that work is an evolution, usually from law enforcement, security, or the military. Along the way the person has learned to accept the risks—or else has rejected them and chosen another line of work. It's not a question of wanting to be shot; it's a matter of accepting the risks that accompany the agent's chosen career.

While the risk of death may seem high, it is not as high as the risk in many other occupations. According to the U.S. Department of Health and Human Services, the industries with by far the highest annual rates of occupational fatalities are mining (31.9 deaths annually per 100,000 workers); construction (25.6); transportation, communication, and public utilities (23.3); and agriculture, forestry, and fishing (18.3).[30]

The occupational fatality rate for EP specialists is unknown. In addition, the risk would have to vary substantially with the type of client protected and the place where the work is performed. (In other words, there's a big difference between protecting a client in Cincinnati and protecting one in Bogota.) It's worth noting that the large occupational group most similar to EP specialists—police—isn't anywhere near the top of the fatality list. The job of executive protection has its risks, but they aren't outlandishly high.

---

[30] *Fatal Injuries to Workers in the United States, 1980-1989: A Decade of Surveillance (National Profile)* (Washington: U.S. Department of Health and Human Services, 1993), p. xiii.

He who exercises no forethought but makes light
of his opponents is sure to be captured by them.
Sun Tzu

Chapter 4
The Advance

The opponents of which Sun Tzu speaks need not be people only—they can be circumstances, logistics, and physical conditions. To enter a situation blindly, to move the principal from a safe position to a position where safety is unknown, is to take unnecessary risk. The alternative to proceeding with uncertainty is to undertake an executive protection practice know as the advance survey, or the advance.

What is an advance? Its definition is the totality of an EP specialist's efforts to learn about an executive's route and destination and all the details that affect the trip and the stay. Its practical effect is a *preemptive strike against confusion and exposure.* Advance work requires that a member of the protection team actually go to the destination and prepare the way. However, advance work does not apply solely to long-distance travel. Any location that the client intends to visit should be advanced—even if it's just across the street. An agent who has done a proper advance has a much better chance of keeping his protectee—and himself—out of trouble. Further, when a threatening event occurs, he knows how to remove the client from the situation, whom to summon for help, and where to get medical or any other type of assistance, depending on the situation.

Experienced EP specialists strongly emphasize the importance of advance work. When two protective agents are available, it is almost always best to assign one to conduct an advance and one to accompany the principal, as opposed to assigning both to accompany the principal. Advance work is that important.

Besides its direct importance in accomplishing the protective mission, advance work has a side benefit—client appeal. While some aspects of protective service may occasionally seem burdensome or costly to clients, advance work is a client pleaser. Why? Advance work saves the client time and trouble. A well-done advance saves the client from the annoyance of driving around searching for the hotel, looking for a parking space, waiting to check in, finding the hotel room, determining whether room service is open, entering an auditorium through the wrong door, looking around for the correct seat on the dais, enduring airport customs lines, waiting for tables at restaurants, etc. Being spared those annoyances makes the client's life more enjoyable, reduces his exposure to threats, and frees him to work more or relax more. Increasing the client's available working time is an especially important cost justification in private sector protection.

A case in point comes from the British gossip magazine *The Tattler*. Describing recent VIP sightings on the island of St. Barthélemy in the French Antilles, the editor writes: [31]

> During dinner at Maya's, the island's most branché restaurant, the talk was of recent visitors such as Giorgio Armani, Romeo Gigli, and a contingent of rich, young Italians;...Brad Pitt and Gwyneth Paltrow, who were surreptitiously photographed starkers by paparazzi lurking in the hills near the exclusive hotel Le Toiny; and [well-to-do executive Mr. X...], who came with his wife and a man called Bob. This Bob arrived everywhere in advance of his boss, surveyed restaurants, and placed all of [Mr. X's] orders. Then there was the embattled TV chat-show host David Letterman, who stayed shut up in his villa like a ghost in the fame machine, making it clear what he needs next Christmas: a Bob of his own.

---

[31] Michael Gross, *The Tatler*, January 1996, p. 104.

The evangelist Matthew, quoting Isaiah, wrote, "Prepare a way for the Lord, make his paths straight."[32] No one should grant executives divine status, but it is a time-honored practice to labor to make an important person's journey and visit go as smoothly as possible—to "let every valley be filled in, every mountain and hill be laid low."[33] Advance work—a key part of facilitation—is a very valuable service that the EP specialist can provide his client.

The advance has many parallels in other realms of life. If an executive's overseas business trip is the EP specialist's exam, then advance work is a semester of diligent study (not all-night cramming). If the trip is a play, advance work is rehearsal. If the trip is a leap, advance work is the "look before." Most simply, conducting advance work is like turning on the lights before entering a room.

Protective Intelligence

Chapter 1, Threat Assessment, distinguished between risk analysis and protective intelligence. The former is more general, looking at types of threats and the risks they pose to the client, whereas the latter is more specific, examining the details of a particular trip or activity. Further, risk analysis focuses on the client (who he is, who wants to attack him), while protective intelligence focuses on the client's immediate surroundings and imminent circumstances. To clarify the relationship, then, risk analysis and protective intelligence gathering are the two legs on which a protective effort stands, and advance work is the most important means of gathering protective intelligence.

The difficulty of obtaining reliable intelligence about potential adversaries and about the principal's destination and all the circumstances and conditions between the departure and arrival points is enormous. Here the military strategist Karl von Clausewitz, who wrote at the beginning of the 19th century, has much to offer: "Many intelligence reports in war are contradictory;

---

[32] Mt. 3:3; Is. 40:3.
[33] Is. 40:4.

even more are false, and most are uncertain."[34] He also observes, "The textbooks agree, of course, that we should only believe reliable intelligence, and should never cease to be suspicious, but what is the use of such feeble maxims?"[35] There are only two ways in which an EP specialist can confidently obtain reliable information: (1) developing it himself, firsthand, or (2) using known, trusted members of his resource network—that is, people who live and work in the area to be visited and who are aware of the general goals of protective operations. Generic information about the site, gathered from a book or from phone chats with casual contacts who are not committed to the protective effort, is not good enough. What's needed is an actual, physical advance.

With the advance knowledge that comes from gathering protective intelligence, the EP specialist can greatly reduce the number of surprises he encounters and the number of opportunities to make a mistake. In theory, moving an executive from Point A to Point B is easy; in practice it is not. Here again Clausewitz's experience in war highlights the challenge: [36]

> Everything in war is very simple, but the simplest thing is difficult. The difficulties accumulate and end by producing a kind of friction that is inconceivable unless one has experienced war. Imagine a traveler who late in the day decides to cover two more stages before nightfall. Only four or five hours more, on a paved highway with relays of horses: it should be an easy trip. But at the next station he finds no fresh horses, or only poor ones; the country grows hilly, the road bad, night falls, and finally after many difficulties he is only too glad to reach a resting place with any kind of primitive accommodation. It is much the same in war. Countless minor incidents—the kind you can never really foresee—combine to lower the general level of performance, so that one always falls far short of the intended goal.

---

[34] Karl von Clausewitz, *On War* (Princeton: Princeton University Press, 1976), p. 117.

[35] Ibid.

[36] Ibid., p. 119.

A proper advance reduces this phenomenon of countless little difficulties by endeavoring to eliminate most of them in advance. Von Clausewitz call the phenomenon "friction." Advance work, like "greasing the skids," reduces that friction.

Principles of Advance Work

Like other forms of intelligence gathering, protective intelligence gathering is heavy on the details. Hundreds, if not thousands, of little facts must be uncovered and then stored in the protective agent's mind and archives.

The types of data to collect for various types of advances will be listed in some detail below; it is enough right now to say that the scope of data collection can seem staggering—and perhaps ridiculous—unless the purpose is understood. Here is an example, borrowed from specialists in advance work, of the types of information an advance agent should gather before a principal undertakes the simple act of going out to eat at a restaurant: date and time of survey; survey preparer; directions to restaurant; whether reservations are required; restaurant's name, address, telephone number, and fax number; name of manager and maître d'; entrances and exits, including emergency exits; location of rest rooms; location of telephones; seating arrangements (convenient and safe for both client and agent; examination of where other high-profile clientele are typically seated); seating capacity; menu and wine list; quality of service; dress code; methods of payment and arrangements to have check paid by agent; availability of private rooms; availability of smoking and nonsmoking sections; parking arrangements (valet, self, or street); other events the restaurant is planning on the day of the client's visit; and name, address, and telephone number of nearest rescue squad, hospital, and police department.[37]

Is that level of information-gathering really necessary? Won't the client end up hemmed in by it? The answers are yes and no, respectively, as an understanding of the reasons for advance work will show.

---

[37] Jerry Glazebrook and Larry Nicholson, *Executive Protection Specialist Handbook* (Kansas City: Varro Press, 1994), pp. 49-50.

The major reasons for conducting an advance are these:

- to reduce the principal's exposure
- to establish a safe area for him
- to preserve his valuable time for more important matters

A good advance *reduces the principal's exposure* by smoothing logistics. If, as mentioned earlier, hotel check-in, billing, baggage handling, parking, and other matters are worked out by the advance agent, then the client can exit his car at the hotel's front door, walk straight through the lobby to the elevators, and arrive quickly at his room. Similarly, if an advance agent has scouted out the route to the client's speaking engagement and properly studied the meeting location, then the agent accompanying the client can lead him into the building through a side door if that is necessary to avoid a hostile crowd at the front door or can take different steps to avoid other unfavorable conditions or circumstances, as recommended by the advance agent. Obviously, these improvements over flying blind keep the principal out of many potentially undesirable encounters and conditions.

A good advance *establishes a safe area* before the client arrives at a new location. In the hotel example, the advance agent reconnoiters the hotel in general and the principal's room in particular, working through a security checklist to make sure nothing is forgotten, in order to ensure a safe haven before the principal ever sets foot inside the hotel. In the speaking engagement example, the advance agent creates or ensures a security zone—the dais, perhaps—by checking for hazards, obstacles, and inconveniences, and removing or working around them, before the client arrives.

A contemporary principle of public safety states that, at least for persons who are not poor, and despite the dangers that lurk on the streets, safe movement is achieved by moving from one private, secured zone or bubble to the next—rather than relying on the forces of law and order to make entire cities safe. For example, a woman leaves her home (which is protected by a security system) in a locked car, drives through the guarded gate at the entrance to her subdivision, travels the highways without opening her car's windows, and parks in her company's guarded garage. If her car breaks down en route, she uses her cellular phone to call her automobile club. That principle is congruent with executive protection, and diligent advance work reduces even further the risks involved by working to eliminate identifiable risks en route and at the destination before the client gets there.

To the extent possible, executive protection keeps the principal in a protective bubble. The bubble is flexible and transparent, but it is still the primary safety zone. Travel, movement, activities— these are instances where the principal may not be able to be kept in that bubble. Therefore, careful EP specialists minimize the time he spends outside the bubble. They do so by not leaving him standing around in unsecured areas and by preparing a suitable security bubble at his destination.

A good advance *preserves the client's valuable time* by eliminating unnecessary waiting time. In the hotel example, the client has no need to stand at the front desk while hotel staffers process his paperwork. In the speaking engagement example, his driver will detour around the traffic jam that the advance agent has warned about and spare the client the annoyance of being stuck in a car for hours. In both cases, aside from the benefits to safety, the advance work has saved the protectee time and relieved him of annoying, costly distraction.

The examples above show that, to answer the questions above, yes, this level of information gathering really is necessary. There's no way to gain the potential benefits of advance work without conducting a detailed advance. And, no, the client doesn't end up hemmed in by the extensive research that an advance requires. On the contrary, advance work liberates him by speeding him conveniently through the world.

A further question arises, however: doesn't all this advance work take too much time and effort? Here the answer is no. There's no denying that it takes some time and effort. However, it's not too much time and effort for two reasons: the benefits outweigh the costs, and over time the advance effort can be streamlined by the advance agent's general experience, by his familiarity with the sites to be visited, and by the notes kept from earlier visits to those sites. Those notes, in fact, are so valuable that every protective operation should establish a formal advance file, where advance surveys and follow-up notes from previous trips can be stored for future reference.

How to Perform an Advance

Although the specific bits of data that the advance agent must obtain differ depending on whether he is advancing a hotel stay, an out-of-town trip, local travel, or any other activity of the client, the general method is the same. First of all, the agent needs a few things before beginning the advance. He needs an energetic, inquisitive, and persistent disposition. At the advance site, the agent cannot count on the local contact to point out all potential hazards and gather all the information the advance agent needs. Rather, the agent needs to reach out, ask questions, clarify vague answers, and speculate about potential problems and solutions, handling matters professionally but firmly. The whole point is to resolve uncertainties, prevent logistical difficulties, and preempt hazards *before* the principal arrives. The benefit of an advance is lost if the agent, in response to lack of cooperation from hotel staff, says to himself, "Well, we'll just worry about that later. There probably won't be any problems."

Before actually going to the site, the advance agent should have a copy of or knowledge of the principal's schedule for the day he will be visiting; background materials concerning the scheduled movement, such as copies of letters of invitation, copies of RSVP letters from the principal, maps provided by the host, admission cards or tickets, itineraries, and any other relevant pieces of information; previous advance sheets that were completed and filed for the same location; and the name of the contact person on-site. It may also be useful to bring along a Polaroid camera to photograph any unusual features of the location so the principal and protective staff will have no surprises.

Once he has collected those materials, the advance agent should telephone the site contact person and arrange a meeting. That way, the agent can be sure to be able to meet with someone who has the authority and knowledge to help him with the necessary arrangements. Much time is likely to be wasted if the agent simply shows up at a hotel with a list of special requests—and no one is able to help him. On arriving at the site, the agent should introduce himself to the contact person, reiterate the need for his visit, hand the contact person a business card to make subsequent communications easier, and set to work.

Typically, an advance agent works from a checklist. Checklists are important, in fact probably necessary; however, they are only tools in advance work and are not the whole of the process. An agent might wish to use a checklist as a starting point or as a wrap-up, the idea being to make sure no obvious points were overlooked. But the entire time the agent is working to complete the checklist, he should be envisioning the principal's arrival, stay, and departure and asking "What if?" Checklists help an agent remember, but they don't substitute for judgment.

The "What if?" process is central to thinking universally about the protective environment. It is an especially important mental exercise for the beginning protective specialist, who will find himself asking the question more often than a veteran agent, for whom many of the answers to the "What if" questions are already a part of his mental landscape. As in any profession, experience replaces the need to question everything all the time with a confidence and certainty born of having done all this before. Nevertheless, most veteran advance people still use the "What if?" scenario as a fundamental method to close the gaps that inevitably open.

Advance Work in Various Settings

Executive protection in each of the following situations consists of advance work, on-site protection, and follow-up activities. This chapter discusses the advance and follow-up work that must be done for each situation; later chapters discuss on-site protection.

Speeches, meetings, luncheons, and social functions

Anytime the principal must make or attend a speech, conduct or attend a major meeting, or participate in a luncheon, the agent should look at it as a venture into the unknown. What are the building and the general site like? How do we get in and out? Who is attending the event? What activities are planned? What resources (restrooms, telephones, medical help, police response) are available at the site? Adventures into unknown territory may be exciting for explorers and tourists, but for EP specialists the unknown is something to avoid. Therefore, if it is at all possible to send an advance agent to survey the location personally, it should be done. Ideally, the advance person would use a map to plot the various routes that could be taken to the site and then actually drive them at the maximum legal speed, writing down the elapsed time between major checkpoints. He would then examine the entrances and exits at the site, looking for choke points, hazards, and other relevant conditions and analyzing their proximity to the parking area.

The agent would also find out who works in the building, who owns it, what goes on in any vacant parts of the building, what the parking options are, what potential hazards might be encountered in the neighborhood of the site, whether IDs or access passes are required for entrance, whom to contact for coordination with any private security staff on-site, whether firearms may be brought into the building by the principal's protective staff or other visitors to the building, etc. The agent should also, shortly before the scheduled visit, ask utility companies about any work planned during the time of travel or visit and check with the police about any scheduled parades or fairs that might interfere with travel.

Of course, a certain amount of discretion is required during all this information-gathering—it would be counterproductive to give absolutely everyone advance knowledge that a VIP is coming to the site on a certain date at a certain time. Moreover, the advance agent needs to display an appropriate demeanor. Unless he is a law enforcement officer, his only authority rests on the reputation or notoriety of his principal and on the agent's own way with people. While most people want to cooperate in an effort to keep a VIP secure, many may never even have heard of a particular principal. Therefore, a degree of friendly persuasion and salesmanship is essential. The agent must not bully his way through an advance, for his actions will reflect on the principal. Willing cooperation is the goal.

The agent can then return to home base and share his findings with the other protective agents. When it is time to take the principal to the site, the advance agent can take one of three positions: (1) accompanying the protection team in transit, (2) preceding the team by just enough of a margin that he can warn them of hazards they are approaching (traffic jams, road construction, protest marches, etc.), or (3) awaiting the team at the meeting site. The third option is by far the best. Truly, the advance is so important that it must be conducted no matter what, even on short notice, in which case the second option above might be all that is feasible.

If only one agent protects a principal, it may not possible for that agent to conduct the advance himself. Doing so might mean leaving the principal unprotected for too long. In that case, it may be possible for the EP specialist to hire out the advance work to a trusted freelancer. A less desirable alternative is to use the telephone to contact a site manager and discuss the protective effort's needs—a lot can be accomplished that way.

Commuting and pedestrian travel

The advance work that affects regular commuting by automobile and such pedestrian excursions as after-dinner walks or fitness running consists of actually traversing the routes to be traveled. Although they may cover familiar ground, regular routes must be reconnoitered thoroughly and routinely because they account for the majority of most clients' travel time. At a minimum, several alternative commuting routes will be continually scrutinized and contingency plans drawn up for potential emergencies en route. Ideally, an advance agent would drive the route, preceding the principal's car by several minutes so that he could warn of any problems along the way.

Among the less obvious matters to check out on an advance are the traffic levels at different times of day and different days of the week; scheduled drawbridge openings (and contacts for how to find out about unscheduled ones); railroad crossings that could hold up the client's drive; and, overseas, what official detour signs look like.

Out-of-town travel

Overseas travel presents probably the greatest challenge to an advance agent. Even domestic out-of-town travel is challenging to advance properly. Details about an agent's own city or country may come naturally (where's the airport, what's a good hospital), but similar information about other locales must be earned, sometimes with difficulty. Additional hurdles exist when the destination is in a foreign country, where differences in language, laws, and customs may present significant barriers to the advance agent's research and understanding.

Although the labor involved in properly advancing an overseas trip may be formidable, at least the facts learned serve a dual purpose. They help the executive protection staff protect the principal, and they give the principal a familiarity with the destination that may help him in his dealings there.

The actual advance for an overseas trip consists of the specific arrangements for the topics discussed above: meeting rooms, restaurants, offices, hotels, automobiles, airports, airplanes, etc. What is different about advance work for an overseas trip is the need to develop a portfolio of country-specific information. Sometimes called the "pre-advance" to distinguish it from the on-site practice runs that constitute a real advance, that portfolio becomes a tool for the protection team and can be used to brief the principal on what to expect.

The portfolio covers such topics as these: country's physical characteristics, natural resources, relationship to U.S., capsule history, religious practices, language, local customs and laws, women's concerns (modesty and restrictions on movement), political parties, major allies, sources of foreign aid, practice of spying on visitors; visa requirements; inoculation requirements; sanitation and hygiene; English-speaking doctors who were trained in the U.S., Britain, or other countries with high medical training standards; money exchange; in-country availability of special medications (especially any controlled substances, which should not ordinarily be transported abroad); medical evacuation arrangements and contacts; special sensitivity about cameras; emergency contacts (embassy, consulate, hospitals); terrorist groups active there; and local crime.

Other matters the EP specialist should research include these: weather; terrain; accommodating special interests of the principal (such as golf or tennis); political problems, strikes, political anniversaries (may be occasions for terrorist activity or riots); and holidays. These portfolio items can be learned through research with the U.S. federal government, in-country contact persons, libraries, on-line sources, or intelligence firms that specialize in providing broad-based country briefings.

Advance work regarding hotels, airports and airplanes (whether private or commercial), and chauffeur services tends to cluster around out-of-town travel. Although much work must still be done after the principal arrives at or begins to use those facilities, much must also be performed in advance.

Hotels. The hotel advance is vitally important. Because the executive will eat and sleep there, security at the hotel must be as good as security at the executive's home. Because he may well conduct business there, security must be as good as the security at the executive's office. But several factors combine to make hotel security especially challenging:

- Hotels are much less private than residences and offices.
- Word of the principal's impending visit may very easily leak out.
- The principal's protective staff has much less control over a hotel environment than it does over his home or office.

The extensive on-site measures that must be taken to ensure security at hotels are discussed in Chapter 7. The advance work that must be done before a protective team brings its principal to stay at a hotel is equally extensive. It would take several pages to list everything an advance agent must do to prepare the way for his principal's hotel stay. For a fuller presentation of the key points of advances in a wide range of settings, it is more efficient to read a book like the *Executive Protection Specialist Handbook* by Jerry Glazebrook and Larry Nicholson (Shawnee Mission, Kansas: Varro Press, 1994).

The following is a list of only the major categories of tasks, including information-gathering, meetings, and physical inspections: before visiting, gather all available facts about the hotel, dates of visit, and key contact persons, and bring along a still or video camera; once there, meet with the manager to make special arrangements and obtain names of secondary contacts (bell captain, maître d', etc.); meet with director of security, doorman, bell captain, maître d', valet parking manager, and others at same time of day at which principal will be arriving (and make sure those same people will be on duty when the principal arrives); conduct physical inspection of hotel layout and safety features; determine range of services offered by hotel; gather information about hotel restaurant and recreational facilities; and determine location and phone numbers of nearest fire department, police department, and rescue squad.

After all that, here's the punchline: a thorough protective team advances *two* hotels in each city to be visited—in case one suddenly becomes unavailable (due to fire) or unsuitable (due to changed conditions in the area around the hotel, such as civic unrest). Note that the hotel work just described applies only to the advance; much more remains to be done once the principal arrives.

Commercial Airports and Aircraft. A number of arrangements can be made in advance that will smooth the principal's air travel and reduce his exposure to risk. The advance agent should, for example, make arrangements for special parking as close as possible to the passenger screening checkpoint, so that the principal will have minimal exposure to other passengers on his way to the gate. The agent can also make arrangements for the principal to stay in the VIP lounge associated with the airline being used. Such lounges, located on the secure side of the screening checkpoint, provide a safe, comfortable, and relatively controllable area in which to await the flight.

The advance agent can also make arrangements for the principal to board the aircraft according to the method the protection team thinks most suitable. One option is to board first, thereby avoiding the crush of other passengers at the entrance to the Jetway. Another option is to board last so that the minimum number of passengers will pass by and notice the principal on the way to their seats. Whichever method the protection team chooses, these arrangements are best made in advance with a flight services representative.

Other matters for the advance agent to investigate are the obvious ones, such as the airport's exits, resources in case of emergency, and availability and location of facilities that the principal may wish to use (telephones, fax machines, computers, restaurants, book shops, etc.). It is a good idea to contact airport police or security staff for special assistance before arriving at the airport. As in the discussion of hotel advances, much remains to be done once the principal arrives at the airport and while he is in transit. That subject, too, is discussed in Chapter 7.

Scenario: A Well-Advanced Excursion

When all advance work has been performed properly, the trip should run as smoothly as a well-rehearsed play. Uncertainty and wasted time are reduced to a minimum. A well-advanced trip might run something like this example from the author's experience:

> In February 1990, I undertook a protection assignment with another EP specialist, Gordon Baer. We were awaiting the arrival of a principal from Europe who was attending a major equestrian event in Tampa. The client was staying at the Wyndham Harbor Island Hotel, a four-star, three-diamond property that sits on the Tampa Bay waterfront. The 12-story hotel had 300 rooms and all the amenities of a first-class establishment.
>
> The principal was the type of person who expected everything to go according to plan and nothing to be left to chance. Of course, we had no intention of leaving things to chance, and we constantly asked ourselves the question "What if?" We had worked together for years and were concentrating on the details, both checking and rechecking our advance. First, we completed the advance on the private air terminal at Tampa International Airport; we ran the primary and secondary routes; and we knew most of the choke points between the airport, hotel, equestrian event, and restaurants that we might be using during the principal's stay.

We then concentrated on the hotel. We reserved parking spaces for the principal's car and our follow-up vehicle. We walked all the corridors, located the fire exits, and determined the type of fire suppression equipment in use at the hotel. We met with the in-house security personnel and walked the outside grounds.

The principal arrived by private aircraft. After he cleared U.S. customs, we did our normal ramp-side pickup and proceeded to the hotel. We has already registered the principal into his room, so we took him directly to the 12ᵗʰ floor executive suite. He was tired from his overseas travel and decided to stay in after ordering room service. Everything had gone as planned.

Next to the principal's bed we had placed two smoke masks, a panic alarm that was connected directly to my room, a 3x5 card that gave our room numbers, hotel security's phone number, and instructions for international dialing. A flashlight sat next to those items, along with a small "fire bag" containing duct tape, a cutting tool, directions on how to survive a hotel fire, and a plan of escape in case we were unable to reach the principal. Such items are routine for our clients.

We rechecked our security brief for the next day's activities and ate dinner in our rooms. My room was adjacent to the client's, and Gordon's was across from mine. As in the principal's room, in our rooms we had laid out emergency equipment at bedside. For each of us, that equipment included clothes, a portable telephone, a portable radio, a fire bag, a smoke mask, a map of emergency exits, a key to the principal's room, and a key to the other EP specialist's room. We wrapped for the evening about 10 minutes past midnight. The principal had arranged a 7:00 am wake-up call, and we planned to be moving by 6:00 am.

At exactly 3:07 am I was awakened by the PA system, blaring that there was an emergency in the hotel and that we should proceed calmly to the fire exits. (Remaining calm takes work—this is the moment when all your homework and training pay off.) I jumped into my clothes, grabbed my equipment, and summoned

Gordon on the portable radio. He was already in the hallway. Before I went out of my room, I grabbed the doorknob to see whether it was hot; it wasn't, so I cracked the door open and smelled for smoke. Since there wasn't any, I opened the door fully and saw that the hall seemed to be free of fire and smoke. To add to the excitement, the alarm kept sounding and the hallway lights were flashing on and off.

We proceeded to the principal's door, knocked, and announced ourselves. We opened the door with one of our duplicate keys and saw the principal in his bathrobe, standing by. We took our equipment and his fire bag, smoke mask, and briefcase, and proceeded out of the room. We went directly to the fire exit. After checking the door for heat, we began to descend the stairs. I saw only one resident look out his doorway to see what was the matter, and we were already on our way out of the hotel.

As we reached the 10th floor, we heard an announcement stating that it had been a false alarm and we could return to our rooms. I made the decision to continue down and out until we could verify the hotel's condition. That type of decision is a judgment call; I wanted the principal outside until I could make sure the environment was safe.

Once we were outside the hotel and at the sidewalk, we could hear fire equipment racing to the site. Gordon verified that it was a false alarm; some kids at a bachelor party had set off the water sprinkler on the ninth floor and sounded the alarm.

This incident was a false alarm, but it proved a good test of the advance work and training. The protection specialists knew where to go and what to do; they hadn't slipped away for a nightcap and left the principal unattended; and even though they were asleep, they were ready.

Follow-up Work

Earlier, this chapter asked whether conducting detailed advances is simply too much work. Two reasons were given for why it is not too much work. The first, that the benefits outweigh the costs, should be clear now. Proper advance work significantly improves the principal's security posture, eases his travels, and spares him much time that would otherwise be wasted. The second reason was that over time the advance effort can be streamlined by the advance agent's general experience, by his familiarity with the sites to be visited, and by the notes kept from earlier visits to those sites. That is where diligent follow-up, or post-advance work, pays dividends.

After a trip, the advance agent should compile a report of pertinent facts he may be able to use again. The follow-up report should note the dates of the trip, destination, purpose of trip, names of security personnel who were involved, ground and air transportation details with contact names and numbers, problems encountered, principals involved, lodging details and contacts, emergency phone numbers, maps and site surveys, and weather experienced.

One more follow-up duty remains. The agent should take care to thank the many contacts who helped him on the trip. Besides being a sign of good manners, which will reflect well on the principal, thank-you notes or letters pave the way for future cooperation and assistance. An EP specialist who protects a celebrity might arrange for autographed photos to be sent to persons—such as drivers, hotel staff, or airline personnel—who helped during the advance work and the actual trip. In other cases, thank-you letters signed by the principal work well.

Think how different it is to be greeted at your destination by someone who knows his way around than it is to stumble around unfamiliar territory on your own. That advantage is what an advance agent can do for a protective operation. Doing something for the first time is always difficult and uncertain. Fortunately, for a principal whose protective staff has done the proper advance work, no time is the first time.

Again, advance work is the equivalent of sending someone ahead to light the lamps. It is one more way in which an EP specialist reduces the unknown. As Samuel Johnson wrote, "He is no wise man who will quit a certainty for an uncertainty."[38]

---

[38] Samuel Johnson, *The Idler* (1758).

*By altering his arrangements and changing his
plans, the skillful general keeps the enemy
without definite knowledge. By shifting his
camp and taking circuitous routes, he prevents
the enemy from anticipating his purpose.*
Sun Tzu

Chapter 5
Automobile Security

It's the rare executive who doesn't spend a good deal of time in
cars—whether his own, his corporation's, or a transportation
company's. He may commute to an office; travel to airports; ride
to meetings and other business activities; and then, after work,
motor to social events. During all those expeditions, the executive
faces a much higher risk of attack or injury than he does in the office or at home. Not only are accident rates surprisingly high, but
most deliberate attacks on protectees occur during transportation—typically car travel. The *amount of time* the client spends in
cars dictates the EP specialist's concern for a pleasant, productive
ride for the client. The *exposure to various dangers* dictates the EP
specialist's concern for a safe and secure ride for the client. Therefore, the intelligent management of auto travel is one of an EP
specialist's larger responsibilities.

Why make a fuss about car travel? Isn't driving an ordinary,
everyday activity? Yes, but it's an ordinary, everyday—and usually
unavoidable—activity that is much more dangerous than one cares

to admit. In 1994, motor vehicle accidents resulted in deaths at a rate of 16.5 per 100,000 population,[39] equating to 43,000 deaths. That's roughly twice the homicide rate. Moreover, those figures do not include the 2.1 million disabling injuries from motor vehicle crashes. By contrast, fire, another familiar danger, caused death at a rate of 1.6 per 100,000—only one-tenth the rate of deaths attributable to car crashes. The major diseases present greater risks than auto travel, but EP specialists have little control over those risks. Among all non-disease causes of death, both intentional (homicide) and unintentional (various types of accidents), motor vehicle crashes present by far the greatest risk.

The other risk faced during driving—that related to the principal's exposure to attack—is worth examining also. One source found, using a proprietary data base, that 37 percent of terrorist attacks against principals were waged while the victims were in their vehicles.[40] As Chapter 1, Threat Assessment, points out, not every principal is a likely target of terrorism. But add to that danger the threat of carjacking, random gunfire, criminal opportunity, and bombing, and motor vehicle travel becomes a risk factor worth some thoughtful countermeasures.

For an executive, what is a car? What are its purposes? Obviously, it's a means of transportation. It's also, for some clients, an office, a social setting, a sleeping compartment, and a living room. For the EP specialist, therefore, the car is both a zone that needs protecting and, fortunately, a protective device in itself. This chapter examines the many responsibilities an EP specialist has in relation to that multipurpose device, the car.

Selecting a Car

Before comfort control, route security, performance driving, and emergency response, there is, at bottom, the car itself. In what kind of automobile should the principal be transported? If the principal regularly travels in his own vehicle, the EP specialist may

---

[39] *Accident Facts* (Itaska, Ill.: National Safety Council, 1995), p. 2.

[40] Anthony Scotti, in R. L. Oatman, *Executive Protection Resource Manual* (Towson, Md.: R. L. Oatman & Associates, Inc., 1995), Ch. 1, p. 2.

not have much influence over the type of car chosen. If a company car has already been purchased, the same may be true. But when the agent does have a say in vehicle selection—for example, when the principal or his company is preparing to buy a new car or when the protective operation rents a car for use out of town—there are a few factors to consider.

For the most part, big is good, up to a limit. A large car provides several advantages:

- a high degree of riding comfort
- generous interior space
- great protective bulk
- a powerful engine

The first characteristic allows the principal to work or rest in the vehicle. The latter three characteristics provide definite protective advantages. Space gives the agent a place to push the client to (the floor) in case of an attack and allows other agents room in which to scramble or, in extreme cases, room from which to fire weapons. Bulk increases bumping and ramming ability and provides greater mass for crash protection, and a powerful engine, obviously, improves getaway ability.

Any car chosen should also have several convenience and safety features that double as security features: electric locks, electric windows, anti-lock brakes, locking gas cap, mobile phone, and an exhaust pipe protected at the end with a screen or other device to prevent deliberate clogging from the outside. The car should also have an alarm system.

Another device to consider is one of the new emergency response systems that summon help and pinpoint the car's location for responders by use of a global positioning system (GPS) and cellular telephones.[41] Some of these systems, which include panic alarms, theft protection, local navigation, and on-line tracking and assistance, may be of more use to an executive who insists on traveling alone than to a full-fledged executive protection team.

---

[41] One example is the ADT Security Services, Inc., cellular/GPS car security system, which provides car tracking, theft protection, emergency police notification, and other assistance. ADT can be reached at (561) 988-3600.

Also potentially useful is a system for starting the car from a distance. One such system provides a remote control device that can be used to start the car's engine, turn on its lights, and activate various accessories (such as the heater, air conditioning, or radio). If an explosive device has been set to detonate when the engine is started or an accessory is activated, it's certainly better to be standing at some distance from the car than to be seated in it when the bomb goes off.[42]

Typical car models that many EP specialists prefer include the Lincoln Town Car, Ford Crown Victoria, Chevrolet Suburban, Range Rover, Jeeps, and larger BMW and Mercedes models. Use of such cars as opposed to limousines holds several advantages: they stand out less, rather than trumpeting the message "Here's a juicy target," and they are much more practical than limos for evasive driving.

For some protectees, armored cars are the best choice. Typically, such cars are larger production models that have been modified with various types of reinforcement, shielding, and security features. Also typically, such cars carry a high price—ranging from $35,000 to $75,000 or more, plus the cost of the unmodified car itself. Because of the price, it makes sense to recommend an armored car only if the threat assessment concludes one is essential. Even if that assessment concludes an armored car is not required for daily use, however, it behooves the agent to know the facts about such vehicles. Why? If the principal plans to travel to a city or event where the threat level is unusually high, it might be necessary to use an armored car temporarily, and the agent has a responsibility to understand all equipment he uses.[43] If the agent is driving such a car and an attack begins, he needs to know how much protection the car gives him, and against which types of weapons; what security features (such as run-flat tires) are at his disposal; and how to drive evasively or ram a blockade in such a heavy vehicle.

---

[42] One such system is the LA-Z-*START* remote auto starter from C&A Control Systems, Inc., 4522 Doris Circle, Knoxville, TN 37918. Phone (615) 922-2148.

[43] Note that renting an armored car is problematic. Among other reasons, there's no way to know whether the armoring still meets the specifications.

An armored car typically provides more than an armored barrier to gunfire, offering a range of other security features that are just as important. Armoring consists of supplemental panels in the doors, roof, and floor and both forward and aft of the passenger compartment (armoring materials include ballistic aluminum, ceramic composites, and other lightweight, exotic materials); reinforced posts, pillars, and rails throughout the car; and specially laminated glass-and-polycarbonate windshields and windows to protect the occupants of the car even if the exterior layer of glass is defeated. (See accompanying exploded diagram of the armoring for a Chevrolet Suburban.[44])

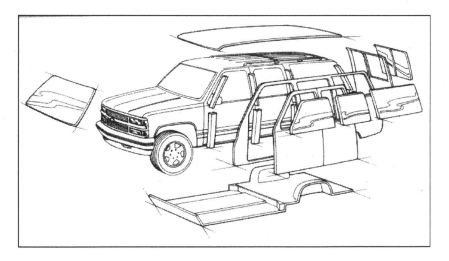

The armoring level is usually rated specifically for the type of weapon it is designed to resist and the anticipated threat. For example, the O'Gara-Hess & Eisenhardt Armoring Company[45] rates its vehicles from protection level II, which resists 9 mm, 124 grain, 1,400 foot-per-second handgun and automatic pistol fire, to level VI, which resists 7.62 mm x 51 mm, 150 grain, 2,625 fps armor-

[44] From O'Gara-Hess & Eisenhardt Armoring Company, 9113 LeSaint Drive, Fairfield, OH 45014. (800) 697-0307.

[45] The author, as an executive protection practitioner, has visited the company's plant, watched armoring taking place, and observed ballistic testing of the cars—and thinks the company's work is the best.

piercing rounds.[46] (See chart.) Armoring like that adds weight (up to 2,750 extra pounds), and weight significantly affects how a car drives. That's why an EP specialist needs some advance performance familiarity with such cars.

	Weapon Defeated	Ammunition Defeated
Levels of Protection		
O'Gara-Hess & Eisenhardt Armoring Company		
Level II	9mm handgun 9mm submachine gun	9mm by 19
Level III	.44 magnum handgun	.44 magnum
Level IV	AK-47 assault rifle	7.62mm ball by 39
Level V	M-16 A2 M-60 machine gun	5.56mm by 45 M80 ball
Level VI	M-60 machine gun	M-61 armor piercing

Other security features, beyond armoring, may include "run-flat" tires, which have a hard vinyl inner core; a foam-filled, anti-exploding fuel tank; a steel-reinforced front bumper designed for ramming; electric dead bolt locks; a dual battery system; an inside/outside intercom; a remote starter; a siren and public address system; and, for principals who face a high risk of kidnapping, a device inside the trunk for opening it. Only if the agent knows what features the car has and understands how to use them can he make intelligent decisions in a crisis. A protective agent should always remember the phrase "Use your resources." If he doesn't fully understand those resources, he can't fully utilize them.

A final note: an armored car buys the executive time but is not a genuine safe haven. The edge it provides is measured in minutes. It may withstand a number of shots, but if it is stopped and the attackers continue to assault it with firearms and sledgehammers, they will eventually get through. As one auto security expert writes, "Armored car or no armored car, keep it moving."[47]

---

[46] Product literature, O'Gara-Hess & Eisenhardt. These levels correspond to levels developed by Underwriters Laboratories.

[47] Scotti, in Oatman, *Executive Protection Resource Manual*, Chapter 1, p. 14.

Preparation

The goal of EP transportation operations is fourfold: comfort, convenience, safety, and security. Comfort enables the principal to make relaxed use of his time; convenience means meeting the principal's schedule; safety means protecting the principal from accidents; and security means protecting him from deliberate or random attacks. Attaining those goals requires the correct mix of the skills and practices that are discussed in the rest of this chapter.

Comfort, convenience, and safety

The goals that are most under the EP specialist's control are comfort and convenience. As a baseline, after which the principal can announce his own preferences, the agent should see that the radio is off, the car is not filled with cigarette smoke, the temperature is set to about 68 degrees, the front seat is moved forward to give the principal ample leg room, and the car's interior and exterior are clean (this last condition also makes it easier to notice signs of tampering).

The next preparatory steps influence comfort, convenience, and also safety. The gas tank should be kept full. In the trunk the EP specialist should keep a box or duffel bag containing a first-aid kit, roadside reflectors or flares, basic tools, jumper cables, a flashlight, flat-tire refill spray cans, an escape device that will enable someone locked in the trunk to get out, and other equipment. The trunk should also contain a real spare tire, not the miniature type, so the car can be driven fast and far after a flat has been changed.[48] The car must be in good mechanical order—that's a comfort, convenience, and safety factor. Therefore, the agent should make sure the car receives proper maintenance, however that is handled in the particular circumstances. Further, he needs to make sure he can properly operate all the car's features: radio, locks, climate control system, alarm system, telephone, etc. The agent should read the

---

[48] An alternative is to use a tire like the Goodyear Extended Mobility Tire, which is rated as being able to operate effectively *at an air pressure of zero* for 200 miles at 55 miles per hour. Among other advantages, it eliminates the need for a spare tire, thus freeing up trunk space for other items.

car manufacturer's manual carefully; Mercedes Benz and BMW cars can be particularly complex, and some study may be required to master the intricate systems. The placement of a suction-cup, convex mirror on the inside of the windshield permits good viewing to the rear for an agent seated in the right front seat. Laminated maps, local hospital guides, pens and note paper, a portable cellular phone, and a list of frequently called telephone numbers can also add to safety and convenience.

Security

One further preparatory measure is the bomb search, a major security factor. Car bombs are a much more likely threat than terrorist ambushes, by far. Though used by terrorists too, car bombs are also placed by family members of the principal, romantic partners, hit men, organized crime groups, disgruntled employees, protesters (in extreme cases), and other parties that a principal might be entangled with. Car bombings are not nearly as rare as one might hope: FBI data record 314 bomb attacks and attempted bomb attacks against cars in the United States in 1994.[49] To put that figure in perspective, that's about the same as the number of bomb attacks against commercial operations and about one-fourth of the number of attacks against residences.

No passenger car, no matter how well armored, is likely to be able to withstand a bomb attack. Therefore, the agent must make sure to prevent such an attack. The two goals are (1) to prevent an explosive or incendiary device from being placed on or in the car, or, failing that, (2) to discover any bomb that might have been placed and keep the principal away from it.

In practice, that means the EP specialist has to search the car thoroughly anytime it has been out of sight and unguarded. Because a thorough search is time-consuming, it makes sense to keep the car in a locked, alarmed garage whenever possible. The idea is that once the car has been searched, it only stays "sterile" if it is continuously locked away or kept under surveillance. When the

---

[49] FBI Explosives Unit–Bomb Data Center, General Information Bulletin 95-2: 1994 Bombing Incidents.

car must be exposed, a member of the protection team should keep a close eye on it—and that cannot be done efficiently from inside the car. Only by standing outside the car and watching it can he be sure that vehicle security has not been compromised.

If a potential bomber knows the principal employs a protection staff, he will certainly take care to conceal any bomb he places. That, plus the fact that explosive and incendiary devices can take many appearances, makes the search for bombs a real challenge. To reduce the difficulty in advance, the agent should keep the car's exterior immaculately clean. A clean surface will more readily show smudges, fingerprints, scratches, and other signs of tampering. Tampering inside is more evident if the interior, too, is kept clean and orderly; even air vents should be kept pointing straight so that any changes will be noticeable. Index marks can be placed on hubcaps to give evidence as to whether a hubcap has been removed and replaced. Such marks can be made with clear nail polish or with clear, frangible evidence tape. Talcum power in the door handle wells reveals evidence of tampering, and clear, 5 x 7 photos of the inside of the engine compartment provide the searcher with a point of comparison for detecting extra items among the mass of wires, hoses, belts, and other parts. Coveralls and gloves make it less unpleasant to crawl under the car and to reach around in grimy areas there. Finally, a flashlight and telescoping convex mirror provide obvious benefits, and a car-search checklist, while no substitute for judgment, may keep the agent from forgetting to search a part of the car.

Once it is time to search, the agent must have some idea what he is looking for. The bomb probably won't be a bundle of dynamite sticks taped to a wind-up alarm clock. It could be a watch attached to something as small as a cigarette pack. It could consist of a blasting cap (which doesn't look much different from a piece of wire) connected to tubes of liquid chemicals, or a plumbing pipe with both ends capped, or a sheet of light-green linoleum (plastic explosive), or many other things. It might not even be a bomb proper—it could be a canister of poison gas, an incendiary device, or a device that disables the car en route by timer or radio control to set the occupants up for an ambush.

A good search procedure is this: Without touching the car, scan its exterior. Look for signs of forced entry; signs of tampering (fingerprints, scratches, fluids or wire clippings on the ground, exposed or hanging wires); marks around the tires and wheel wells; and the condition of any index marks or tell-tales (such as frangible tape) that were placed. Next, inspect the car's undercarriage, systematically checking from front to back, and look at the gas-fill door. Before opening the hood, trunk, or any door, look inside the cracks for tripwires, then gently slide a folded dollar bill through those cracks, stopping if the bill catches on anything. On opening the hood, trunk, or any door, do so slowly, feeling for any catches or tripwires. Then search the engine compartment and the trunk.

Move inside and check the doors, door panels, seats, speakers, dome lights, fuse box, dashboard, vents, ducts, controls, radio, lighter and ashtray, glove compartment, sun visors, and headrests. Start the engine and operate the horn, lights, brakes, heater, air conditioner, power seats, radio, etc. Check the fuel level to see if it has changed. The search requires concentration and thoroughness, but after gaining some experience, a searcher should be able to perform the task in about 10 minutes.

In the real world, of course, the principal is not going to stand around while the car is examined bolt by bolt. The detailed car search just described should be performed at the start of the day or after the car comes back from being serviced. Periodically throughout the day, however, the EP specialist should conduct more cursory searches. As for overnight security, by far the best procedure is to store the locked, alarmed car in a locked, alarmed garage.

If, by chance, the agent finds something suspicious, he should remove the principal from the bomb, not the other way around, and summon expert help (typically the local police department's bomb squad). It is important to stay well away (350 feet or more) from the suspected bomb, to keep others at a safe distance, too, and to turn off all cellular phones in the area (they could trigger the bomb). Bomb experts emphasize that no one should let himself be talked into moving, manipulating, or ignoring a bomb.

Moreover, it is foolhardy to assume that because one bomb has been detected and defused, no other bombs are present.[50]

Security en Route

In protection work, one of three persons will drive the car: the principal, a chauffeur, or an EP specialist. From a security standpoint, the principal—who may own the car, love the car, and feel he is entitled to drive the car—really should not drive the car. The likelihood that he is trained in defensive driving techniques is slim, and there is no way he can duck for cover while he is at the wheel. In addition, he has probably not spent time studying alternate routes, safe havens, and the physics of ramming blockades. Of course, the principal is the boss, so if he wants to drive, he drives. Nevertheless, it is a good idea for the EP specialist to emphasize what a pleasant, useful service it is to be driven by a professional. He should encourage the client to take the rear seat, sit back, and enjoy the ride. However, the EP specialist shouldn't make that suggestion unless he is certain that he can provide a comfortable ride. Few things are more irritating to a principal than to be driven by someone with a spastic foot—to endure the kind of ride that causes the principal's head to jerk backward or roll forward with every touch of the gas or brake. The EP specialist who intends to drive should get someone to perform a critical evaluation of his driving-comfort skills.

As for chauffeurs, they are usually trained to provide comfort and convenience rather than security. If a chauffeur is a permanent part of the protection team, of course, he can be trained in evasive driving and other security measures. If the EP specialist has to contract for a chauffeur—for example, in the process of hiring a car service to transport the principal in another city—it pays to develop a relationship with a single company in each city

---

[50] A recent example is the bombing of an office building in Atlanta on January 16, 1997. An hour after the first explosion, which occurred inside the building, a second device exploded in a trash container outside, next to the crowd that had gathered to see the initial damage. Six people were injured, including a federal agent investigating the first blast.

and to request the same driver each time, so he can learn what the EP specialist wants him to do. It is also important to investigate the chauffeur; he might lack a driver's license, or he might have a criminal record.

If it is necessary to hire a chauffeur for out-of-town travel, or if a chauffeur is a permanent part of the protection team, he should be trained or at least be given a few guidelines. For example, he should keep the gas tank at least half full at all times; arrive 30 minutes before scheduled departures; have two sets of keys; lock all doors once everyone is inside the car; obey traffic laws; use the horn only in an emergency; close doors and the trunk lid firmly but without slamming; and watch the car when it's not in use to guard it against tampering. He should also keep his mouth shut. Verbose town guides or local characters are not appreciated, and they can be very distracting to the protection mission and irritating to everyone. The chauffeur must also be instructed that if a problem arises, the EP specialist will take charge and must be obeyed.

The best driver, from a protection standpoint, is the EP specialist himself. If more than one agent accompanies the principal, all the better—one can drive while another sits next to him in the front seat and assists with observation, logistics, directions, and other matters. The EP specialist is likely to be trained in defensive or evasive driving and to know alternate routes and safe havens.

Secure routes

Once the car is ready and a driver has been selected, it's time to go somewhere—that's what the car is for, of course. Transporting the principal safely from point A to point B requires the driver (who is here assumed to be the EP specialist) to take a number of special measures. First is to develop, before the drive, familiarity with the route to be traveled. If the advance work described in Chapter 4 has been performed, the driver knows a route that is fast, does not pass through dangerous areas, and requires a minimum of stopping; several alternate routes; safe havens at which he can stop along the way; the location of hospitals, police stations, and other potentially vital resources along the route; the time it will take to reach various stages along the route; the likely level of traffic; road conditions, construction work, drawbridge openings, and other temporary factors that could affect the trip; and other facts about the route.

Along the way, the driver will keep the car doors locked and windows closed. By making sure he can always see the bottom of the rear tires of the car ahead of him, he will avoid being boxed in while stopping for a traffic light, leaving himself room to maneuver the car to escape. He will avoid stopping to help at accident scenes, instead using his portable phone to call the police for help. Minor, rear-end collisions will make him suspicious—if someone seems to have stopped deliberately in front of him, causing a minor crash, or has smashed into the principal's car's rear bumper without skidding in an attempt to stop, the driver will consider not stopping and instead drive to the nearest police station.

Furthermore, it is important for the EP specialist to reduce or eliminate the need for client-requested detours that risk taking the car through dangerous areas. One way the agent can do so is to anticipate any of the principal's needs that might cause a request for such a detour. For example, what if, on the way to a meeting, the principal announces he absolutely must have some chewing gum? Chances are that the agent could have known and predicted the principal's desire. If the agent is fully prepared, he can hand over a stick of gum and prevent the whole motorcade from having to detour from its safe, carefully selected route just to stop at a convenience store. This preemptive need-satisfaction comes in handy in many other protective settings as well—at the principal's home, on travel, etc.

One of the great keys to reducing risk is reducing exposure. To reduce the principal's exposure during car travel, the driver will, when driving on the highway, most often use the passing lane. The problem with the slowest, rightmost lane is that cars are constantly trying to merge into it to enter or leave the highway. Using the middle lane, if there is one, leaves open the possibility of being approached on both sides of the car at once. Using the leftmost lane puts the driver in a protected position and exposes only one side of the car to traffic. Furthermore, in the extreme and highly unlikely case that attackers attempt to shoot at the principal's car on the highway, being in the leftmost lane leaves open the possibility of employing two non-driving shooters (one in the right front seat and one in the right rear seat) to defend the car, while the attackers can only field one non-driving shooter (in the left rear seat of their car).[51] It is important to watch out for motorcycles, however: they can easily pull alongside the car on either side, they move very fast, and they may even enable attackers to plant a bomb or incendiary device on the principal's car. Again, that is not a likely scenario for most principals, but reducing exposure can even help protect a principal against more random attacks, such as bump-and-robs, by making the principal less noticeable and less accessible.

The most important factor in reducing exposure on the road is speed. As Ralph Waldo Emerson wrote in his essay "Prudence": "In skating over thin ice, our safety is in our speed."[52] The driver should obey speed limits but do everything else that is legal and safe to keep his speed up. Knowing the route well helps. It is much harder for an assailant standing by the road to shoot successfully at a car that darts by quickly than to hit one that lumbers. During the time he was stalking President Nixon, Arthur Bremer stood outside a Canadian military airport, from which he knew the President would emerge by car. He stood along the road, in the rain, with a gun hidden in one of his galoshes. He later noted in his diary:

> [As the motorcade approached,] people jumped from their cars. Would the assassin get a good view? Everyone moved in close (about 20 people). We were the only people other than cops for a few blocks. He went by before I knew it. Like a snap of the fingers. A dark shillowet [sic], waving, rushed by in the large dark car. 'All over,' someone said to no one in particular.... I had missed him that day. The best day to make the attempt was over, I thought.

---

[51] An alternative is the slingshot technique. If, on a fast road, passengers in a car driving alongside the principal's car begin to behave threateningly, perhaps pulling a gun, the principal's driver should stop his car abruptly and change directions. The other car will likely continue to rocket ahead for several seconds at least.

[52] Ralph Waldo Emerson, "Prudence," in *Essays, First Series*, 1841.

Street-level criminals—those who commit carjackings or cause minor crashes followed by attempted robberies—might be foiled by the driver's use of a fast, relatively safe route and knowledge of alternate routes in case of heavy traffic or some other obstacle. However, if the threat analysis suggests that a more professional attack on the principal's car (by kidnappers, terrorists, or hit men) is a realistic possibility, then an additional route consideration arises: that is, unpredictably varying the route driven.

Every route presents some security concerns, whether they be narrow roads, long stoplights, blind spots, or isolated areas. By varying the route driven to, say, the principal's office, the driver makes it much more difficult for attackers to lurk in those areas with any certainty that the principal will come by. Unfortunately, no matter how much the driver might vary his route, there are some stretches of road that he must predictably drive on, such as the public street at the end of the principal's driveway, the main road out of a subdivision, or the entrance ramp to the only highway that leads to the office. A measure that reduces the predictability of being in those places is to vary the time at which the driver passes those spots. If the principal's schedule allows it, and the threat analysis suggests it is important, the car can depart the principal's premises at a slightly different time each morning. It is unfortunate but true that the area at or just beyond the end of a principal's home's driveway is one of the most dangerous parts of the trip. In the last few years, many of the executives who have died in ambushes or been kidnapped were attacked within a few hundred yards of their driveways.

One effective technique for enhancing the security of routine drives to the office is to send an advance route car out 15 minutes ahead of the principal's car. The advance car conducts a countersurveillance effort and checks for traffic tie-ups and other hazards. The EP specialist in the advance car watches to see whether the same cars or people turn up along the route day after day; if so, a surveillance effort against the principal may be under way.

Choreography of people and cars

It's hard for an adversary—whether a carjacker, mugger, stalking fan, or assassination-bent zealot—to confront the principal while the principal's car is flying down the highway. Vulnerability to a face-to-face incident is far higher when and where the principal is entering or leaving the car. Moreover, in most cases, that vulnerability must be faced several times each day. A well-rehearsed drill among the protective staff and the principal greatly increases the principal's safety in those situations.

This discussion of choreography assumes that the driver is a permanent member of the protection team and that another EP specialist is a passenger in the car—that arrangement is desirable and feasible for day-in, day-out driving. In a typical arrival scenario, the principal is riding in the back seat of the car, on the right side. Why that side? That's the sidewalk side, and it's safer to enter and leave the car from that side. As the car slows in front of the principal's destination, the EP specialist in the right front seat says, "Sir, I'll get your door." That agent then opens his own door first. The driver immediately relocks all the doors as the EP specialist climbs out of the car and closes his door. The agent looks around to see if everything seems safe, signals the driver to unlock the doors, opens the principal's door, lets the principal out, and closes the door. He then accompanies the client into the building. The driver stays behind the wheel to facilitate a quick getaway if necessary. Note that if a follow-up car is used, the process of exiting from the lead car (if that is where the principal is riding) should wait until the follow-up car arrives—unless the follow-up car has lagged far behind.

It is just as important to choreograph the principal's return to the car. A few minutes before the expected return of the principal, the driver should inspect the vehicle for signs of tampering, position it at curbside, keep the motor running, and give the car's interior a chance to reach a comfortable temperature. He may wish to stand outside the vehicle to maintain surveillance on the site and the car, but he should position himself right next to the open driver's door and should keep all the other doors locked. When the principal emerges from the place he has been visiting, the driver should get behind the steering wheel, close his door, unlock the other doors, and remain ready to drive away—in a hurry, if necessary. Once the EP specialist who is accompanying the principal has placed him in the back seat and taken up position in the front passenger seat, and after all doors are closed and locked, the driver should pull away.

Choreography applies to cars, too. When the principal is transported in a convoy or motorcade, keeping the cars together can be a challenge. The only solution is practice. The drivers should be in radio contact with each other, though minimal talking is required. Most of the cars' coordination can be done more easily and discreetly through signaling with various lights. For example, when it's time to change lanes, the follow-up car signals the lead car by turning its directional signal on. The follow-up car moves over, then creates room for the lead car to join it in the new lane. It's also important to consider the positioning of the principal. It's unwise to drive along aimlessly in parallel traffic in such a way that the principal is exposed for long periods to the driver or passengers of the adjacent car. That is especially important if the principal is well known and recognizable to the general public.

Many convoy configurations can be used, depending on the level of security required and the number of cars in use. In a two-car motorcade, typically the lead car will contain a driver, one or two EP agents, and the principal, while the follow-up car will contain other EP agents and serve as a spare car for the principal. In a three-car motorcade, it is common for the principal's car to be sandwiched between the lead and follow-up cars.

Performance Handling

Many people consider themselves good drivers, but risky, nonchalant, overly aggressive, or illegal driving does not make one a good driver. A good driver, in general, is one who drives safely. A good driver in the executive protection field is one who drives safely *and*, when necessary, aggressively. As mentioned earlier, protectees face two kinds of risk when traveling in cars: the routine but surprisingly high risk of an accidental crash, and the risk (at different levels for different protectees) of harm from a deliberate attack. The skill of the principal's driver can reduce both these risks.

There's a huge difference between playing a little touch football with the guys at the company picnic and playing for the NFL. The two activities may be more or less the same game, but the levels of training, skill, understanding, and commitment involved in the two activities are worlds apart. The same holds true with driving. Really driving, with eyes and mind busily working the changing conditions, the driver knowing what the car can do when pushed to its limits, and knowing—actually having tested—the limits of his own skill: that's the kind of driving from which a principal deserves to benefit.

That level of driving ability doesn't come from years of commuting or even from reading an executive protection book. This chapter can introduce the concepts important in performance driving, but the only way to learn the actual techniques and be able to use them both daily and in crises is to attend a driving school. Some schools are geared to defensive driving for ordinary citizens who wish to reduce the risk they face every time they turn the ignition key. Other schools are geared specifically to law enforcement officers, EP specialists, and others who must use their driving skills to save lives, including their own, and who may have to escape from deliberate attacks, not just accidental collisions.

Driving theory

Routine driving is so simple to most adults that they rarely consider the physics of driving and the factors that affect their control of the car. However, an EP specialist, whose head may already be filled with mountains of protective data, must know, understand, and internalize the facts about human reaction time, physics, weight transfer, skids, and speed. Mastering those subjects requires much study and practice—in fact, much more than can be given here. Whole books and schools specialize in the subject. What follows is merely a brief lesson in the dynamics of protective driving.

Cars, by themselves, do nothing. If they proceed safely, the driver deserves credit; if they crash, it's his fault. Driving experts distinguish between driving *out of control*, which occurs when the driver exceeds the vehicle's limitations, and suffering a *loss of control*, which occurs when the driver exceeds his own limitations. Both conditions should be avoided, and it is up to the driver alone to do so.

The major human limitation is reaction time. Before the driver can stop, turn, or take any other action, the brain must receive appropriate data from the senses, the brain must make a decision on what to do next, the message must be transmitted from the brain to the muscles that are need to move the controls, and the muscles themselves must respond. All this normally takes about three-quarters of a second. The process can take much longer if the driver is tired, distracted, or frightened to the point of indecision. Alternatively, the process can be performed a little faster if the driver is especially well trained. But isn't three-quarters of a second more than fast enough? Not really—a car traveling 65 mph travels about 71 feet in that period. And that 71 feet just counts the reaction time; only after that distance can the car begin to stop or turn.

Stopping distance depends not only on the driver's reaction time but also on the road surface, brakes, and driver's braking experience. The equation for stopping—where S equals stopping distance, V equals velocity in feet per second, μ equals the coefficient of friction, and G equals the acceleration of gravity (32.2 feet per second per second)—is this:

$$S = \frac{V^2}{2\mu G}$$

The driver need not memorize this equation, and he certainly won't have time to compute it while driving, but a quick look at it shows that the relationship between speed and stopping distance is nonlinear. That is, a doubling of speed results in much more than a doubling of stopping distance—in fact, the distance quadruples. For example, a car traveling at 30 mph on a road surface with a friction coefficient of 0.8 (that of a dry concrete surface) requires 38 feet in which to stop. A car traveling twice as fast (60 mph) on a similar surface requires four times the distance—152 feet—to stop. If that same car is traveling at the same speed (60 mph) but on a slippery surface—say, ice, which has a friction coefficient of 0.1—then it will need 559 feet to stop. That's a tenth of a mile. To these stopping distances must be added the distance covered during the driver's reaction time: 33 feet at 30 mph, 66 feet at 60 mph.[53]

Obviously, even the most conscientious driver isn't going to calculate these numbers as he drives down the street. But in general, under average conditions, a driver should allow himself a good two seconds in which to stop his car, or a little more if he is driving especially fast or is on an unusually slippery road. The practical expression of the two-second rule is to make sure the car is at least two seconds behind any car in front of it and that the driver can, in bad weather or on curvy roads, always see ahead at least the distance he covers in two seconds. Therefore, if the car is moving 30 mph, or 44 feet per second (fps = mph x 1.47), the driver should leave at least 88 feet free ahead of his car.

Along with stopping, the other two major operations a car performs are *going* (forward or backward) and *turning*. Knowing how a car stops is important mainly for avoiding accidents. Knowing how a car goes and turns is important for both avoiding accidents and escaping from ambushes. The physics of turning is more complicated than that of stopping, but it is extremely important. In a nutshell, when a car is parked, each wheel bears a certain amount of the car's weight. When the car is driving through a turn, a weight transfer occurs, redistributing the amount of weight each wheel bears. The force that causes that transfer is lateral G-force. As the G's increase (from turning, braking, or accelerating), the car's steering is affected more and more; once too much force is applied to the tires, they lose their grip on the road, and the driver may be able neither to stop nor steer.

---

[53] This discussion of stopping distance is inspired by the chapter "Braking Control" in Anthony Scotti, *Driving Techniques for the Professional and Non-Professional* (Ridgefield, New Jersey: PhotoGraphics Publishing, 1995).

The equation for lateral G-force, or lateral acceleration, where V equals velocity in feet per second and R equals the radius of the car's path in feet, is this:

$$LA = \frac{V^2}{RG}$$

Again, there's no need to memorize the equation, and certainly no time to use it in a pinch, but it shows, once again, a nonlinear relationship between the car's speed and the lateral force exerted against it. In other words, doubling the speed at which the driver takes the turn quadruples the force exerted on the car. There's a lot to learn about understeer, oversteer, maintaining control in turns, and regaining control in skids. The executive protection team's driver should also know about kinetic energy, the effect of different tire and car designs on performance, G-force ratings of various cars, and other technical matters. That's why driving school is so important.

Though this chapter cannot address all the relevant technical topics, it can offer some of the nontechnical practices that contribute to controlled driving. One of the most important observations is that, when under stress, drivers tend to focus on the outcome (impending crash) rather than the process (what can be done to avoid hitting a tree). The best technique is to think one's way out of the problem by focusing on the *process*. That way the driver will be too busy to panic. Knowing the way cars behave, the way weight shifts among wheels in turns and skids, and other mechanical relationships gives the driver something concrete to think about, to work with in getting out of the problem.

Another key to success behind the wheel is called "ocular driving." In ocular driving, the driver chooses a goal with his eyes and drives toward it. It is natural to drive where one is looking, but not everyone realizes the implications of that fact. When a car starts to skid, the driver should not stare at the tree he thinks he is about to hit but should instead look at his positive goal—that is, the roadway. His natural reflexes will take him in the direction in which he is looking. Similarly, when swerving around an obstacle or attempting to squeeze the car through a tight space (such as a narrow alley), the driver should look not at the obstacle or the alley walls but at the patch of road where he wants the car to go. This is a simple technique that actually works.

This section on driving theory has presented several complicated topics. If the formulae seem confusing, the EP specialist should at least remember these important points:

- Doubling a car's speed quadruples its stopping distance.
- Doubling the speed at which a driver takes a turn quadruples the lateral force exerted on the car. (This lateral G-force causes cars to skid).
- When in trouble, a driver should focus on the process (what can be done to avoid crashing into a tree) rather than the outcome (mental images of crashing into the tree).
- A driver should perform "ocular driving"—looking at the place he wants the car to go rather than the obstacle he wants to avoid hitting. One naturally guides the car where one is looking.
- A driver should take care not to slip up on the basics: remaining alert, observing other cars around him, keeping his hands at ten and two o'clock on the steering wheel, etc.

Emergency Response

The preceding section, "Performance Handling," provided an introduction to why cars behave the way they do. This section describes some of the actual defensive or evasive maneuvers an executive protection specialist might have to perform. This discussion is directed solely at countering deliberate attacks on the principal, not at avoiding common, accidental crashes. As above, this treatment only introduces the concepts of security driving; to learn them well, a driver must attend a professional driving school.

The threat of ambush is not a high risk to most protectees, yet it cannot be ruled out. Many prominent businessmen have been kidnapped or killed in automobile ambushes, both in the United States and elsewhere. Ambushes, while not exactly predictable, are more likely to happen in some locations than others. Locations in which EP specialists should pay special attention to the signs of an incipient ambush are places near the protectee's home or office; one-way or narrow streets; places where the protectee's car must drive very slowly, such as a sharp curve in the road or a median gap at which the car stops to make a turn; and blind spots like hills or corners.

At such places, and at any others of the attackers' choosing, a car may swerve in front of the protectee's car, blocking forward motion; attackers may jump out of cars or step from behind bushes and begin firing weapons; or some other, as yet undreamed-of type of ambush may occur. If the ambushers are on foot and do not block the protectee's car with a car of their own, there's no reason to stop at all; the driver should simply drive away as fast as possible, not worrying at all about the safety of the attackers. (Practice on a slalom track may help the driver execute a serpentine escape.)

An exception to the automatic drive-away rule is carjacking: in an unarmored vehicle that is stopped, if a carjacker points a gun at the driver or principal, it is time to give the car up. The driver is unlikely to be able to accelerate from the scene before the carjacker shoots through the window. However, if no weapon is showing or the vehicle is armored, it's time to burn rubber. If the car's doors are already locked, as they should be, it is unlikely that the principal can be harmed.

One further point about driving away from a threat is this: traffic laws are meant to be obeyed, but not at the cost of the principal's life. If the car is stopped at a red light and evildoers start approaching the car in a threatening manner, the driver should—carefully—drive through the light. Likewise, backing up onto a sidewalk in order to turn the car around to escape danger is a minor infraction compared to carjacking.

Once the driver realizes an ambush is about to take place, he may have only a second or two—literally—to decide what he will do. His options are limited: he can drive around the barricade, as noted above; he can turn around, using the bootlegger turn, J turn, or two-point turn; or he can ram through the barricade. The choice of response depends on the conditions of the ambush and the skill of the driver. There's so little time to decide what to do, however, that the various ambush scenarios should be practiced in advance. That way the driver may be able to react automatically, which is what he will have to do to react in time.

The bootlegger turn consists of driving forward (toward the barricade), turning sharply to spin the car 180 degrees, and driving back in the direction from which the car came. It's an exciting maneuver seen often in action films; like other aspects of executive protection represented in movies, it is not very true to life. The bootlegger turn requires a driver with a high degree of skill, a large area in which to perform the maneuver, and a car that is physically capable of doing the turn. Even if all those conditions are satisfied, the maneuver leaves the car temporarily stopped right in front of the attackers. In most instances, the bootlegger turn is not practical—the driver is likely to crash into something or end up in a vulnerable position close to the ambush.

In a J turn, the driver who sees a barricade ahead of him stops the car fast, throws it into reverse, drives backwards away from the attackers at high speed, turns the steering wheel sharply, and, while the car is spinning 180 degrees, throws the transmission into drive and speeds away. Its advantage over the bootlegger turn is that the maneuver takes the car away from the ambush immediately. However, like the bootlegger turn, it is difficult to do and it requires more room than the driver is likely to have. A safer maneuver is simply to drive quickly in reverse and then, once the car is a safe distance from the attackers, perform a two-point turn, backing into a driveway or even up on a curb, then driving away forward.

In some situations, it may not be possible to turn around and leave the scene of the attack. The road may be too narrow, or another car may be blocking the road behind the principal's car. In those cases, since it is important even in an armored car not to come to a halt and become a sitting duck, the only option may be to ram the barricade. Ramming a parked car doesn't have to be suicidal; in fact, it can be a very effective alternative if done correctly. The first thing to note is that the principal's car can probably push the ambushers' car out of the way at a surprisingly low speed. That's good, because a high-speed crash between the principal's car and the parked blockade car could have as destructive an effect as any other high-speed crash. The reason a moving car can push a parked car out of the way at a low speed is kinetic energy, which the moving car is well supplied with. The formula for kinetic energy (KE), where W equals the moving car's weight, V equals velocity, and G equals gravity, is this:

$$KE = \frac{WV^2}{2G}$$

That formula shows, for example, that at 10 mph, a 3,500 lb. car has enough energy to lift a 10,000 lb. object one foot off the ground. Like the other formulas in this chapter, this one is nonlinear; that is, doubling the car's speed will quadruple the kinetic energy produced.

The following is a good, step-by-step description of how to ram a parked vehicle:[54]

1. First, determine whether it is an attack. If it is, slow the vehicle as if to stop. You must make the attackers think you are going to stop at the barricade. As you approach the barricade, pick a possible ramming point.

2. When you are about one to two car lengths from the barricade, brake to a sudden stop. When you stop, your car will rock fore and aft. Try to time the acceleration as the bumper on your car rises. Floor the accelerator, striking the blocking vehicle at the center of one of its wheels with your right or left fender. Strike either end of the blocking vehicle.

3. Keep the accelerator on the floor until you are past the barricade. If you take your foot off the gas, you release the energy you have built up in the car. Hold the steering wheel straight, and do not swerve away at the last moment. You will be going no more than 5 to 15 mph.

4. Beginning the run too far back will allow the attacker to figure out what you are planning and will also let you

---

[54] Adapted from Scotti, in Oatman, *Executive Protection Resource Manual*, Chapter 8, pp. 3-4.

build up too much speed. At the recommended speed you will hardly feel the shock. The barricade vehicle will spin violently out of the way.

One last response to an ambush must still be discussed. If the protectee's car cannot go forward, cannot go backward, and cannot go around—in other words, is trapped—and the attackers are advancing on the car with the intent to kill the passengers, there is only one option left: shooting from the car. Doing so is truly a last resort, but if the principal faces the risk of kidnapping or assassination, either because of who he is or what part of the world he is traveling in, the EP specialist had better know how to take this drastic measure.

Shooting from inside the car is such an extreme, unfamiliar, and unnatural-feeling measure that an agent is unlikely to be able to do it well without at least a little practice. During such practice, the agent would learn the fine points. Here, however, are just the basics. It's unlikely that the principal could safely run away from the attackers if they are already bearing down on the car. Therefore, he should stay in the car and keep the doors locked. Also, rolling down the windows only increases the passengers' exposure, so the shooting must be done right through the windshield, side windows, or rear window. The technique is to bring the gun's muzzle close to the window and then fire a double tap. The first shot breaks the window, and the second shot goes through. This is a messy, highly dramatic step to take—it may even temporarily damage the hearing of the car's occupants—and it should be done only if there is no alternative but to sit there and be shot. It is the last resort in the worst of all possible scenarios.

A principal's exposure to attack runs particularly high when he is traveling by automobile. Moreover, principals, like most people, spend a large amount of time in their cars. That raises the risk to a relatively high level. Fortunately, by taking care to select an appropriate car or having one modified as needed, by learning how the principal's car works and how to drive it to maximum protective advantage, by practicing good route security, and by knowing how to respond in an emergency, a protective agent can significantly reduce the risk to the principal.

*You can ensure the safety of your defense if you
only hold positions that cannot be attacked.*
Sun Tzu

Chapter 6
Home and Office Security

This chapter's opening quote may sound like a tautology: obviously, a principal who is kept in a location that cannot be attacked may be assured of a good defense. However, Sun Tzu is cleverer than that. If his statement is taken as ironic, he may be saying that since no position is ever completely immune to attack, no defense is assuredly safe. Alternatively, he may be alluding to the desirability of maintaining such strong positions that no attack is made— that is, hardening the target so well that attacks are discouraged and its hardness need never be put to the test.

Either way, security at a principal's home and office is a major undertaking for an executive protection specialist. The risk faced per minute may be greater during travel, commuting, or public appearances, but an executive spends far more hours in the office or at home than anywhere else. Therefore, security for those locations is essential. This chapter examines security measures that must be undertaken to protect homes and offices, first presenting considerations and practices that apply to both settings, then detailing measures that apply specifically to home security, and finally describing office-specific protection practices.

Home and Office

Many protective measures apply to both home protection and office protection. Among them are the following:

- threat assessment
- rings of protection
- security engineering
- intelligence and surveillance
- life safety precautions (primarily fire and first-aid considerations)
- bomb prevention and response

Threat assessment

Chapter 1 covered threat assessment in some detail, but it is important to realize that threat assessment is not a one-time exercise. The threat assessment process is actually a continuous operation in which the EP specialist collects and analyzes new data constantly. Most of the time, he can use the new pieces of information to tweak the protection program. For example, if a small group of protesters is planning to march back and forth across the main entrance to the executive's office building, it might be wise to use a different entrance for a few days.

However, when an EP specialist sets out to establish an initial security plan for the executive's home and office, something a bit more intense than that sort of fine-tuning is required. What the protective agent must do is conduct an expanded threat assessment, essentially rebuilding it from the ground up. The reason is that an accurate measure and understanding of the threats is the foundation on which the home and office security plans will be built. If the foundation is weak, the security plans will be weak, too. A thorough assessment of the threats against the principal helps the agent gauge not only the *range* of threats that must be defended against but also the *level* of the threats. For example, if there is reason to believe that the principal could be a target of kidnapping, it also helps to estimate the level of that threat—that is, are the would-be kidnappers likely to be clumsy crooks who developed a half-baked plan after reading about the principal in *Forbes* magazine, or are they highly motivated, well-financed, international terrorists? The potential crime may be the same no matter who commits it, but the defenses to be erected would differ enormously. Often, of course, there is no way to know who—and how able—the adversary might be. In such a case, a responsible EP specialist would assume a middle-of-the-road security posture and would build in the flexibility to ratchet the defenses up or down as needed.

If it has been possible to maintain a threat file—meaning a collection of notes regarding unwanted visitors, threatening telephone calls and letters, and tips about other dangers—the diligent EP specialist would check through that file now. It also pays to take a fresh look at local crime risks, analyzing the types, locations, and times of various types of crimes around the home and the office. Such information may be obtained from the local police, from the crime analysis units of state law enforcement agencies, or from commercial services that track reported crime data and geocode it to draw crime maps.

What about publicity? Is it well-known where the principal works or lives? The answers to those questions affect whether the security measures must primarily defend against opportunistic crimes or well-planned ones. For example, if a financial, society, or life styles magazine has recently profiled the protectee, hundreds of thousands of readers may have learned the location of the protectee's house or office, perhaps seen interior and exterior pictures of those locations, discerned the protectee's general commuting route, and so on. Such an article may also have shown a photograph of the protectee and published his net worth. Certain adversaries might find such intelligence useful. (In fact, protective specialists sometimes refer, with chagrin, to magazines' detailed lists of the rich and famous as "hit lists.") Protective measures may have to change after an article like that is published.[55]

---

[55] The kidnapping of Charles Geschke, described in Chapter 1, was inspired by newspaper articles describing an act of philanthropy by the Geschke family. The idea to kidnap Geschke developed when two young men living in the San Jose area

Adversaries can gain other intelligence from the executive's trash, finding travel plans, personal mail, security information, and other data. A threat assessment might reasonably conclude that the risk of burglary, blackmail, robbery, or kidnapping could rise if sensitive materials were thrown away in unsecured trash. That finding might then lead to specific preventive measures at the home and office, such as secure trash collection or routine shredding or burning of documents.

Rings of protection

Chapter 3, Working the Principal, discussed the theory of concentric rings of protection as it applies to protecting a mobile individual as he walks about and travels through his day. In the context of home and office security, concentric security refers to the layers of physical and procedural security measures that surround the kernel of the house or office in which the principal spends so much of his time. Also called defense-in-depth, the idea of concentric rings of protection can be likened to the protective measures surrounding a medieval castle. From the outside, heading inwards, the layers would include vassals living in the village outside the castle, who must defend their lord; a moat; the castle's outer walls; armed men inside the castle walls; and a fortified tower in the center of the castle, to which the lord and his family might retreat in times of crisis. Those protective layers, which would have to be fought through, one after another, would deter many aggressors altogether and would certainly slow the progress of those who were more determined.

As this book has explained elsewhere, executive protection is not the art of imprisoning a protectee in a gilded cage. Concentric protection, however, is the most effective means of safeguarding anything, whether a person or a thing, and at the home or office it can be done in such a way that the principal sees or feels very little

---

read that he had given $50,000 to upgrade computers at San Jose State College. Concluding that Geschke must be wealthy, the conspirators found out the location of his company (Adobe Systems, Inc.) and his home. Then, one morning, as he pulled into his corporate parking space, the kidnappers abducted him at gunpoint.

of it. The theory of concentric protection affects most of the topics that follow in this chapter; certainly it influences physical security, surveillance, fire prevention and first aid, and bomb protection.

Overwhelming force can push through any number of rings of protection, but very few protectees face the risk of overwhelming force. More typically, an adversary plans to make his way into the home or office through stealth. No matter how clever or dim the bad guys are, whether they are highly skilled kidnappers or drug-stupefied burglars, the need to penetrate numerous rings of protection will slow most of them down, stop them, or prevent them from ever attempting the crime in the first place. The last thing any EP specialist wants to see is the case in which an intruder manages to slip through layer after layer of security to the protectee's inner sanctum, such as occurred at 2:45 a.m. on November 5, 1995, when Aline Chretien, wife of Canada's prime minister, came face to face with an intruder who was standing at the couple's bedroom door with an open jackknife.[56] Police said the man broke into the official residence, which is surrounded by a wall made of stone and wrought iron, by smashing a window with a rock. It can only be assumed that the concentric rings of protection, which included the wall, exterior lights, various sensors, Canadian Mounties, and of course locked doors and windows, were not numerous enough, contained significant gaps, or were not properly monitored. Such incursions are not common at well-protected homes and offices, and even though they apparently show a failure of the defense in depth concept, in reality they merely show what happens when the rings of protection are not circular but C-shaped—that is, open with wide gaps.

The intrusion into the Canadian prime minister's residence presumably occurred because the intruder slipped through gaps in physical protection. However, it is also possible for adversaries to slip through other gaps in the protective rings: namely, gaps in procedures. That occurs most often when a member of the house-

---

[56] Associated Press, "Man with knife arrested in Canadian leader's home," *The Washington Times*, November 6, 1996.

hold or office staff falls for a ruse and simply lets the intruder in, making it unnecessary for him to defeat such physical barriers as walls, access control systems, or locked doors. Ruses include dressing in the uniform of a police officer, delivery person, or utility worker or posing as a family friend or business associate. Such impersonations can be made more convincing if the adversary has had access to the principal's trash or has otherwise gathered personal and business information about him. An adversary who knows the name of the principal's daughter who is away at college can put on a realistic act by dressing as a police officer, knocking at the door, and announcing, "I need to speak to the parents of Chelsea Jones. It's an emergency."

Of course, visitors must be positively identified before they are let in. If the protection team does not clearly recognize a visitor and know him to be safe, the person must be checked out with a phone call to the organization he represents. And naturally, the number dialed must be one the protection team finds on its own, not one suggested by the visitor. When positive identification is not possible, the person must not be let in, regardless of the inconvenience. These are not special measures but common ones that even people who face only the average level of risk—actually, everyone—should take. However, for executives and other protectees, the issue of positively identifying visitors is especially important because (1) the protectees face an above-average level of risk and (2) there are so many domestic staff, office staff, and other persons who could fall prey to a ruse. The second reason dictates the need for training not just protective staff but all staff in proper security procedures. It is not unheard of for a well-secured home to be invaded because a maid untrained in security procedures opened the front door for a criminal who claimed to be a plumber.

A recent example of adversaries entering a building by posing as legitimate visitors involves Tupac Amaru, a terrorist organization in Peru. On December 17, 1996, Tupac Amaru took over the Japanese ambassador's residence in Lima. The terrorists were able to enter the building by dressing as waiters who were coming in to serve at a large party. At first they took hundreds of people hostage; later they released all but 72, whom they offered to free in exchange for the release of some 450 of their comrades in Peruvian jails. On April 22, 1997, more than four months after the takeover, Peruvian troops stormed the residence. Seventy-one captives were rescued, and one died during the assault, as did two soldiers and all 14 captors.

Several lessons can be drawn from that incident:

- Screen *every* cook, waiter, and other person who enters the principal's home or office, no matter how inconvenient that may seem. If the building is not under the EP specialist's control, and he has doubts that people are being screened properly, he'll have to try to get the local security staff to improve their screening. Otherwise, if the threat assessment justifies doing so, he may have to recommend that the principal not attend.

- Keep servers and other support workers at a distance from the principal, allowing them near only when they are needed.

- When a building's rings of protection are penetrated, don't hang around to see if everything turns out all right. The agent needs to know all the ways of getting the principal out of a building. At the beginning stages of a takeover, it's highly unlikely that the perpetrators can have every single exit covered. That's the time to make an immediate escape.

Later sections of this chapter will describe techniques for interviewing unwanted visitors and will emphasize the importance of following security procedures.

Security engineering

The specific physical security measures required for a home or office cannot be prescribed broadly—the selection and placement of equipment is a custom job that depends on the features of the location to be secured and the level of security needed. Obviously, such equipment as solid doors, locks for doors and windows, alarm systems, fences and gates, closed-circuit television, exterior lights, and other items would feature prominently in most physical security schemes. But strictly speaking, each security application is unique and specialized.

That is why the EP specialist, who is typically a generalist, may well wish to contract with a security engineer. The probability of obtaining optimal physical security is greater when the process is handled by someone who specializes in designing physical security systems, who knows about the latest and best types of equipment, and who can specify systems that vendors will then bid to provide. With this approach, the EP specialist avoids relying on a security equipment vendor who tries to sell him everything the vendor thinks he needs and not necessarily what the circumstances require. A consultant with engineering expertise can design the best system for the EP specialist, leave procurement and installation to others, and serve as a watchdog over the entire project.

Physical security at the executive's office is typically not the purview of the EP specialist alone. Rather, he may have to insert his own special considerations into the overall corporate security effort. At the executive's home, the EP specialist may have a freer reign, being able to have installed whatever security features he and the protectee agree on. In either case, using the services of a consulting security engineer can improve the likelihood that the security equipment selected and the way in which it is installed will produce the level of security the EP specialist desires. In this context, the EP specialist is like a film director who knows how he wants the light to look in a particular scene but relies on the gaffer to select the right lamps and placement.

Contracting with a security engineer carries a cost, but it is much less than the cost of the security equipment, and without expert help the EP specialist runs the risk of selecting inappropriate equipment or deploying it ineffectively.[57]

---

[57] One especially well-regarded security engineering firm to consider is Systech Group, Inc., headed by John J. Strauchs. Systech can be reached at 11260 Roger Bacon Drive, Suite 501, Reston, VA 22090. (703) 759-9600.

Intelligence and surveillance

At both home and office, a great advantage can be gained through aggressive intelligence-gathering, including surveillance. In general, it is easier to defend the principal if the agent has some idea what to expect in terms of threats. The importance of refreshing the threat assessment was mentioned above; this section describes specific measures the EP specialist should take to ensure a regular flow of intelligence into his decision-making scheme.

A key step is to increase the number of eyes and ears gathering potentially useful information and passing it along to the agent. Obviously, it is important to develop a liaison with representatives of local, state, and federal law enforcement agencies. The agent will want those law enforcement insiders to alert him of specific threats, general crime trends, and other developments with security value. Less obvious is the need to bring other people into the greater protective team, both at home and at work. Housekeepers, personal secretaries, gardeners, neighbors, doormen, office cleaners, and many others can be brought on board and encouraged to report suspicious persons, packages, and other sightings. They can become a passive surveillance network, reporting useful information they come across in the course of their normal activities. For example, a gardener might report a suspicious lurker who spends an unusual amount of time watching the executive's house from across the street, or an office cleaner might report the presence of someone who appears to be an employee but is tampering with office locks.

Another type of intelligence network consists of electronic surveillance. Both at the executive's home and at his office, video and sometimes audio surveillance of key areas can provide several advantages. Video surveillance recording and archiving can help protective staff discern whether a suspicious person who has been reported as hanging around the front entrance to the home, or the rear entrance to the office, or any other key location has been there before in the preceding days or weeks and what he did during any of those visits. Such surveillance can also help protective staff spot vehicles that do not belong near the executive's office or home.

A third type of intelligence-gathering consists of the careful interviewing of unwanted visitors to the executive's home or office. At home, the executive's family, domestic staff, and anyone else who opens the door or answers the phone should be trained in the methods of dealing with such visitors, as should, at work, the executive's secretary, receptionist, and other gatekeepers. When a person tries to approach the protectee—at home, at work, or in a public place—in order to speak with him, shake his hand, or obtain an autograph, the EP specialist (or another party at the office or home) needs to determine whether the person is merely curious, a nuisance, or an actual threat. This is not a minor concern; stalkers latch onto many types of protectees and can be dangerous, determined, and difficult to shake.

An assessment of the visitor's general behavior gives one set of clues as to which category he belongs in. For example, a bystander who notices that a prominent person has just stepped out of a luxury car in a motorcade might step toward the principal to see what is going on and perhaps to ask for an autograph. If the person stops his quest when the EP specialist gives him the cold shoulder and escorts the principal into a building, then the person is likely to be seeking no more than a little satisfaction of his curiosity. Most likely, that will be the end of his interest.

Now, if a person shows up uninvited at the protectee's home or office, repeatedly places himself in public locations that the protectee frequents, or otherwise pays unwanted attention to the protectee, that person has shown a higher level of interest. He might fall into the category of nuisance; maybe he's an enthusiastic fan, or perhaps he has an unresolved grievance against the principal. If he has been shut out from communicating with the principal by telephone and mail, he may simply be trying to speak to the principal in person. His behavior may be annoying, even deliberately so, but he may or may not be dangerous, and it may not be possible to determine much just by looking at him.

To estimate intelligently whether the person is dangerous or merely annoying, an interview is needed. When the principal is safely out of the visitor's reach, the EP specialist can stop to ask the person a few questions. The person will probably want to state his case in the hope of gaining access to the principal. The interviewer can simply ask a few questions that encourage the visitor to talk. In addition to listening to the answers, the interviewer should study the visitor's manner: Does he seem mentally ill? Does he seem violent or desperate? It is also fruitful to ask him what exactly he wants from the principal and why. A sympathetic ear and reassuring or apologetic tone from the interviewer may be enough to satisfy the visitor that he is not the victim of a hateful conspiracy. A further step is to ask what the visitor will do if he does not get what he wants from the principal. Indications that the visitor feels backed into a corner with no way out or that his grievance is profound and unbearable are signs that he may be dangerous. Of course, there is no way to be certain of who is and who is not dangerous, but a threat file packed with hundreds of names is too unwieldy to be of much use, so the EP specialist has to focus on the people who are the mostly likely threats.

If the EP specialist deems the person to be a potential threat, he should build a file that contains the person's photo, a description of his grievance or desire, and a list of where and when he has tried to approach the principal in the past. With that information, the protective agents will know who to watch for and will be better able to predict when and where he is likely to turn up. Although the dangerous visitor to a protectee's home or office is obviously a great cause for concern, keeping even the benign nuisance visitor at bay is an important duty.

Stalkers. In recent years, the threat of stalking has gained much attention. News reports describe incidents in which television and film stars and other celebrities have been the object of intense, unwanted attention. (The long list of objects of stalkers' attentions includes such familiar names as Jody Foster, David Letterman, John Lennon, Michael J. Fox, and Michael Landon.) When that attention consists of too much fan mail, it's a nuisance. When the stars are physically stalked like prey, when an inappropriately interested person follows the principal around, lurks at locations where the principal is likely to appear, or actually sneaks or breaks into the principal's house or office, it's a major problem and one that, unfortunately, is difficult to solve.

Interestingly, it is not necessary to be nationally famous to attract a stalker. A principal need only be prominent in the circles he inhabits. If the stalker feels the principal occupies a higher social, economic, or other plane than the stalker does, that impression may be enough reason to become fixated on the victim.

Though they may not appear mentally ill, stalkers typically have developed an irrational love for or hatred of their victims. The stalker may feel his prey loves him deeply, even if the two have never met. That feeling may be based on the most casual contact between the two, on an exchange of glances, or on nothing at all. The stalker may even feel that the victim's current rejections are a test of his love. Other themes that may motivate him are destiny—the idea that fate has decreed that the stalker and the victim should be together; revenge against a former employer, a business partner, or a politician; and narcissism, in which the stalker is motivated by rage over an insult or slight.

Some research suggests that the great majority of murderous stalking cases involve jilted lovers—most often, spurned men stalking the women who rejected them. Clearly, jilted-lover cases could apply to many types of protectees.

How can an EP specialist protect his client from a stalker? First, the agent must identify whether the person is in fact a stalker. Several techniques of home and office security help with that: archived video recordings (which allow the EP specialist to see whether and how often the suspect has visited or lurked), interviews with suspects, etc.

Second, the agent must attempt to rid the principal of the threat and annoyance posed by the stalker. In some cases, working to have the stalker arrested, jailed, or committed to a mental institution may be appropriate. Doing so requires paying significant attention to record keeping (details of encounters and communications with the stalker) and evidence handling (saving gifts, letters, voice-mail messages, and other forms of evidence in a way that preserves forensic information such as fingerprints, postmarks, etc.). However, many persons who have relied on the justice system to rid them of stalkers have found that method slow, cumbersome, and sometimes ineffective. There is also reason to believe that restraining orders and peace bonds only challenge the stalker to try harder. Arrest and incarceration may help temporarily, but a stalker who hasn't killed anyone is unlikely to be jailed for life—he'll get out, and he'll be back.

An executive protection-oriented solution is to view stalking as yet another threat against which the target must be hardened. That means preventing the stalker from seeing, communicating with, or following the principal. Severing those contacts serves several purposes: it insulates the principal from annoying, frightening, and potentially dangerous encounters; it prevents the occurrence of encounters that might encourage the stalker (such as one-to-one conversations in which the victim attempts to dissuade the stalker from his activities); and it hardens the target for the purpose of making it more desirable for the stalker to move along to another target. The EP specialist's goal, of course, is not to steer the stalker toward another victim but merely to steer him away from the agent's own protectee.

Stalking continues to draw attention in the media and in criminal justice circles, particularly as it relates to domestic violence. The era of stalking is still developing—there are now cases in which police and prosecutors have construed aggressive e-mail communications as stalking.

Safety

Preventing injuries and minimizing their impact is a key part of protecting the principal and facilitating his activities at the office and at home. The two safety considerations most in line with an EP specialists' responsibilities involve (1) fire prevention and survival and (2) first aid. In well-constructed, well-managed homes and offices, it is not as if fires break out constantly, but when they do they can be fatal, obviously, and even when not fatal they are extremely inconvenient and disruptive. In other words, a fire that doesn't represent a failure to protect the principal's physical well-being may, considering the damage and other inconvenience, still represent a failure to facilitate the principal's work and personal activities. The other major safety consideration, first aid, provides the EP specialist with the opportunity to perform heroic service, keeping the principal alive or at least preventing further injury or reducing pain. First aid skills, when applied to guests or associates, can also make the principal look like a hero for keeping such a useful person as the EP specialist around. Moreover, because minor injuries are fairly common, there's a good chance the protective agent will be able to use his first-aid skills.

Fire Prevention. Preventing fires at the principal's workplace and home is not an onerous task. That stands in contrast to the challenge of ensuring fire safety in facilities over which the EP specialist has almost no control, such as hotels. That particular challenge is discussed in Chapter 7, Domestic and International Travel. At the office, most fire prevention will already have been attended to by building codes, inspectors, and facility managers. (However, the protective agent had better make sure fire prevention has been attended to properly. If in doubt, it might be worthwhile to hire a fire safety engineer to check the environment carefully.) The EP specialist can take the extra step of providing the protectee with packaged smoke hoods, some brands of which enable the wearer to breathe safely for up to 15 minutes while escaping a smoky building;[58] an additional smoke detector beyond those provided by the building designer or facility manager; an escape ladder (if feasible); an extra fire extinguisher; and, above all, practice in escaping the building by several different routes. Such practice should include crawling along the floor to avoid breathing smoke and poisonous gases and making one's way out in darkness.

At the executive's home, the EP specialist may have even more control over the situation. If the home is large or old or for some other reason a little more susceptible to fire than other houses, it might pay to hire a fire safety engineer to assess the situation and recommend equipment, practices, and building modifications that would reduce the likelihood of fire. If the home has a security alarm system, it might make sense to integrate fire detection and notification with the security console.

---

[58] One type is QuickMask®, which is effective against smoke, tear gas, OC (oleoresin capsicum, or pepper) spray, and the nerve agent sarin, which was used in the March 20, 1995, attacks on the Tokyo subway. Contact Fume-Free, Inc., P.O. Box 1680, Stuart, FL 34995. Phone (800) 386-3373.

Certainly there are many simple measures that the principal, being an intelligent person, may already have taken. However, human nature tends to leave many obvious precautions undone, so the EP specialist should double-check on the household's fire-readiness. In terms of equipment, the gear is much the same as described above for the office: smoke hoods, smoke detectors, escape ladders, and fire extinguishers. In terms of practices, the principal, along with his family and domestic staff,[59] should be trained in a number of matters: the best means of escape (specific windows and doors to use, rope or chain ladders and permanent fire escapes, the importance of crawling down low, and how to escape in darkness); the importance of checking the temperature of doorknobs to see if they are hot before opening any door; rendezvous points outside the house; how to report fires (by shouting and by calling the fire department as soon as the fire is noticed, not after waiting for the fire to grow); safe smoking, cooking, and heating procedures; the necessity of reporting suspicious-smelling appliances; and what to do when clothing catches on fire (stop, drop, and roll). Most people are generally aware of these practices, but by having the principal and other members of the household rehearse them occasionally, the EP specialist will be following Sun Tzu's advice to "make no mistakes."

With a little effort, the EP specialist can help bring the risk of fire down to near zero and also greatly reduce the principal's risk of injury if there is a fire. There are enough threats over which a protective effort has little control: plane crashes, cancer, suicide. It certainly makes sense to minimize the threats one can.

First Aid. First aid is discussed in this chapter on security at homes and offices because those are the places where the principal spends, by far, the most time and therefore where he is likely to be

---

[59] Why the domestic staff? Can't they take care of themselves? Probably, but goodwill and prudence demand that they be trained, too. Undesirable publicity can result when an employee of a famous person dies or is injured. One example is the news coverage that resulted from the shooting and stabbing of a security guard at Sylvester Stallone's estate in Miami on July 17, 1996. No one suggested Stallone had anything to do with the incident, yet the news creates a sour association in the public mind.

when he injures himself, falls ill, or for some other reason requires first aid. If the EP specialist wishes to protect the principal from harm and help him operate productively, statistics support the relevance of being able to apply first aid.[60]

It isn't necessary for the EP specialist to be a doctor, an emergency medical technician, a battlefield medic, or a registered nurse. While a protective agent must be a good generalist and possess a wide range of knowledge, in-depth, expert medical training is too much to ask. What is required is a sound understanding of "10-minute medicine"—that is, the steps required to assess and stabilize a person who has suffered an injury or the sudden onset of illness, such as a heart attack.

The EP specialist should not attempt to learn 10-minute medicine solely from a book. Much better is to take a short course in emergency medicine or first aid, CPR, and the Heimlich maneuver. A good course would cover, at least, the primary survey of a patient (checking airway, breathing, and circulation; performing triage), the secondary survey (assessing the patient's spine, scalp, face, chest, abdomen, back, pelvis, and extremities), injuries (soft tissue, fractures, trauma, medical emergencies), and the proper contents of a first-aid kit (see box).

First Aid Kit Contents		
triangular bandages (cloth)	splints (several different sizes)	pocket (Swiss army) knife
rolled bandages	pillow	CPR barrier mask
eye protector	blanket	face masks
occlusive dressings	blood pressure cuff	towel
adhesive tape	stethoscope	sugar or candy bar
shears	gloves	plastic wrap
Diphenhydramine (Benadryl) capsules, 25 mg.	convenience drugs, such as aspirin, antacids, or burn cream	plastic or paper cup (to place over object protruding from body)
gauze pads and dressings	adhesive bandages	

---

[60] See Chapter 1, Threat Assessment.

The EP specialist's skills accompany him wherever he goes, of course, and so should his first aid kit. The chapter on automobile travel mentioned the importance of placing a first-aid kit in the car. It is also important to keep such a kit both at the principal's office and at his home, and to bring one along when traveling. In addition, the EP specialist should carry a fresh supply of any prescription drugs required by the principal and be familiar with and able to respond to known medical problems of the principal and his family.

Emergency medicine skills help a protective agent assist both the principal and those the principal cares about. If one of the principal's family members or guests should require first aid (because of, say, a kitchen accident or a heart attack), the EP specialist can step in and save the day. This is an example of the agent's global responsibility to the principal's world.

Note that some legal questions arise regarding the provision of first aid. If the person requiring first aid is one to whom the EP specialist owes no duty of care, then no legal blame can be laid upon him if he refrains from assisting the person. If the EP specialist does assist that person, he assumes some responsibility, varying from state to state, for providing first aid ably and at least doing no harm.

It is up to the EP specialist and the principal to decide whether such risk should be taken; however, it doesn't look good, and is possibly immoral, not to assist an injured person whom you could obviously and reasonably help. Because of the variation in states' Good Samaritan laws, this question is one that the EP specialist, the principal, and a lawyer should iron out in advance.

Bombs

Bombings, sad to say, are common. (See sidebar.) The big ones make the news all too frequently; the little ones are so common they don't get much attention. Some bombs or incendiary devices (the distinction being that the former primarily explode with great force, while the latter explode and produce an intensely hot fire) are easy to make. The recipes can be found readily in books, on videos, and on the Internet, while the ingredients can be found in hardware stores and chemical and farm supply houses.

Powerful homemade bombs (such as pipe bombs) can be quite compact. Highly powerful homemade bombs tend to be large (like the bomb carried in a rental truck outside the federal building in Oklahoma City). Amateurs who want bombs that are both compact and highly powerful can steal bomb materials from construction or military sites; terrorists, of course, can obtain the most exotic, miniature bombs in the world. In short, to anyone with such a desire, building a bomb is well within reach.

FBI Bomb Report

Bombing is on the rise. According to "FBI Explosives Unit-Bomb Data Center, General Information Bulletin 95-2: 1994 Bombing Incidents," the latest FBI report available, 3,163 bombing incidents were reported to the EU-BDC in 1994. That is a 6 percent increase over 1993.

Explosives accounted for 77 percent of the incidents; the rest involved incendiary devices. In 78 percent of the incidents, the devices successfully detonated or ignited. Only 4 percent of the actual and attempted bombings were preceding by a warning or threat.

The top five bombing targets were residences (52 percent of incidents), commercial operations and vehicles (both 11 percent), open areas (7 percent), and academic facilities (4 percent). Bombings injured 308 persons and killed 31.

The trend is clearly upward, as the chart on the next page shows:

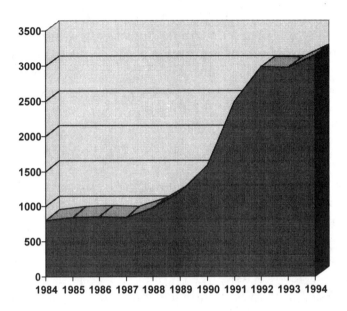

Bombing Incidents, Explosive and Incendiary,
Actual and Attempted
(FBI Data)

States with especially high numbers of bombing incidents include California (545), Florida (312), and Illinois (353). Populous states with relatively low numbers of incidents include New York (109) and Texas (193).

As for knowing what to look for, pipe bombs account for 39 percent of all improvised explosive devices.

The techniques for preventing, detecting, and reacting to bombs are similar for both the home and the office. Good, ongoing intelligence will help the EP specialist determine the relative likelihood of a bomb attack and the types of attacks that might be expected. For example, a protectee who faces the wrath of an ex-spouse's boyfriend could be targeted for a pipe-bombing or mail-bombing, while a protectee who, through dealings in international business, has been targeted by terrorists might instead have to be defended against an explosives-packed car parked against his home or office or the detonation of a bomb placed under a bridge over which he drives. (Chapter 5, Automobile Security, discussed protection measures against bombs planted in or on the executive's car.) The source of the threat does not positively determine the type of bomb attack to be expected, but it might give some probabilities based on past events. Certainly, not everyone is a likely target of a bomb attack, but having some knowledge of what to expect helps the EP specialist determine where to focus his preventive efforts. This section on bombs is extensive; fortunately, many of the protective measures specified below for bombs also protect the principal against other assaults and hazards.

Prevention. Absolutely preventing a bomb attack against the principal's home or office is impossible, but the EP specialist can take several steps to make such an attack more difficult. This is another instance of target hardening, whereby the EP specialist makes it more challenging for an attacker to harm the principal, under the theory that certain attackers will, in effect, take their business elsewhere. In discouraging the placement or delivery of a bomb, target hardening consists of forcing the bomb to surmount numerous security rings before reaching the principal. A number of measures can be selected for both home and office, depending on which are deemed necessary and which are physically feasible. These measures also increase the level of security against other intrusions. For bomb prevention, target hardening measures include the following:

- selecting a building that is set back from the street
- surrounding the property with a fence or some other barrier, such as a row of trees or bushes
- eliminating or minimizing hiding places against the building (foundation plantings, trash bins, mailboxes, etc.) and inside the public areas of the building
- controlling access to exterior building doors, parking lots, and garages (via guards, card systems, or other means)
- controlling access within the building (through interior control of access to the principal's floor, suite, or personal office) to make it difficult for anyone to leave a bomb close to the principal

In high-threat environments, the installation of bomb-proof glazing material designed to minimize the effects of shattering glass can be an effective injury-reduction measure. Bomb-proof sheer curtains also minimize glass damage.

The measures just listed make it hard, though probably not impossible, for a bomber to park a car loaded with explosives right next to the principal's home or office, to place a bomb up against the building, or to place a bomb right in the principal's personal office or other room.

If physical barriers are in place and procedural access control is enforced, no one is likely to be able to hand-carry an explosive device right into the principal's office or bedroom. However, where a person might be prevented from going, a piece of mail might be carried right into the principal's hands. If that mail is a bomb, the concentric rings of protection will have been penetrated just as successfully. The term of art used to be "package bombs," but sophisticated, new bomb materials are thin enough and light enough to travel easily even in slim envelopes. There's no particular preventive measure an EP specialist can take against the sending of mail bombs; instead, he must rely on detection and interception.

Detection. If the principal is to be protected, it is simply essential to establish mail bomb safety procedures. The mail must not go to the principal before it has been screened. Screening, however, does not necessarily involve expensive equipment. It is a multi-stage process that escalates for suspicious pieces of mail. Because the overwhelming majority of letters and packages are routine and benign, what is needed is a screening process, a sort of triage in which the mail checker decides which few pieces require further study. At work, the mail-checking responsibility might fall to a mail-room clerk or to the EP specialist. At the home, probably the EP specialist will have to handle it.

Over time, bomb experts have discerned certain characteristics that may indicate the presence of explosives. Whoever is given the mail-checking responsibility should be trained on the right procedures for performing the first-level examination and for reporting questionable items to a superior. No mail should reach the principal before it has passed the screener. It is important, however, that the screening process be quick. The protective effort will lose the support of the principal and his staff if the mail is delayed inordinately. The only time they understand and support this process is when the news reports a bombing, and that only lasts for a week or so.

Despite advances in bomb materials, plastic explosive is still not as thin, light, or pliable as paper. That means a paper-thin, letter-size envelope, weighing less than an ounce and carrying correct postage, is probably OK. Anything over an eighth of an inch thick may need further checking, as would any envelope that is marked to the principal's personal attention, is mailed from a foreign country, bears misspelled words, shows grease spots or strange smells, or bears an illegible return address. Another red flag is excess postage: typically, the bomber prefers not to hand his envelope to a post office employee for weighing and therefore places too much postage on the envelope to be on the safe side. In the initial screening, the mail-checker should also feel the envelope, gently, trying to detect the presence of any strings or wires. The mail screener should also examine the envelope's weight symmetry. The weight should usually be evenly distributed, like a stack of papers. If the weight is all in the middle or on one end, that could be a bad sign.

If an envelope fails this first cut, it needs further checking before it can be passed to the principal. First, the mail-checker should inquire whether the principal was expecting anything from the apparent sender. Next, the sender listed on the return address should be contacted to see if he sent the item. If neither method satisfies the mail-checker's concerns, he should notify the protection or security staff.

The technology involved in bomb-detection machines changes rapidly, and there's no sense buying yesterday's technology. Therefore, before asking the principal or his company to lay out the money for one of those expensive devices, the EP specialist should gather as much information as possible from police bomb squads, vendors, and possibly consultants who are knowledgeable about such equipment. Some machines can detect most bombs, but none can detect all, and many machines require substantial training before their results can be interpreted correctly. Also, some technologies harm magnetic storage media, so they might not be practical to use if the principal often receives computer diskettes or tapes by mail. Among the types of bomb-detection equipment are computed tomography, ion vapor characterization, neutron stream, nuclear magnetic resonance, thermal neutron activation, vapor trace analysis, x-ray (dual-beam, backscatter), and quadrupole resonance. It's not a simple matter. The most commonly used device is the x-ray scanner. It is simple to operate, is relatively inexpensive, and gives a visual read of package contents. Even at $5,000, it's cheap insurance.

Because of the greater ease of concealing a bomb in a package, as opposed to an envelope, and the greater difficulty of observing suspicious signs about them (weight distribution, etc.), packages need a greater level of scrutiny. Any package could be a bomb, but usually the number of packages received by the principal is relatively small (in relation to letters). The triage process for packages includes directing extra suspicion to a package that is not expected, that carries a return address that is illegible or proves impossible to check with a phone call, that is marked to the personal attention of the principal, or that was not (or, in a case of uncertainty, may not have been) delivered by a postal worker or legitimate delivery service employee. If a package does not pass this first level of scrutiny, the mail-checker should follow the steps already outlined for letters.

Of course, the need for detection also applies to bombs that do not arrive through the mail. At work, security staff should be on the lookout for "orphaned" boxes, bags, briefcases, or other objects that could contain bombs. The number of watchful eyes can be greatly increased if the EP specialist or corporate security staff instructs employees to be alert to such items and report them at once. At home or on the estate, staffers can be asked to report suspicious items found on the grounds. Protective personnel, especially any patrolling guards, should routinely scrutinize places where bombs could most readily be placed, such as against the house or next to or inside any important outbuildings. If the threat level rises because of an important event on the premises, bomb-sniffing dogs may need to be brought in. Local law enforcement agencies may be able to provide that service, depending on their capabilities and the EP specialist's or principal's relationship with them.

Reaction. If a bomb is discovered or a bomb threat is received, well-rehearsed responses should be initiated. At the workplace, the discovery of a suspicious object may be grounds for an evacuation, or it may not. The decision depends on the threat level, the degree of suspicion about the object, and the difficulty, danger, and expense of evacuation. The decision tree should be established in advance, so that the EP specialist or corporate security staff know for certain, in a potentially tense situation, who should make the decision and using what criteria. If there have been bomb threats recently, the object looks very suspicious, and it is not too difficult to evacuate the building, then naturally the building should be emptied. (The evacuation route may have to differ, however, from that used in a fire in order to keep people away from the location of the possible bomb.) It is also important to consider whether, in a high-rise building, evacuating people from floors far above the bomb will only bring them closer to danger as they pass the bomb floor. If, by contrast, the current threat analysis suggests bomb risk is minuscule, the object is only a little questionable or can be neutralized or safely removed by explosives experts, and evacuations in the past have often resulted in unacceptable disruption, then perhaps the building should not be evacuated. It is hard to make the decision, but thinking through the various considerations in advance, during calm moments, will help the EP specialist make that call.

At the executive's home or estate, evacuation is usually not as problematic. At the home, too, the EP specialist is likely to have more control over what response is made in reaction to the discovery of such an object, not having to contend with corporate security and large numbers of employees. Of course, the evacuation of the residence must be done cautiously; the bomb could be a decoy designed by adversaries to draw the principal out of his secure enclave.

Sometimes suspicious objects are simply discovered on the premises, but other times the question of bomb response arises from a telephoned bomb threat. In cases where bombers or their associates call ahead to say a bomb has been placed and will be detonated, the goal may be not mass destruction but mass disruption. If such a call comes in, much can be gained by attempting to question the caller. At an office with a central switchboard, it might be sufficient to supply the telephone operators with a list of questions to ask the caller. If a caller can easily reach anyone to leave his message, it may be necessary to supply all employees with the bomb questionnaire. At the executive's home, the questionnaire can simply be placed next to or under all the phones in the house. In both locations, those who are expected to use the questionnaire must be instructed, in advance, on how to do so. A little practice goes a long way during a tense situation.

Bomb call questionnaires aren't long; it's unlikely the caller will hang on the line for a long conversation. The list can be printed on a small card or a sheet with blank spaces to be filled in. The following is one version of such a questionnaire, but the EP specialist will want to tailor the one he uses to the specific threats and circumstances faced by his protectee:

Bomb Call Questionnaire

Ask the caller:
1. When is the bomb going to go off?
2. Where is it?
3. What does it look like?
4. What would cause it to go off?
5. Why would anyone want to hurt us?

Note about the caller:
6. Quality of voice: accent, pitch, speed, nasality; presence of stammer, lisp, or other feature.
7. Apparent emotion: is caller calm, nervous, crying, excited, angry?
8. Does the voice sound familiar? Who does it sound like?

It may not be possible to obtain much information, but every little bit helps. If the bomb threat is real, the smallest nuggets of information may help in finding the bomb or catching the bomber. If the threat is a hoax, clues written down by the person taking the call may lead to the caller's capture.

Once a threat has been received, it may be necessary for the protective staff to search for the device. That is not a highly desirable assignment—who wants to find a bomb?—but it is necessary.

129

If a bomb is found, the local military or law enforcement EOD (explosive ordnance disposal) team should be called in; if no bomb is found, the executive can resume using his home or office.

One good bomb-search technique is for two agents to search each room. They divide the room into horizontal layers, typically four (floor to waist, waist to chin, chin to ceiling, and above a false ceiling, if any). Standing back-to-back, they begin to search the first layer, working their way around the room until the layer has been searched by both agents. Then they search the next layer, then the next, until the room is judged clean. The procedure is repeated in every room that requires searching. One reason it is so important to ask a bomb threat caller where the bomb is located is that it can take a long time to search a home or office building. If the caller can help narrow the search, so much the better.

If the searchers find a suspicious object, they should personally notify the situation leader or call him by using the internal phone system. Use of radios could detonate certain types of bombs. The executive protection team should create a safety zone with a radius of 300 feet or more—not just outwards, but also upwards, in the case of a high-rise building. Naturally, they should not touch the object but leave it to the EOD experts. One factor to beware of, however, is that the object found could be a decoy designed to distract the search team while the real bomb explodes elsewhere in the building.

Procedures

The preceding precautions—threat assessment, rings of protection, security engineering, intelligence and surveillance, fire and first aid measures, and bomb safety—are wasted if they are not converted from one-time activities to regular, consistently followed procedures. Almost any protective measure can be defeated, but protective measures that are not employed are especially easy to defeat. For example, a threat assessment that is performed once and then forgotten is worth little. Security alarm systems don't do much good if they are turned off or if repeated false alarms are assumed each time to be false. And a first aid kit is no help if it has been left at home and the principal suffers an injury at work or if the EP specialist hasn't reviewed the contents in a year. In fact, procedures are important not just in home and office security but in all facets of executive protection.

When it comes to making no mistakes, established, rehearsed, and sound procedures are everything. The EP specialist should make a point of training his own agents, the principal's family and domestic staff, and the principal's office staff about proper procedures regarding all the security measures discussed in this chapter. The training has to cover specific steps to take when someone comes to the door, when a package arrives, when tradesmen arrive, when the fire alarm goes off, and so on, plus one all-important rule: that the procedures must be followed *always*. Why should the rule be so strict? The reason is that the visitor who strongly requests an exception is more likely than others to be an adversary, and the incident that seems to merit an exception is more likely than others to have been staged just for the purpose of causing an exception to security procedures. Most people understand that offices and households have rules. People who push for exceptions to those rules or procedures may have a harmful motive.

The principal himself in many cases needs reminding of the importance of protective procedures. While protection service carries some benefits in the convenience department, it also carries some unavoidable inconveniences. A principal might wish to detour from a planned, well-checked travel route. Eager for a certain piece of mail, he might step forward to grab all the day's mail before it has been screened for bombs. He might even prop a secured door open for convenience. The best approach is for the EP specialist to anticipate these "violations" and work around them. The EP specialist can't usually insist that the principal comply with procedures, but he can tell the principal that those actions may increase the risk to the principal's life. He should intervene only under circumstances that present a clear danger.

The Home

The EP specialist has some control and influence here. Presumably, if the client is interested in personal protection, he will also be willing to let the EP specialist suggest modifications to the physical attributes and the procedures followed at the client's home or estate. The client might not accept all the agent's suggestions if he believes they are too inconvenient or expensive. However, from the EP specialist's point of view, securing the home is usually less problematic than protecting a corporate site. He has only the client to please (not a whole company); the amount of traffic into and out of an estate should be much less than at an office; and if any place can be made into a fortress, or at least a comfortable version of one, it is an estate.

Note that the foundation for determining the security needs of the residence is a full security survey. Such a survey should cover fire protection, access points, neighborhood environment, police and emergency responses, lighting and alarms, etc.

This discussion will focus on securing the principal at a detached house on a piece of land at least large enough to separate the house from the street and other houses. If the protectee lives in an apartment, the agent's ability to make physical modifications for security is much more limited because he probably cannot control the whole building. In that case, only some, not all, of the following discussion applies.

Range of threats

At the beginning of this chapter, the discussion of updating the threat assessment emphasized the importance of calculating the risk that a particular principal might reasonably face. The threat assessment might determine that likely threats consist primarily of burglary, vandalism, and car theft—problems that most other residents on the block face. In that case, the EP specialist can take the appropriate cautions and then concentrate on the facilitation side of executive protection. On the other hand, if the threat assessment determined a very high level of threat, such as bombs, kidnapping, terrorist attacks, or sophisticated surveillance for purposes of industrial espionage, political gain, or blackmail, then the EP specialist will have to edge his efforts toward hardening the target. The EP specialist should look over the measures and procedures that are listed below and, perhaps with technical help, choose those that are appropriate to the protectee's location on the threat-level spectrum.

Physical security

An earlier section of this chapter described the advantages of hiring a security engineer or other security consultant to select physical security equipment. There are so many technical details involved in selecting and effectively deploying security equipment that an average EP specialist is unlikely to be able to keep up with all of them. However, even if the agent plans to hire out the detail work, he had better understand the basics of security hardware and systems—at least enough to know the vocabulary and the general options. Below are some recommendations that apply particularly to protection of the estate.

Using the previously described theory of concentric rings of protection, security should begin not at the house but at the property's perimeter. Depending on the threat level, the land should be demarcated as being private. However, the ways of doing so are not always self-evident. A security concept known as "crime prevention through environmental design" offers several good ideas.

CPTED is the use of physical design features to simultaneously discourage crime and encourage legitimate use of an environment. Originally developed to reduce crime in public housing projects, CPTED can be applied to any space from a home or office building to an entire city.

CPTED offers protection without the fortress mentality. Use of heavy-duty security construction is minimized, and when it is used, it is integrated into the overall design, reducing negative visual impact.

Major concepts in CPTED include these:

- defensible space
- surveillance
- lighting
- landscaping

Defensible space. In the defensible space concept, areas are designated as public, semi-private, or private. Those terms designate the appropriate use of each zone and determine who may occupy it and in what circumstances. Public zones are generally open to anyone and are the least secure of the three zones—for example, the street in front of the estate. Semi-private zones create a buffer between public and private zones. They are accessible to the public, but are set off from the public zone. At an estate, the route to the mailbox or wherever packages are delivered might be a semi-private zone (and then only open to delivery persons, not the general public); at an office, an example of such a zone would be an interior courtyard. Private zones are restricted. Access is controlled and limited to specific people or categories of people.

Zones are divided by barriers, either physical or symbolic. Physical barriers include fencing, walls, gates, some forms of landscaping, and locked doors. Symbolic barriers—low, decorative fences; flower beds; or changes in sidewalk patterns or materials—do not prevent physical movement but indicate that a transition between zones has taken place.

Surveillance. A space can be designed to maximize surveillance by its legitimate users, and criminals are reluctant to act if they feel they will be seen. Informal or natural surveillance can be maximized by designs that minimize visual obstacles and eliminate places of concealment for potential assailants. Formal surveillance methods, such as closed-circuit television, electronic monitoring, fixed guard posts, and security patrols, are used when natural surveillance must be supplemented. Public and semi-private zones that are isolated or concealed from view may require formal surveillance.

Lighting. Proper lighting discourages criminal activity and enhances natural surveillance opportunities. The necessary amount of lighting varies, but the key attribute is evenness—bright spots and shadows should be avoided. Highly vulnerable areas and those that could conceal a potential attacker should be lit especially brightly. It's also important to light up the criminal without spotlighting the potential victim.

Landscaping. Landscaping performs several CPTED functions. Features such as decorative fencing, flower beds, ground cover, and varied patterns in cement work can clearly show separation between zones. If more substantial barriers are needed, shrubbery such as evergreen hedges or dense, thorny plants (trifoliate orange among them) can be used to create formidable obstacles. Visual surveillance corridors can be maintained by limiting shrubbery to a

134

maximum height of three feet and trees to a minimum height of six feet at the lowest branches. That way, visibility between three and six feet from the ground will remain unimpaired. Even the growth rates of various plants should be taken into consideration, as a bush too small to hide behind this year may be just right next year if trimming and pruning fall behind schedule.

CPTED works best when its precepts are integrated into new construction. Nevertheless, even for a property that is already built, the EP specialist can keep CPTED in mind when deciding (1) how the principal should enter and leave the estate, (2) where on the estate various activities should take place for greatest security, (3) what security hardware should be purchased and, especially, where it should be installed, and (4) what would constitute optimal surveillance, lighting, and landscaping.

Working from the outside in, the EP specialist will have to be familiar with and make decisions about the following security equipment. Of course, high-end security would require many of these devices, while moderate or low-end security would require only a few. In addition, some of this equipment would look offensive or unattractive in areas of the estate that are seen daily but might be acceptable in concealed areas. Here are the major categories of physical security equipment:

- **fences:** wooden, chain link, wrought iron; topped with spikes, barbed wire, razor ribbon
- **fence sensors:** taut-wire, strain, flex, shock, fiber-optic
- **gates:** vehicle, pedestrian, automatic, manual, high security, decorative
- **vehicle barriers:** bollards, tire traps, pneumatic or hydraulic anti-ram devices
- **lighting:** visible, infrared, motion-activated
- **closed-circuit television systems:** pan-tilt-zoom controls, low-light, infrared; various housings (outdoor, extreme weather, indoor, concealed, domes)
- **perimeter intrusion sensors:** capacitance field, electrostatic field, infrared beams, fiber-optic continuity, microwave motion, passive infrared, buried pressure,

seismic geophone; tamper-evident seals (for utility access panels, manhole covers, etc.)

- **high-security apertures:** metal or solid wood doors; windows made of security glass, plastic, or wire-glass or covered with security film (possibly blast- or bullet-resistant); grilles; door viewers; hinges with non-removable pins; window-locking hardware; locking skylights
- **building-intrusion sensors:** passive infrared, magnetic, mechanical, mercury, continuity loop, glass-break, piezoelectric, shock; for windows, doors, walls, skylights, ceilings
- **interior-intrusion sensors:** passive infrared, CCTV motion detectors, infrasonic, microwave, photoelectric, ultrasonic, vibration
- **access control systems:** locks (manual, electric strike, pneumatic, electromagnetic); cards, keys (regular or noncopiable), digital touchpads; for doors, windows, gates, garages, manhole covers
- **safes:** fire, weapons, valuables
- **security equipment monitoring:** monitoring station (on-site, long-distance); integrated security, fire, and utility/process monitoring; CCTV switchers, recorders, monitors, multiplexers, video printers
- **fire detection, notification, and suppression systems:** detectors (independent, hard-wired, smoke, heat, ionization), alarms, sprinkler systems (water, clean agents)
- **communications:** radios; intercoms; panic buttons; distress codes on keypads or phone numbers; cellular phones; personal duress transmitters that pinpoint principal's location—in shape of pen, beeper, name badge on chain; scrambled telephones, cellular phones, fax machines, radios

To gain a cursory understanding of the categories just listed, the EP specialist should take some time to read a book or two on the basics of physical security equipment and perhaps make a habit of reading a security magazine regularly. Appropriate books can be ordered by mail from specialty publishing houses or found at libraries, especially those at colleges with security or criminal justice degree programs.

Special considerations

After the major physical security matters, a number of special concerns merit attention. Such considerations arise mostly because of the principal's personal wealth, valuable property, or desirability as a kidnapping target.

First among the special considerations is the safe room. A safe room is a place in which the principal and, if necessary, his family can "hole up" if intruders invade the house. The idea is that the principal and his family would lock themselves in the room, contact a source of help, and await rescue. A safe room needn't be large—a bathroom or walk-in closet would be fine—but it needs a fortified door with a dead bolt lock that is hard to defeat, must not be vulnerable to break-ins through a window or other portal, and, of course, should have in it some means of communication with the police or security staff, such as a land-line or cellular telephone, a citizen's band or other two-way radio, or a panic button wired to a central monitoring station. Based on the level of threat and the principal's self-defense capabilities, the EP specialist and the client can discuss whether it would be a good idea to keep a firearm in the safe room, too. Aside from that, the safe room should contain smoke hoods, water, duct tape, a signal whistle, pepper spray, a first-aid kit, flashlights, and batteries.

When police respond to an incident, they want to know whether anyone on the scene is carrying a firearm. EP specialists have the same need. An agent who rushes into the house to answer a panic alarm from the principal needs to know whether the principal or one of his family members is likely to be armed. The EP specialist should know the location and type of all firearms in the house.

A few other items that need to make the estate security checklist are these:

- Make sure security measures apply to the estate's out-buildings and garage, not just the main part of the house. The garage may prove a less-observed route to the house. Also, if the garage is well secured, then once the principal's car is searched for bombs it can stay searched and not have to be rechecked constantly.

- For both security and quality of life reasons, it might be worthwhile to set up an emergency power generator on-site. If assailants cut the electricity, security systems will still operate, and if a storm knocks the power out, the venison won't rot and the wine cellar won't get too hot.

- If the principal has any special collections (such as art, guns, or wine), they may need customized protection against theft or damage.

- The use of a shredder to destroy personal documents (letters, bills, bank statements, itineraries) greatly reduces the likelihood that anyone who snooped through the estate's garbage could learn anything useful.

- Examine the security of the telephone service. A cut phone line can seriously hamper security—it prevents the principal from calling for help, and it keeps the alarm system from sending a signal to the police or the alarm monitoring company. First, find out where the telephone company line runs into the house (usually at the interface box). Make a judgment on the security of the box itself and the lines that run from it to the house and away from the house. Ask the phone company to move the interface box to the inside of the home. Most phone companies don't like to do so, but if the principal's security concerns are explained to them, they will usually comply. If the phone line runs overhead, it can be covered with guarding material at the residence and at the pole location. The idea is to make it very difficult for someone to cut (or tap into) the line. A backup plan is to purchase a cellular backup. That way, if the land-line phone system goes out, due to tampering or any other problem, the house phones will switch to cellular and calls can still be made.

A final, very important consideration for home security is K-9 assistance. Even in an era of sophisticated technology, an age-old helper—the dog—is one of the best tools available for detection and deterrence.[61]

The main assets a K-9 adds to a protection detail are its extraordinary senses of hearing and smell, which allow the dog to detect an intruder long before a human could. The dog's sense of smell is at least 100 times better than man's, and its hearing is easily 10 times better than man's. In addition, a dog can detect a greater range of sounds than its human counterpart. Those assets make a dog an excellent aid to a protection detail.

The dog is also useful for detecting explosives. It can be used to check for explosives throughout the home, in addition to cars, aircraft, and any other area or form of transportation that the principal will use. In fact, a single dog can be cross-trained to detect explosives and serve as a patrol dog.

By far the best use of a K-9 is a handler–dog team, in which the handler is ultimately responsible for the actions of the K-9 and serves as the reasoning part of the team. On a tracking, apprehension, search, or patrol assignment, a handler–dog team can do the work of several human patrol officers. Around the estate, the handler can also ensure that the K-9 behaves in a way that does not cause the principal any embarrassment.

In some cases a K-9 should be used inside the home. For example, if the principal is a woman and she wants privacy from her male EP specialist in the evening, a dog can serve as the agent's ears (and nose) literally right next to the principal's bed. That

---

[61] For this section on K-9s, the author wishes to acknowledge the help of Karen Freeman Duet and George Duet of K-9 Companions Dog Training and K-9 Security and Detection Int'l, L.L.C., 13703 J.J. Lane, Lake Matthews, CA 92570. They are also authors of *The Home and Family Protection Dog: Selection and Training* (Howell Book House, 1993) and *The Business Security K-9: Selection and Training* (Howell Book House, 1995). The Duets can be reached at (800) 870-5926.

works, of course, only if the principal likes the arrangement and the dog is properly trained for such an assignment.

The use of a dog by itself in a perimeter protection situation is somewhat effective but less than optimal. The dog without a human partner is vulnerable to a number of dangers because of its inability to reason. A person on the other side of the estate's fence can plan for the defeat of the dog, whether by poisoning, shooting, cutting the fence and luring the dog, or cajoling with food. Outdoors, alone, the dog is at a disadvantage to humans.

By contrast, a dog inside the home has a distinct advantage over a human intruder. The dog can hear the intruder before he even enters the house. The dog also has the drop on him because of the dog's familiarity with the environment. Those factors, coupled with the element of surprise that the dog can have on its side, puts the intruder at a real disadvantage when a dog is in the house.

A protection operation may wish to use K-9s for temporary assignments, such as at the principal's vacation home. In that case, a local K-9 handler may be used. Alternatively, for ongoing use of a dog at the principal's main home, it might be better to purchase the dog. K-9s require special care and handling, and it is important that anyone who plans to use, and especially to own, a K-9 be properly trained.

The Office

The task of protecting a principal at his office poses some interesting challenges that differ from those faced at the principal's home. For one, the EP specialist may or may not be in charge of security for the whole office building. The principal's company might use only part of a large building, or the company may employ a corporate security director who is part of a different chain of command and over whom the EP specialist has no control. Another challenge is the volume of human traffic and the wide range of activities, which make the workplace a much more fluid, complex, unpredictable, and uncontrollable environment than the home. Although the following section describes some of the office-based threats from which a principal must be protected, one threat is frightening enough and complicated enough to merit its own chapter (Chapter 8). That threat is the range of dangers that come under the heading of workplace violence.

Corporate protection program

As mentioned above, protecting a principal at the office raises some special challenges. Those challenges extend beyond those associated with actually performing the job and reach into the realm of corporate culture, politics, and structure. These latter challenges are especially acute in situations where the EP specialist is funded by the corporation that the protectee works for, and not by the protectee himself. A corporate executive protection program will only succeed if the company supports it both financially and psychologically.

The existence of an executive protection program in the corporate environment may constantly be under scrutiny; its permanence is not guaranteed. Both the corporation and the executive may have certain disinclinations to continue the program. Why? First of all, executive protection raises unpleasant thoughts of danger and death. Second, executive protection doesn't contribute to the bottom line; it isn't a profit center. Third, if the executive protection operation runs 24 hours a day, the corporation might not fully support its budget, requiring the principal to cover some costs himself. Fourth, the principal may feel the EP specialist's presence is burdensome; fellow CEOs may look at him as an oddity when they themselves go about their day unprotected. Fifth, the executive may worry that others think he isn't man enough to take care of himself. In some settings, the executive protection program is on firm footing only as long as the principal remembers the latest kidnapping headline.

Without a doubt, the preceding objections are hard to counteract. However, the EP specialist can minimize them by learning and working within the corporate culture. If the agent knows the rules of the game, he can survive, even thrive, and perform a vital service for both the principal and the company. Perhaps the fundamental rule of the game is to maintain the confidence of corporate leadership, and that requires making sure the protection program is perceived positively. No matter how efficacious and cost-effective the program is, if key corporate figures believe—even ignorantly—that the program is not worthwhile, then the operation is sunk, just as surely as if it were a victim of its own incompetence.

How should the EP specialist build a favorable reputation for the protection program? He should take the trouble to show the corporate decision-makers the high quality of the program and its personnel and of his own ability as a *corporate officer*, not just as a narrowly limited protection specialist. Skill in executive protection is, obviously, a central requirement, but it is just as important that the EP specialist be perceived as a respected, effective, well-informed, and articulate executive who can represent the CEO and the corporation in their best light. Developing personal comfort and dialogue with the major players, keeping them informed, seeking their advice, and being accessible pays huge dividends.

Executive protection in the corporate environment does not exist in a vacuum. The EP effort has to fit into the corporate mission. That's why the EP specialist needs to understand the corporate big picture and accommodate himself to it. Where is the company headed? What are its resources? What motivates corporate leadership? If the EP specialist can answer those questions and integrate the answers into the EP effort, he won't go wrong. It is also wrongheaded for an agent to believe that his special access to the principal exempts him from having to conform to corporate rules.

When corporate accountants claim that the executive protection program is an expensive, intrusive extravagance, the rebuttal must be this: EP permits the chief executive to live safely in and move efficiently through a dangerous world—and to concentrate fully on the business at hand. The same rebuttal can be given to an executive concerned about the unavoidable quantum of inconvenience that EP imposes on him.

Range of threats

The EP specialist's ongoing threat analysis tells him what to protect the principal against and approximately how likely various threats are. However, an agent thinking primarily of protecting a principal physically could overlook some categories of concern. At the workplace, threats to the principal are of two types: those that could harm him physically (robbery, bombs, kidnapping, harassment, etc.) and those that could cause him or his company serious inconvenience or embarrassment (computer crime, drug use and sales, industrial espionage, etc.). The first category is familiar territory for an able EP specialist; the second category may require that a specialist be called in. A principal's body and property are valuable, but so is his reputation, which could suffer severe damage if, for example, drugs were found in his office, a hacker violated his computer, or a visitor absconded with vital trade secrets from the principal's desk.

Physical security

In many cases, the EP specialist will not be in charge of overall corporate security. If he is, he has a great deal of control over the security of the work environment and can choose from the many security equipment options listed in the section on physical security for homes, above.[62] But more likely, the EP specialist can at best *influence* the security of the workplace. In that case, he should focus his efforts on the locations where security will make the greatest difference to the principal's safety: the parking lot or garage and the executive suite. The security of other areas, such as the main entrance, may not be customizable to the needs of the principal, but the EP specialist should still check to make sure security equipment and procedures there are sufficient. The concept of providing concentric rings of protection still holds.

The principal's parking space should not be graced with a large sign announcing "President" or any other title. Any value such a sign may have for purposes of vanity is far outweighed by the fact that it tells everyone exactly where to find the principal and his car.

---

[62] Some additional options that might be useful in a workplace setting are biometric devices (fingerprint, hand geometry, iris pattern recognition, palm systems, retinal scans, signature comparison, voice comparison), which are normally too expensive and elaborate for home use. Such devices, a high-security alternative to keys or cards, are used to control access to buildings, rooms, and computers.

The best arrangement is a locked garage or else an aboveground parking space that is constantly under surveillance. These protective measures guard the car from theft or vandalism, prevent anyone from planting a bomb in it, and reduce the chances of an ambush as the principal enters or leaves his car.

It is also useful for the principal to be able to enter and leave the office building by a relatively surreptitious route when necessary. The client might prefer to enter through the front door most of the time, but if something causes the threat level to rise suddenly (such as a mass of protesters at the front door), it would be advantageous to be able to take an elevator straight from the garage to his suite. In addition, to whatever extent is feasible, the EP specialist should map out alternate exits from company property in case one gate or driveway is blocked.

As for the executive suite, depending on the threat level, the EP specialist can consider access controls at the outer entrance to the suite. For examples, at some offices, a visitor stepping off the elevator must be buzzed in through locked glass doors even before reaching the receptionist for that floor. That ring or layer of security can be complemented with protection at the door to the principal's room, with locked rest rooms, with a panic button at the desk of the principal's secretary or administrative assistant, and perhaps even with a safe room adjacent to the principal's office. The physical protections must be supplemented with procedural measures (such as keeping couriers at a distance, double-checking that maintenance workers are who they purport to be, etc.) to ensure that no one who shouldn't be there ever reaches the principal's office.

The full range of protective measures presented in this chapter, working in concert, can greatly reduce the risk posed to a given principal. By conducting careful threat assessments, setting up rings of protection, arranging for high-quality security engineering, gathering intelligence, making thorough safety preparations, instituting proper bomb procedures, and establishing responsible security routines among office and domestic staff, the protection specialist can get as close as possible to Sun Tzu's goal of holding only those positions that cannot be attacked.

When in difficult country, do not encamp....
Do not linger in dangerously isolated
positions. In hemmed-in situations, you
must resort to stratagem. In a desperate
position, you must fight.
Sun Tzu

Chapter 7
Domestic and International Travel

To the contemporary executive, travel is inefficient. The sort of person who needs executive protection is typically accustomed to rapid and convenient satisfaction of his goals and needs. In the business arena, he can use the latest, fastest equipment and the ablest support staff to get the job done. In his personal life, he can maximize his enjoyment of time away from work with the latest and best in personal comfort and recreation. But travel puts him in an environment that's not so easy to control. Although travel has its pleasures, it can also be difficult, time-consuming, and frustrating.

Fortunately, an EP specialist can greatly increase the efficiency of travel for the principal, providing both protection and facilitation simultaneously. In business travel, smooth connections, check-ins, pick-ups, and drop-offs can easily add two or more hours per day of good working time or needed resting time. That's worth a lot. Even during pleasure travel, efficiency can be raised. If the EP specialist can make sure a pleasure trip is pleasurable, that makes a big difference to any client. Considering the cost of recreational trips, both in dollars and in the client's time, the EP specialist's actions to smooth the way are valuable. And that is only on the facilitation side. Protection is more than valuable—it's priceless.

This chapter covers trip preparation, security in transit, hotel and resort security, general personal security, health considerations, communications, privacy, and dealing with crises. Some of the advice given here could well be employed in the principal's home town, not just on trips. For example, guidelines on fire safety, surviving a kidnapping, and protecting business information are useful anywhere. However, that information is presented here because, during travel, the likelihood of fire, kidnapping, and industrial espionage is especially high, and the necessary countermeasures are especially difficult to employ.

Threat assessment and the advance

As soon as he has reason to think the principal might wish to travel, the EP specialist should perform or update a threat assessment and an advance for the proposed destination. (Much of the advice in this chapter is tailored to foreign travel, but many tips will clearly apply to domestic travel as well.) The threat assessment must be specific to the city and country of destination, not just generically applicable to the region. The reason is that the risk faced in traveling to different countries varies enormously. It's not just that the principal may be *slightly* more at risk of, say, kidnapping in one place or another. Sometimes the contrasts are extreme. For example, in 1996 numerous newspapers reported that more than 45 percent of the world's kidnappings were taking place in Colombia, with someone abducted almost every two and a half hours. Those figures were said to make Colombia, with 3,600 abductions in 1995, the kidnap capital of the world. A significant number of those victims were U.S. businessmen. Columbia's number of kidnappings was three times that of Mexico and five times that of Brazil. In 1997, Colombia was reported to have the highest murder rate in Latin America (895 per million inhabitants—more than eight times the U.S. rate), followed by Jamaica, Brazil, Mexico, Venezuela, Trinidad and Tobago, and Peru.

Detailed advice on conducting an advance can be found in Chapter 4, The Advance. In general, however, the protective agent should do the following:

- Obtain a country briefing (whether a written briefing or advice from a trusted contact in that country) to learn the basic history and current affairs in the country (including attitudes held there about the United States and its citizens).

- Become familiar with the country's climate, health conditions, time zone or zones, and currency rates. Fodor and similar travel books are useful sources for such basic information.

- Learn the key points of local social customs.

- Clarify why the principal is going on the trip, how he wishes to travel, and who he will meet with.

- Touch base with local contacts.

A proper advance will guide the EP specialist to the best decisions in all aspects of the trip. By contrast, an agent who performs poor advance work is like a carpenter with a crooked T-square—he's working with a faulty tool that will warp the entire project.

Whether to Travel at All

During the Second World War, posters in Britain asked passersby the question, "Is your journey really necessary?" The EP specialist, too, should keep that question in mind. If the threat assessment and advance work suggest that the risk involved in a particular trip is relatively low, then the question may not need to be asked. However, if the risk of injury, kidnapping, serious inconvenience, robbery, or other problems is relatively high, the EP specialist might have to query, gently, whether the principal actually must travel. Of course, that decision is up to the principal, so he should be fully informed about the unsatisfactory findings of the threat assessment and advance work. If the proposed trip is for business, perhaps its goals can be satisfied just as well or nearly as well through phone calls, teleconferencing, or some other means. If it's meant to be a pleasure trip, the EP specialist can hope that, after the executive is informed of the dangers, he will opt for a trip to a safer destination.

Preparation

There is much for an EP specialist to attend to before accompanying his principal on an out-of-town trip. Trips inside the United States require a strenuous amount of planning; trips to other countries require much more. There are so many considerations that some could fall through the cracks of a busy agent's schedule. To keep any area of concern from being overlooked entirely, the following list presents the key subjects to remember. Still, it is just an aid to memory, and each subject contains many subordinate issues. Some will be mentioned later in this chapter, but others must be conceived by the EP specialist as he asks himself the question, "What if?"

- Review or perform a threat assessment for the proposed destination.
- Review notes from the most recent advance mission to the proposed destination. Update the advance information if that has not been done recently.
- Consider whether the trip is necessary. That's up to the principal, of course. The agent should assume the trip is necessary but should be prepared to suggest alternatives if the advance work shows an inordinately high risk. Sometimes travel can be avoided if arrangements are made for the business to be transacted electronically, closer to home, or by someone else.
- Make reservations strategically (choosing the safest lodgings and modes of transportation) and discreetly (not advertising to potential adversaries that the principal will be traveling).
- Arrange appropriate travel documents (such as visas, passports, and itineraries).
- Pack intelligently, not randomly. The less the agent and principal pack, the less time they will have to wait to pick up any checked luggage.

- Rehearse (mentally if not physically) security measures for travel by all modes that could be used (commercial and private planes, autos, boats, ships, and trains).
- Review and refresh notes from the last advance of the hotel or resort at which the principal will stay. If no advance was performed, do so now. Devise a detailed security and safety plan specific to that property.
- Review personal security tips with the principal.
- Examine health aspects of the trip. Pack appropriate health-related items and information, and develop or refresh the plan that will be followed in health emergencies. Line up all necessary emergency assistance, such as hospitals, trauma centers, medical transportation, and suitable doctors.
- While traveling, communicate frequently with the protective operation's home base (typically at the principal's office or home).
- Take steps to safeguard the principal's privacy on the trip. Review information security measures with him.

There's one category of preparation that involves deliberately leaving some items behind. In case an emergency occurs on the trip, the EP specialist should make sure the principal's will, insurance policies, and power of attorney are readily accessible by the appropriate person at home.

Travel may seem like a perk of the job of executive protection. However, it is really much, much more work than fun. The number of details that must be attended to in unfamiliar territory is enormous, and every little step of the trip has the potential to be difficult or disastrous. As the travel writer Paul Theroux once put it, "Travel is glamorous only in retrospect."[63]

Making reservations

Something as simple as making hotel reservations can have a significant impact on the whole trip. If the principal is protected

---

[63] *The Observer*, "Sayings of the Week," October 7, 1979.

primarily in his capacity as a corporate executive, it might be the corporate travel department or the principal's personal secretary who makes reservations. If the principal has hired protection on his own, the EP specialist may well be in charge of making reservations. Regardless, the person in charge of making hotel and transport reservations must do two things. First, he must do his homework and select providers that are up to the EP specialist's standards for security and safety and the principal's standards for comfort and convenience. Second, he must exercise discretion, keeping to a minimum the number of people who know about the trip. In particular, when making reservations it is best not to name the company that the principal represents. If the principal's own name is well known, it is advisable to make reservations in the EP specialist's name whenever feasible and legal. (Airline reservations must be made in the actual passenger's name.) Reservations for a female protectee should use only the first initial and last name, such as E. Jones instead of Edith Jones, so that the protectee will not immediately be identified as a female (and therefore, in some adversaries' minds, an easier target).

Packing

What should the EP specialist pack and what should he make sure the principal packs for an out-of-town trip? As for the EP specialist, he faces the challenge of packing both lightly and completely. He must balance two requirements: (1) the need to transport his bags without adding significantly to the principal's travel logistics and without drawing attention to himself or his needs, and (2) the need to bring along all necessary security and safety equipment. Even the necessities can add up to a very heavy load, so it is important to pack and think efficiently, especially when traveling on commercial airlines.

The EP specialist should bring at least the following:

- smoke hood
- first-aid kit (including latex gloves and mouth-to-mouth cover)
- 3 x 5 cards and pen

- electronic organizer or other means for taking notes and accessing corporate and security contact information
- miniature flashlight and spare batteries
- travel clock
- correct clothing for weather and activities, including an umbrella
- credentials and copies of credentials
- duct tape (for a multitude of purposes)
- toiletries kit (a new set so the client can use the agent's if necessary)
- pocket secretary kit
- multiplex tool
- portable passive infrared intrusion detection system or other supplemental security devices
- health-related items (see "Health" section for details)
- fire bag or hotel room bag, a small container that includes items for the principal to use in an emergency and that can be placed at his bedside during the room sweep on arrival

If the client travels to the same foreign countries over and over, the EP specialist can cut down the luggage burden by storing some of the above items there instead of transporting them back and forth. It can also be useful for the agent to carry on his person several hundred dollars' worth of the currency of the country to be visited (or, more specifically, the currency that locals like to receive—that may actually be U.S. dollars) as a tool for getting himself and the client out of awkward situations, or simply for use where credit cards are not practical. That is something for the agent and client to discuss in advance, however. In a business setting, it can be difficult to document such expenditures; in any setting, the principal may prefer to be the one handling cash transactions, even though that is something better left to the agent.

There's another reason to carry, while traveling, a supply of the currency of the destination country. If no currency exchange facilities are available at the point of arrival, the EP specialist can still pay for necessaries, such as transportation and meals, that may not be payable by credit card.

Then there's the paperwork. The EP specialist should leave a complete itinerary with the home base but not spread the information around any more than necessary. A copy of the itinerary should also be filed with the U.S. embassy or consulate in Third World countries to facilitate evacuation in a crisis. For several reasons, including convenience and the policies of various governments, the passports of anyone traveling should have at least six months of validity left on them. As a backup, it helps to make three copies of the passport page that contains the principal's photo, storing one in a carry-on bag, one in luggage, and one at the home base.

Visas are required before travelers can enter certain countries. The EP agent should make sure all the necessary visas have been obtained. It may sound obvious, but everyone in the principal's entourage, including the principal himself, must take care to answer truthfully on any visa applications. The last thing anyone wants is to be challenged and delayed (or refused entrance) on arriving at a foreign country. Also, if the principal and agent are traveling back home on a private aircraft, the agent should make sure that any foreign nationals coming along have the necessary visas, if needed, in addition to their passports. Improper entry can cause inordinate delay and may result in seizure of the aircraft.

Another key paperwork item is proof of inoculation, if required (see "Health" below). In addition, to avoid being charged import duty when bringing the principal's own goods back into the United States, the EP specialist should complete customs declarations for any valuables being taken out of the country. Alternatively, the EP specialist can carry proof (such as receipts) that the items were purchased in the United States.

Finally, because some countries have special requirements for foreign drivers, it might be necessary to obtain international driver's licenses and insurance certifications for both the client and the agent. Sources of information on foreign driving include the American Automobile Association and foreign countries' embassies and consulates in the United States. However, it is better to use contract drivers overseas. That way the agent needn't be distracted trying to figure out local driving patterns and can focus on the job of safeguarding the principal.

Business papers and information on diskettes and notebook computers should be brought only if necessary. The EP specialist should make clear to the principal that any such information that he might bring on the trip could be seized or copied. Therefore, he should only bring what he must and should follow the agent's advice for protecting it. Details on information protection during travel are offered below in the section called "Privacy."

Another packing consideration concerns luggage tags, which should not bear the principal's company's name. If the principal's own name is not well known, the tags should bear his name and his business, not home, address. If his name is well known, less attention will be attracted if the luggage tags carry the EP specialist's name. Another alternative is to use hard, lockable luggage with concealed luggage tags. A color-coded tag can then be attached to the suitcase handle for identification at the baggage carousel.

Because the EP specialist is a vital part of the principal's trip, the way he packs for himself is also important, although for the most part it affects the principal's convenience more than his security. If possible, when the trip is by air, the agent should carry on his garment bag, briefcase, and toiletries; that way, they won't get lost, distracting the agent from his protection duties or adding a delay at baggage claim.

The EP specialist should also bring along medicines that he himself will need—and not just for serious conditions. Although he must be stoic and work well no matter how he feels, a bad case of hay fever, diarrhea, nausea, or motion sickness can definitely make him a less effective agent, so he should bring medications for all those ailments. If the agent is traveling alone with the principal, he should have a foreign alternative security representative in mind in case he becomes incapacitated by illness.

In addition, the agent should be practical in his choice of footwear. Regardless of how he and the principal travel, the agent will be on his feet most of the time. Good walking shoes are essential.

In Transit

The key security concept while in transit is to keep a low profile—the client shouldn't look too much like a prime target for criminals. The easiest way to blend in with a crowd is to dress like the crowd. If the travel will take place entirely in private vehicles that begin, pass through, and end in private locations, the principal and EP specialist can safely wear whatever they want. However, if the principal will be using a commercial airport, airplane, train, or other public conveyance or facility, it makes sense to dress in a style that matches the occasion and environment. The alternative is to take active steps to look like a hard target, but that approach is difficult when the environment is an airport or airplane, where firearms are illegal and, practically speaking, it may be impossible to maintain a distance from others or surround the principal with agents. By far, the better approach is to keep a low profile in transit.

By car

It's unlikely the principal would wish to travel between cities by automobile. If he does, most of the security consideration in Chapter 5, Automobile Security, will apply. It's likely, however, that the principal and EP specialist will use a car at their destination. Ideally, the agent should arrange for a driver trained in defensive, security-oriented driving. Of equal importance is that the driver speak fluent English and that he know the principal's travel destinations and how to get around. American embassies can make recommendations for good car services. If it's necessary to use a driver who has not been trained in security, the EP specialist can still brief him, from a security standpoint, on where and how to park, how to handle the car and doors at drop-off and pickup, and the importance of locking up the car and watching it closely when it is not being driven. It is also important, when abroad, to avoid cars that clearly identify the principal as an American, particularly steering clear of overly flashy cars.

By air

Some protectees travel exclusively by private aircraft; others use common carriers. From an executive protection standpoint, each method has its advantages. However, the protective measures for each differ significantly.

Commercial, public aviation. First of all, the EP specialist is going to have to conduct an advance of, or gain some familiarity with, all airports to be used. A typical airport advance would cover at least the following subjects:

- availability of express service at customs
- airport name, international code, and location
- location of airport's security office, first aid station, parking, ticket counters, baggage claim, customs area, telephones, newsstands, airline clubs, currency exchange, taxi stand, and security checkpoints
- airport's FAA classification and any relevant alerts
- length of time to allow for check-in, baggage pickup, and customs[64]

Next, the agent should try to avoid having the principal travel by commercial airline on terrorist anniversaries. Some dates that are significant to terrorists are known well enough by U.S. citizens: April 14, the date in 1987 when U.S. naval attack planes bombed targets in Tripoli, Libya, and July 3, the date in 1988 on which the U.S.S. *Vincennes* shot down an Iranian civilian airliner over the Persian Gulf.

Revenge for those incidents could take place anywhere in the world. However, there are many other anniversaries that have a more local significance. It would pay for an EP specialist to build a general, worldwide terrorist anniversary list and supplement it, as needed, with dates that are significant in the particular countries to which the principal intends to travel. That information should not alarm the principal or discourage travel; it is merely intended to keep the agent on his toes and help him anticipate potential problems.

In addition, if terrorist anniversaries or current events have raised the threat to a relatively high level, it is worth considering flying on airlines that have not typically been targeted by terrorists.

---

[64] This list inspired by Glazebrook and Nicholson, pp. 31-32.

American, British, Israeli, German, and French airlines have most often been the subject of terrorist attacks. By contrast, such carriers as Swiss Air, SAS, Singapore Air Lines, Cathay Pacific, KLM, Air New Zealand, Thai International, Qantas, Gulf Air, and Malaysian Air are historically much less likely to be attacked.

Several other tips apply to travel via commercial airports. Travelers should stay away from unattended baggage and maintain close custody of their carry-on items (to prevent others from placing dangerous or illegal materials into the principal's or agent's luggage). Also, the agent should check the principal in quickly and escort him through the security checkpoint, on the other side of which there is less danger of attacks involving weapons. At all times, the agent should know how to find the nearest exits and secure areas.

If the trip to the airport has been properly coordinated, it is unlikely that the principal will need to spend much time waiting inside the facility. However, delays can spring up at the last minute. For example, everyone may be about to board the plane when a maintenance problem is discovered and the passengers must wait several hours until a repair is made or a replacement plane found. In such a case, the EP specialist should encourage the principal to stay in secured areas of the airport only, especially avoiding waiting areas, stores, and rest rooms on the unsecured side of the security checkpoint. An airline club makes a comfortable, secure place to pass the time. The agent should seek private or corporate memberships in the clubs run by the airlines the principal uses most often. In a pinch, the agent should ask whether a needed club offers a one-day membership.

While en route, if the EP specialist and principal are traveling together on a commercial airliner, there is fairly little the EP specialist can do to protect the principal. Activity on airplanes is highly regulated and physically constricted. Still, it's good for the agent to sit close to the principal. One recommendation is for the agent to reserve, through the airline passenger service representative, an aisle seat a couple of rows behind the principal. If the principal flies first class and the agent doesn't, the agent should sit in the first row behind first class. If the principal and agent are any farther apart, they might get separated during the crush of deplaning.

In the (fortunately rare) event of a hijacking, the EP specialist may not be able to do much for the principal. However, before such an event, the agent can reinforce safety-enhancing behavior in the principal. Advice that the agent should give the principal in advance includes the following:

- Reserve a window seat. It is harder for hijackers to inflict indiscriminate violence on passengers seated there.

- Review the flight safety information card in the seat pocket in front of you. Learn about the exits and emergency equipment on that particular plane.

- Memorize your passport number so you won't have to reveal the passport itself when filling out landing cards.

- Stay calm, and encourage others to do the same. Avoid eye contact with your captors, and follow their directions. Remember that the hijackers are nervous and may be scared. If shooting starts, keep your head down or drop to the floor.

- If you are singled out by the hijackers, be responsive but do not volunteer information. Keep answers short and non-political, and speak in a regulated tone. Downplay your importance, the importance of your job, and your reasons for traveling.

- Do nothing to attract the hijackers' attention; limit fluid intake so you will not have to use the rest room, and don't alter or mutilate your passport. Remember that other hijackers may be mixed in with regular passengers, so be discreet no matter what you do.

- Carry a family photo. At some point you may be able to appeal to the captors' family feelings.

- During a rescue, stay low. Expect the rescuers to treat you roughly until they determine you are not a hijacker. Get out fast if told to do so.

Airport security personnel may ask questions about the agent's and the principal's luggage. The EP specialist should know what has been packed and be able to describe all electrical items.

While in an immigration or customs enclosure, neither the EP specialist nor the principal should do anything that attracts attention, such as changing lanes repeatedly, moving items between bags, or disposing of items. Such areas are under surveillance, and that type of behavior may attract unwanted official attention. Also, it's important to be accurate in declaring any items purchased; in some countries, store clerks may furnish information about buyers to the authorities. If a conflict arises during screening, the EP specialist and principal should cooperate politely. This is one area where it's impossible to "fight city hall" and win. If necessary, the EP specialist can attempt to take up the matter with higher officials later.

Private and corporate aviation. The principal's private or corporate plane has the potential to be the most secure means of travel available. The only catch is that the security of such a plane is the responsibility of the flight crew and EP specialist. In other words, travel on a private plane is as secure as the agent and flight crew make it. It's a big responsibility: aside from the threat of a bomb, even minor tampering or an unreported ramp accident can have disastrous consequences.

As with travel on commercial airliners, a good advance is vital to a safe private or corporate flight. First, the agent should meet flight crew members and ask them to walk him through flight security measures. The agent should obtain, or see that the flight crew knows, the following details:

- the airport's name, address, phone number, hours of operation
- runway length and restrictions on night landings, noise, and type of aircraft
- availability of mechanics, fuel, de-icing, security, and catering
- police jurisdiction airport resides in
- ambulance response time and nearest hospital with trauma unit
- aircraft's owner, year, make, tail number, and hours of flight time
- number of hours to next maintenance

- fuel range and luggage and passenger capacity
- presence of flight attendant on aircraft
- aircraft's interior layout and facilities
- number of pilots needed to fly aircraft
- name and phone numbers of pilot and copilot
- availability of plane-side drop-off and pickup
- alternate arrival sites in case of bad weather (and ground transportation options from those sites)[65]

Looking into those details is important, but the agent needs to remember that he isn't in charge of the aircraft—the captain is. It's important to be polite and work well with the captain and flight crew.

Beyond the advance, the EP specialist needs to protect the plane itself. Among other duties, he should establish procedures to ensure that no unidentified package is brought aboard the aircraft. Besides the risk that a bomb could be brought aboard, someone might use the plane as a narcotics carrier. That is more common than one would hope. In September 1996 in Bogota, more than eight pounds of heroin were found stashed aboard Colombian President Ernesto Samper's Boeing 707 as the plane was being readied for Samper's visit to New York. He was heading there to sell the U.N. General Assembly on a global anti-drug strategy. Besides the obvious embarrassment that a principal would suffer if drugs were found to be smuggled aboard his plane, two other unpleasant consequences could result: confiscation of the aircraft and, possibly, prosecution of the principal. From an executive protection standpoint, any of those outcomes would represent a grave failure on the part of the EP specialist.

The key to keeping unwanted items off the aircraft is to instruct the crew to accept no item unless the principal has told them to expect it. Further, only passengers or crew should load items onto the plane. A backup measure is to instruct the pilot or crew chief to draw up a manifest of the aircraft's cargo and have the EP specialist approve it before takeoff. The manifest will also be useful when it's time to clear customs.

---

[65] This list inspired by Glazebrook and Nicholson, pp. 32-33.

Baggage is not the only route through which an adversary can place an explosive device on an aircraft. Planes have a number of vulnerable external areas, including wheel wells and other cavities, which can be accessed when the plane is parked unattended, either in a hangar or on the ramp. To prevent or detect the placement of a bomb, the EP specialist or flight crew should do some or all of the following:

- Inspect the plane's exterior and interior, using techniques similar to those for searching an automobile.

- Replace the locks that came with the plane. Have high-quality locks professionally installed to reduce the likelihood that someone with a key to other planes made by the same manufacturer could let himself in.

- Insert telltales into cracks of doors or windows in a way that they will be dislodged if those apertures are opened. A telltale may be something easily observed (such as frangible anti-tampering tape or stickers) or something barely noticeable, such a match stick.

- Install a door counter, which is a device that counts the number of times a door has been opened. Look to see whether the counter reading is higher than it was when the plane was secured.

- Have an aircraft security system installed. One type of on-board system can monitor sensors on all the aircraft's apertures. System users can use a hand-held transceiver to query the aircraft from a distance and ascertain the time and date of all legitimate entries and the identities of those entering. If illegitimate entries have been made or attempted, the device will report their location. The system is also capable of transmitting an alarm by radio.

- Establish perimeter security. One device, a portable microwave fence kit, consists of four sets of transmitters and receivers that provide an invisible "fence," an interruption of which generates an alarm signal.

One time when the aircraft is not safely stowed away from strangers is during fueling. To prevent any harmful behavior when the plane is being fueled, the flight crew should oversee that operation. In addition, once engines are started, the EP specialist should be suspicious of any attempts to delay, stop, or otherwise impede the departure from other than air traffic control authorities.

A number of security advantages accrue to traveling by corporate aircraft. For one, there is no obligation to publish schedules, itineraries, or passenger lists. In fact, the agent should make such information available only on a need-to-know basis. Also, a private jet can be anonymous. There is no need for it to display the company name or insignia; that applies to crew uniforms, too. In addition, the EP specialist can request that pilots communicate special and routine radio messages to help coordinate arrival procedures on the ground.

EP specialists should note that the Aircraft Owner and Pilot Association offers a "pinch hitter" course designed to enable the student to land a small plane in an emergency if the pilot can't. (The course would not enable the agent to fly larger, more sophisticated aircraft, however). The course is offered around the country, takes only four hours, and costs about a hundred dollars.[66] That, plus perhaps 10 hours of flight training, would be a good idea for an EP specialist who wishes to protect his principal—and himself—no matter what.

Helicopters. Protecting a principal during helicopter travel is similar to protecting him during travel by plane. A few important differences exist, however:

- The ceiling—the highest altitude under particular weather conditions from which the ground is still visible—makes all the difference in helicopter travel. Rain, snow, overcast skies, and flying around mountains influence helicopters much more than fixed-wing aircraft. If the weather is foggy or icy, it is much better to change plans and travel by plane.
- The safest arrangement is to use two pilots on a twin-engine helicopter. The EP specialist should work with

---

[66] Aircraft Owner and Pilot Association, 421 Aviation Way, Frederick, MD 21701. (800) 638-3101 or (301) 695-2172.

them to satisfy safety and security needs. He should be inquisitive, asking them to demonstrate the helicopter's features and capacities.

- The EP specialist might have to lay out a landing pad. If so, he must know the terrain, be confident there are no overhead wires nearby, arrange for the use of a suitable flat surface, and set up low-profile lighting that illuminates the pad but doesn't blind the pilots.

- The agent should be familiar with the seating and luggage capacity of different models of helicopters. None of them have much room for luggage, and even the best ones are loud. The agent may want to bring along earplugs for the principal and his guests.

- The approach to a helicopter requires some forethought. The agent should ask the pilot the best way for passengers to board. Will the engine be shut down? Will the rotors be engaged? It is imperative for the agent to instruct the principal and his guests not to wear hats or other items that might be lifted off by the updraft underneath the rotors. A person's natural tendency is to reach up and grab the clothing—risking the loss of an arm or worse. Furthermore, passengers should follow several other safety practices: never approach a helicopter from the rear, as the vertical tail rotor is nearly invisible when spinning; always enter and exit the helicopter on the downslope side of any land mass; lower your body height by leaning at the waist until arriving at the nose of the helicopter; and, once strapped inside a helicopter, stay put and don't slide from one side of the helicopter to the other to improve your view of the scenery.

Most professional helicopter services give ample safety guidance for passengers. For the most part, the protection specialist should allow a competent air crew to manage the safety issue.

Hotel and Resort Security

If the EP specialist has already performed an advance for the particular hotel or resort the principal will be using, he should refer to it as soon as trip planning begins. If it needs updating, that should be done immediately. If no advance has been performed for the property, it's now time to do one.

As part of that process, the agent should take several steps:

- Meet with the hotel manager and get to know him.
- Obtain a hotel floor plan.
- Meet the hotel security director and find out what he has at his disposal, such as cameras, guards, and security systems. Find out how he can help protect the client.

In general, the best type of hotel at which to book a protectee is one operated by a large, high-quality lodging chain based in a Western country. Such hotels are especially likely to take security and safety seriously and to offer the types of facilities and support both the client and the agent will need. The best type of room to book is the largest possible suite by the end of a hall, where there is likely to be the least traffic. For fire safety, the room should not be too high up. A room between the second and seventh floors is high enough that intruders can't easily climb in the window but low enough to be reached by fire department ladders.

The concept of taking care of check-in before the principal arrives was already discussed in Chapters 3 and 4. An additional step to speed and safeguard the entry process is to place color-coded tags—without any names—on all the luggage. (For airline travel, luggage might need name tags, but they can be removed at their airport before the principal arrives at the hotel.) That way the EP specialist can say to the bellman, "Take the bags with red tags to room 320 and the bags with blue tags to room 322." There won't be any need to mention the principal's name in the lobby or at the curb. In addition, the agent can keep the principal's vehicle immediately accessible by laying a heavy tip on the hotel valet service.

In some countries, the hotel clerk is obliged to obtain the passport of anyone who checks in. In some cases he will record certain information from it; in other cases he will hold it until the police can review it personally. If the principal must part with his passport, the EP specialist should make a point of retrieving it as soon as possible. In any event, the agent should always carry a copy of his and the principal's passports or at least know the passport numbers.

The protection specialist should take a room adjacent to that of the principal, or at least on the same floor. When the agent and principal arrive at the principal's room, the agent should always search the room quickly but thoroughly, then let the principal in, say goodnight, and secure the room.

The agent should quickly familiarize himself with the location and availability of essential hotel services, restaurants, meeting rooms, gift shops (to purchase convenience items), and other areas. It's also a good idea for the agent to telephone the hotel security manager for any information that would be useful (such as recent criminal activity) and to identify himself as being responsible for the protectee. The agent can ask the security manager to call if anything that the agent should be aware of occurs.

Two key aspects of protection once the principal is safely in the hotel are access control and fire safety. Some protection specialists use portable travel locks as a supplement to the locks already on the hotel door. Why? Hotel key control is not always reliable. In effect, the EP specialist is placing the principal in a building that anyone can enter and a room to which any number of people have a key. The built-in dead bolt lock might do the job fine when the principal is in the room, but when he is out many people may routinely enter the room. Rather than allow that, the EP specialist can arrange for cleaning and repairs to be done at a scheduled time, under supervision. The agent should also remind the principal to keep his room door closed, dead-bolted, and chained whenever he is in it. The agent should have a spare key to the principal's room. If the rooms adjoin, the agent should ask the principal to keep his adjoining door open while the agent closes his own. That arrangement allows the EP specialist access without having to deal with a dead bolt and chain in a nighttime emergency and still gives the principal privacy.

The agent may also wish to use telltales, as described in the section on corporate aviation security. For hotel use, less easily observed telltales are better because they don't draw attention to the room.

A more high-tech method is to use a system that monitors room entry with portable sensors. One such system, called The Agent,[67] is a portable, programmable alarm system for use where hard-wired systems are impractical. It can be used with numerous types of wireless sensors, such as panic buttons, door contacts, tilt sensors, and passive infrared motion detectors. The system consists of a briefcase that contains a computer, a communication link, a receiver, the system charger, several sensors, and, if desired, a hand-held, two-way radio. At a hotel, conference room, or other area in which the principal requires portable protection, the EP specialist places as many sensors as he likes at points of entry to the area. As the principal travels, the sensors can be removed and placed in new locations. When a sensor is triggered (for example, if someone enters the protected space or the principal pushes his panic button), the sensor sends a signal to the receiver in the briefcase. The receiver interprets the alarm, and the computer then sends the protection team one of four pre-selected messages by radio, pager, or cellular phone. With such a system, the EP specialist can provide the traveling executive with a level of intrusion detection like that offered at home.

Regardless of whether a portable alarm system is being used, all deliveries that are destined for the principal's room should come to the agent's room first so he can check out the delivery cart, the goods on it, and the people delivering them. He can then be present when the items are delivered to the client. If the protection specialist has a rapport with the principal, it should be a simple matter to learn the "out time" for the next morning. If not, the agent can call the hotel's front desk to ascertain whether the principal has arranged a wake-up call. (That information would help the agent determine when he should be up and ready.) Alternatively, the agent can ask the principal whether he would like the agent to make the wake-up call himself.

As Chapter 1, Threat Assessment, demonstrated, an EP specialist will be doing an incomplete job if he only protects the principal

---

[67] The Agent is available from Intellitech, 1300 Shiloh Road, Kennesaw, GA 30144. (770) 514-7999. A smaller version offered is call The Spy.

from intentional harm. Accidents of various sorts cause death and injury far more often than intentional causes do. In hotels, a key part of accident prevention is fire safety. As part of the advance, the EP specialist should have checked out the hotel's fire safety features, such as exits, emergency lights, and fire extinguishers (including whether they have been inspected recently). Once the principal is at the hotel, the agent should take a second to show or tell the principal how to get out of that particular hotel in a fire.

The agent should also take the trouble to determine how many doors there are from his room to the principal's room and to the fire exit—doorways can be felt in a dark or smoky corridor. Another measure is for the agent to make sure the client knows how to open the hotel's windows; it can be difficult to unlatch and open an unfamiliar window in the dark. The window may not even open at all, and wrestling with it in an emergency would just waste time.

The case study in Chapter 4 mentioned placing a "fire bag" in the principal's room. The bag was described as including duct tape, a cutting tool, and a survival plan in case the EP specialist was unable to reach the principal. An example of directions that the EP specialist could provide the principal are as follows:

- Don't waste time. Act as soon as you have any indication of a fire in your hotel.
- Keep calm. Call the front desk and state the location of the fire.
- Before leaving your room, check the door by placing your palm on the door and then on the door knob. If they are cool, grab your room key (so you can get back in if necessary) and head for the stairs. If the hall contains smoke, crawl to the exit. (Count the door knobs between your room and the exit. If you have to retreat and the hall is dark, you can count backwards to the safety of your own room.) Take care to check the stairwell door, too; the fire could be behind it. Do not use the elevator.
- Don a portable smoke hood. Note: this is not the time to try it out—you should have practiced putting it on before an emergency.

166

- If your room door or door knob feels hot, do not open the door. For fresh air, open a window, but do not break it, as you may need to close it again if smoke starts to enter from outside.
- Call the front desk and say you are in your room awaiting rescue. Also call 911 and leave your room number, and call someone in your family to tell the authorities where you are.
- Fill the tub and sink with water; soak towels and blankets to block vents and openings around the door to keep smoke and fumes out. Try to keep the walls, doors, and those towels cool and wet. If necessary, swing a wet towel around the room to clear smoke. It may help to cover your mouth and nose with a wet cloth.
- As an alternative to wet towels, use duct tape to seal door cracks and tape magazines over smoking air vents.
- Stay low, but keep alert to any signs of rescue from the street or halls. Let fire fighters know where you are by waving a towel or sheet out the window. You can also use duct tape to spell "HELP" on your window.

Another service the EP specialist can provide—one that is not particularly security- or safety-oriented but may be appreciated anyway, is to leave the principal some simple instructions in the hotel room. For example, some agents leave one adhesive-backed note attached to the television, listing the news channels, and another note next to the phone, listing dialing instructions (local and long-distance, including international) and the agent's phone number and room number.

It's also a good idea for the agent to make similar preparations for himself. He should always prepare for an emergency before retiring for the night. Good practices include laying out—on an unused bed or cleared-off table—his hotel room key, a key to the principal's room, a flashlight, and a smoke hood. The agent's shoes, shirt, and pants should also be ready. To speed middle-of-the-night operations, he should leave the bathroom light on when going to bed. What's an easy way to remember to do these things?

167

The agent should just imagine the panic and confusion he would feel if he woke up from a deep sleep at 3:00 a.m. to the sound of a fire alarm—and was unprepared to protect the principal.

General Personal Security

The regular security measures that apply at the principal's home and office and during local activities were discussed in most of the preceding chapters. Those measures include conducting an advance before any outing, keeping a low profile, varying the principal's schedule and route, and knowing the location of the nearest hospitals and police stations. During travel, those same considerations apply, but they may be more difficult to perform than at home. Moreover, additional considerations arise during travel, especially in foreign countries.

For example, in some countries, the police or members of an intelligence agency may detain the client, agent, or both for no other reason than curiosity. Whoever is detained should ask to contact the nearest U.S. embassy or consulate. A U.S. citizen has the right to make such a contact, but that right may not be granted immediately. The detainee should ask periodically until the "hosts" comply. It is important to stay calm, maintain one's dignity, and not provoke the arresting officers. Further, the detainee should admit nothing, volunteer nothing, and sign nothing. Finally, no one should be accepted at face value. When a representative from the embassy or consulate arrives, the detainee should request some identification before discussing the situation.

Chapter 1 mentioned that the risk of kidnapping is much greater in countries other than the United States. Unfortunately, it is not necessary to go far from home to be in harm's way. Here is one recent account: [68]

> A kidnapped Sanyo executive from suburban San Diego was found unharmed Monday in Tijuana, Mexico, after a Mexican police officer delivered a $2 million ransom in a nighttime rendezvous with gunmen. The abductors

---

[68] "Sanyo Pays $2 Million Ransom; Kidnapped Exec Found Alive," *Chicago Tribune*, August 20, 1996.

remained at large with the ransom—unmarked U.S. currency—but investigators believe they know who committed the crime…. Hours after Sanyo provided ransom money to police, Mamoru Konno, 57, was found in the basement of an abandoned house where the kidnappers said he would be. Konno is president of Sanyo Video Component Corp. USA…. [T]he kidnappers are six members of a ring operating in Tijuana and Ensenada. All are believed to be Mexican.

Gunmen abducted Konno, a plant manager in Tijuana, on Aug. 10 after a company baseball game. A state police officer driving a Sanyo company car and carrying a suitcase filled with money was met by two gunmen in the La Joya section of Tijuana who took the ransom money and left….

Konno lived in the San Diego suburb of Chula Vista and, like other Sanyo executives, regularly traveled between corporate headquarters in San Diego and the company's television-parts factory on the south side of Tijuana. Shuttling across the U.S.-Mexico border regularly may not have seemed like foreign travel, but it was—and the destination, Mexico, is known to have an enormous kidnapping problem.

Of course, the EP specialist will take proper precautions to prevent kidnapping wherever the principal may be, depending on the level of threat. Nevertheless, because for U.S. protectees the risk is higher during foreign travel, advice on how the principal should behave if kidnapped will be presented here. A principal who has hired executive protection certainly is planning not to be kidnapped. However, when the threat level is high enough, it is not impossible for a protectee to be abducted. The following are some guidelines the EP specialist should share with the principal in case the unthinkable should ever occur:

- The moment of kidnapping provides one of the best opportunities for escape. If you are in a public area, make a commotion to attract attention. If you are in your hotel room, try to arouse the suspicion of the EP specialist, hotel staff, or persons in neighboring rooms.

At least someone might report the abduction so a search for you can begin.

- If you have one, use your panic alarm to call the agent.
- Concentrate on surviving. Notice and remember sounds, movements, and smells as you are transported. At your destination, pay attention to room and building details. Keep track of time, and attempt to gain a knowledge of your captors' schedule, behavior, and weaknesses. Use all this information to seek opportunities to escape.
- If you are interrogated, retain your pride but cooperate. Divulge only information that cannot be used against you. You can expect to be accused of working for the government's intelligence service, to be interrogated extensively, and to lose weight. Still, do not antagonize the interrogator with obstinate behavior.
- Stay physically active, even if your movement is limited. Try isometric and flexing exercises.
- Plan on a lengthy stay. Keep track of the passage of time.
- Manage your time by setting up schedules for simple tasks, such as exercises, daydreaming, or housekeeping.
- Keep your mind active. Read anything available. Write, even if you are not allowed to retain your writings. If materials are not available, mentally compose poetry, try to recall Scripture, design a house, even "play tennis" (as one captive did).
- Try to establish some kind of rapport with your captors and fellow captives.
- Do not be uncooperative, antagonistic, or hostile toward your captors—you will only be asking for longer captivity or harsher treatment. Your best defense is passive cooperation.
- Remember, the more time passes, the better are your chances of being released alive.
- Still, if the opportunity to escape arises, go for it. As long as you're a captive, plan to escape; if nothing else,

it gives you something to think about. When the chance comes, be ready to seize it quickly.

Health

An agent should keep in mind two categories of health concerns when his principal plans to travel: first, dealing with medical situations that could have occurred at home but happened to occur out of town or in a foreign country, and second, dealing with medical situations that are particularly related to the country being visited. The precautions and reactions are approximately the same for both, but being aware of the two categories can help the agent make sure he has considered all possible risks.

In general, health considerations are minor for domestic travel. Good medical care can be obtained in almost all parts of the United States, and rarely are diseases rampant or food and water impure. For domestic travel, the EP specialist need only do a few things: make certain he knows where the nearest hospital is and how to get there; see that the principal has packed an extra quantity of any important prescription medicines (ideally, in original containers so they won't be confused with illegal drugs), along with extra eyeglasses or contact lenses; and, if applicable, make sure the principal has his insurance card with him. Special medical conditions on the part of the principal might require a few extra steps, but those concerns probably do not differ from concerns at home.

However, foreign travel can be more complicated. In the best of destinations, the major problems are matters of insurance, language, and convenience. That is, if the principal needs medical care in Germany, his insurance might not pay for treatment there, he might not be able to communicate with the doctor (though that is unlikely), and his trip may be ruined. However, if the principal's itinerary includes developing nations—or even countries that are otherwise sophisticated but do not offer medical care up to American or Western European standards—things can get much more complicated.

A travel agent or the State Department can specify whether certain shots are required for legal entry into various countries, but that is a bare minimum requirement. More detailed information on health precautions can be obtained from the U.S. Public Health Service[69] or the Centers for Disease Control's international traveler's hot line.[70] Still, those sources may not be able to provide the inside scoop about which diseases are prevalent at the principal's destination and how to avoid them. For example, there might be no legal requirement that the principal obtain a yellow fever immunization before entering a certain country, but that doesn't mean it's safe to drink the water or eat certain foods there. In fact, even in first-class hotels, the tap water may not always be suitable for drinking—and that means ice cubes, too.

To get more detailed health information about a destination, some travelers visit travel clinics, which are medical facilities that focus on treating international travelers before they leave the United States and after they return. Depending on the risks uncovered in the threat assessment, the EP specialist may wish to advise the principal to visit such a clinic before traveling abroad.

A visit to a travel clinic allows medical staff to relate the principal's particular health status to his itinerary, mode of travel, and activities planned. Travel clinic staff are up to date on the latest research and information on diseases and epidemics abroad and keep in stock vaccines that the principal's general medical practitioner would not have. The Johns Hopkins University International Travel Clinic describes health risks overseas as follows: [71]

> Diseases like malaria and typhoid, almost unheard of in the United States, and others like polio and diphtheria, which Americans routinely prevent through immunization, are common in the developing world. Unlike you, most of the citizens of the developing world have acquired an immunity to these diseases. In developing nations, common foes include unusual strains of organisms that cause colds, other respiratory infections, and

---

[69] The U.S. Public Health Service's book *Health Information for International Travel* is available for $7.00 from the Superintendent of Documents, U.S. Government Printing Office, Washington, DC 20402.

[70] CDC hot line: (404) 332-4559.

[71] *Traveler's Handbook* (Baltimore: Johns Hopkins University International Travel Clinic, 1989), pp. 4-5.

diarrheal diseases. Allergies sometimes cause problems too, especially when the visitor is not aware of the seasonal differences. For example, in the southern hemisphere the spring and fall seasons are reversed; therefore the pollen seasons are reversed also.

The EP specialist should look into vaccinations early; some shots may need to be spaced a month apart, while other injections must be taken within a week or two of departure. In addition, the EP specialist should pack or see that the principal packs the following:

- a wallet card identifying blood type, allergies, required medications, insurance company, and name and telephone number of person to contact in an emergency
- mosquito repellent containing DEET
- water-purification tablets (halazone or tincture of iodine)
- anti-diarrheal medication
- any prescription or non-prescription drugs the principal uses regularly, including analgesics and antihistamines
- sunscreen and sunburn lotions
- extra eyeglasses, contact lenses, or the prescription
- altitude sickness preventative (if principal will be in areas above 10,000 feet)
- motion sickness pills
- feminine products, if applicable

Aren't these items available in most destinations? That depends. In some places, the only problem will be identifying what to buy because of the foreign labeling, but in many destinations, the products the principal wants will simply be unavailable. It's not necessary to travel to central Africa to be unable to find those items; they may be unobtainable even in South America or central and eastern Europe.

One other important item to bring doesn't go in a suitcase: a good protective detail includes at least one member with a blood type compatible with the principal.

Most travel goes well, but the range of possible problems is so large that the EP specialist should know basic emergency medicine, at least to the level of a "first responder" type of training (described in Chapter 6). It is good to know what is and is not a medical emergency. For example, if the principal is bitten by a dog, should he be concerned about rabies? The answer is yes, but that concern doesn't necessarily translate into an abrupt end to the trip. Because rabies is ultimately fatal and is endemic in most developing countries, the bite should be taken seriously. Here's what the Johns Hopkins Travel Clinic advises: [72]

> If the animal in question is a family dog, tie it up and watch it for 10 days. Assuming your tetanus immunizations are up to date, no other measures need to be taken immediately, except thorough cleansing of the wound with soap and water. If you cannot locate the dog or the restrained animal develops symptoms, such as unusual behavior, you must consult a physician and receive rabies immunizations, either the primary series or boosters. Contact the American consulate for advice. Avoid using locally made vaccines because of their serious reactions. The long incubation period (several months) allows you time to return to the United States immediately if no safe, approved vaccine is available locally.

Maybe a dog bite seems an unlikely event, given the principal's activities and the places he frequents. Nevertheless, the dog-bite scenario illustrates the type of decision chain the EP specialist should be able to follow after a medical incident. There may be no need to rush the principal home; on the other hand, there might be. The EP specialist will want to consult with competent medical advisors in the decision-making process.

If the principal has a heart condition, it could be critical for the agent to carry and know how to use a portable defibrillator. Such devices range from the size of a book up to the size of a briefcase and can weigh as little as four pounds. To use a defibrillator, an agent needs training but needn't be a doctor. Having such a device on hand gives the principal a chance of receiving help within the optimum time of five minutes, greatly increasing his likelihood of surviving ventricular fibrillation or tachycardia, the two cardiac

---

[72] *Traveler's Handbook*, p. 19.

rhythms that can be reversed by defibrillation. Among the portable defibrillators available are the Heartstart 1000s from Laerdal Medical and the Forerunner from Heartstream.

Reportedly, several hundred passengers die each year aboard U.S. air carriers. Observers claim many of those deaths could be prevented if better medicines and medical equipment were aboard the aircraft. That makes medical readiness one more criterion on which to judge an airline. In November 1996, American Airlines purchased 300 Forerunner defibrillators to carry on its overseas flights and announced plans to place them on all flights eventually. It trained flight crews to operate the devices when no physician is available to help.

What about medical insurance? It is wise to review the principal's health insurance policy (and the agent's own) before a trip. In some places, particularly at resorts, medical costs can be as high as or higher than in the United States. If the principal's insurance policy does not cover him in a foreign country, the EP specialist should recommend that he change to a policy that does or purchase short-term insurance designed specifically to cover travel. There are even policies and medical services that will provide for immediate, assisted evacuation to the United States in case the principal suffers a medical emergency. As part of the coverage, such programs typically offer emergency consultation by telephone, referrals to the nearest hospital, and even translation of the principal's instructions to a health care worker on the scene. A common option is self-insurance, assuming the principal's resources are sufficient. If that is the case, the agent must know how to get the principal home in an emergency, regardless of the resources that need to be expended. If the medical emergency occurs while the principal is flying in a corporate aircraft, an emergency medical service could recommend a country to fly to for the best medical care.[73]

---

[73] One useful resource is MedAire, Inc., which provides medical support to flight crews, ground personnel, international travelers, and others who find themselves isolated from medical assistance. The company offers a worldwide emergency medical hot line service, medical training courses, and first-aid kits. MedAire can be reached at 1301 E. McDowell Road, Suite 101, Phoenix, AZ 85006. Phone (602) 263-7971.

Communication

The essence of any successful human endeavor is good communication. Executive protection is no different, and the efficiencies of modern technology permit someone from New York to directly dial a pocket phone in Milan or Paris. Radios, pagers, fax machines, and satellite location technologies allow a protection team to keep up with a fluid environment. Communication technology is more important than any other item in the protection inventory.

Twenty-four-hour communication requires a 24-hour command center, which can make the difference between a successful operation and disaster. One instance that illustrates the practical value of a 24-hour command center is the need to alter travel plans while overseas and on the run. The agent can't spend time chasing down flight schedules, hotel bookings, and all the other resource-consuming factors involved in a change of plans. However, with a 24-hour command center, there is someone on the other end who does have the time. A quick call from the cellular phone to the command center sets the wheels in motion, allowing the agent to continue focusing on the principal's immediate needs. The same benefit applies to message handling, business faxes, emergencies, and other situations. A well-managed, static, and operationally flexible headquarters can do wonders for logistics.

The command center should already have a copy of the principal's itinerary. As the itinerary changes, the EP specialist should keep the command center staff posted. In turn, those staffers can tell the agent about any news at the principal's company, which in turn might cause the itinerary to change again or indicate a higher threat level for the principal. Staying connected with the command center (that is, communicating with staffers there once or twice a day) also provides access to any news about the client's family. Further, if the principal and agent were to disappear while traveling, their last known whereabouts would be accurate to within hours.

As for specific equipment, the usability of different devices varies according to the principal's destination. For example, in Europe, the use of two-way radios is prohibited without proper credentials. However, cellular telephones are common there, and the use of such phones draws less attention to the principal and agent than does the use of radios.

Privacy

During travel, two kinds of privacy that are always important to the principal become especially crucial: personal privacy (maintaining a low profile) and the privacy of information belonging to the principal's business. How well the EP specialist protects the principal's *personal privacy* may very well affect the principal's personal safety. How well the agent protects the *privacy of proprietary corporate information* may well affect the company's prosperity.

On the personal side, guarding the principal's privacy means helping him blend into situations, not widely revealing any travel plans, and protecting him from the unwanted attention of invasive visitors. By helping the principal lower his profile as he travels, the agent makes him a smaller target—and as was pointed out in Chapter 1, a small target is also a hard (that is, difficult) target.

On the business information side, industrial espionage or business intelligence-gathering is always a concern, but information may be at especially high risk of compromise when the principal is traveling. Why? Among other reasons, business papers and notebook computers face greater exposure to legal and illegal searches (at customs, in checked luggage, and in hotel rooms), and electronic communications, both voice and data, typically have to travel over equipment and lines that the security team has little ability to secure (public and hotel phones in foreign countries). In many foreign countries, one must assume that telephone and fax transmissions are being actively monitored by police and government authorities.

This concern is not something out of spy books; it's for real. Perpetrators may be operatives working for corporations or even for foreign governments. Means of gathering the principal's business information are many. Sometimes a friendly foreigner will strike up a conversation with the principal and then proceed, subtly, to ask questions about the principal's business. At other times, a competitor of the principal's will bribe hotel staff to photocopy any fax messages that the principal sends or receives through the hotel's front desk.

As R. Patrick Watson, assistant director of the FBI and head of its counterintelligence division, has observed, "It's one thing for a company to deal with another company, but quite another for it to deal with a sophisticated intelligence apparatus of a foreign power."[74] In the last few years, several governments have admitted assigning their intelligence agencies to gather information on U.S. corporations, using such methods as searching checked baggage at airports or installing eavesdropping devices in first-class seating compartments aboard airplanes.

The scale and sophistication of business intelligence-gathering can be intimidating. A recent FBI report stated that the Bureau was investigating 800 cases of foreign economic espionage directed against American companies—and that's a 100 percent increase in its caseload from a year ago.[75] FBI Director Louis Freeh said recent investigations have found that 23 countries are engaged in covert economic espionage activity to obtain advanced technologies from U.S. industries, and 100 others have spent public funds to help companies obtain American technology.[76]

Some such intelligence-gathering takes place in the United States, but much occurs overseas. Sometimes U.S. targets find out before the damage is done. For example, in 1993, Hughes Aircraft Company and other American aerospace companies pulled out of the Paris Air Show after being warned by the CIA that French intelligence agents were after their industrial secrets.[77]

Getting down to specifics, there are several precautions the EP specialist and principal should take when traveling. Jim Royer, di-

---

[74] Ronald Yates, "Cold War: Part I: Foreign Intelligence Agencies Have New Targets—U.S. Companies," *Chicago Tribune*, August 29, 1993.

[75] "Corporate Cloak-and-Dagger Spying—Either By Rival Businesses or Foreign Governments—Can Cut Right to the Heart of a Vulnerable Corporation, But Congress Is Considering Ways to Strike Back," *Chicago Tribune*, September 1, 1996.

[76] Ibid.

[77] "French Spy Charges Highlight Trade Wars," *Chicago Tribune*, February 23, 1995.

rector of corporate security for FMC Corporation in Chicago, points out, "When you register in almost any hotel in Europe, you can expect that your registration card will wind up in the hands of the local intelligence agency, so if you have any sensitive material, you'd better not put it in the hotel safe. You're better off either sending it to yourself via a service like Federal Express or DHL, or taking it to the U.S. embassy and asking them to hold it there."[78]

Not every hotel room is under surveillance, of course, but the agent should err on the safe side. If the threat analysis gives the EP specialist reason to suspect that the principal might be under surveillance, he should warn the client not to do or say anything in the hotel room that he would not want to see printed on the front page of *The New York Times*. If the risk is great enough, and if resources allow, the EP specialist might wish to bring in technical surveillance countermeasures (TSCM) specialists to check the hotel room for surveillance equipment. However, during travel that is inconvenient, and even then TSCM experts can only do so much in a hotel, where they cannot control access to all adjoining rooms.

If eavesdropping is suspected, the agent has alternatives to a TSCM sweep. Because bugging a room takes time, and checking a room for bugs takes even longer, a quicker and easier approach is for the agent to switch the principal to a different room than the one that was reserved. The agent can also switch the principal's telephone with one from another room, making sure to change the telephone number written on the phone.

The EP specialist should also warn the principal to be careful about what he says within earshot of any interpreters provided by a foreign government or business competitor. The interpreters might later report on private conversations or other statements not intended for public consumption.

If the principal works for a large corporation, the company should join the Overseas Security Advisory Council (OSAC)[79] of the U.S. Department of State. That body, consisting mostly of corporate members, collects and shares information about safety

---

[78] Ibid.
[79] OSAC can be reached at (202) 663-0533.

and security conditions for U.S. business travelers in other countries. OSAC also publishes a number of useful publications about business travel and facilitates networking. Before a trip to a certain country, the agent can call other corporations and ask what their experiences were during recent travel to the same place and how they handled business information security.[80]

The following are a few tips that are not difficult to employ and that should probably be used even when the risk of information theft is relatively low. They can be passed along to the principal for use even when the agent is not present.

- Beware of non-electronic eavesdropping. Discussions you have on airplanes and in restaurants and bars may be overheard—accidentally or very deliberately.

- Beware of electronic eavesdropping. Any voice, fax, or data transmission over telephone lines is vulnerable.

- Beware of physical information compromise. Business documents left in the hotel room are not safe. Carefully evaluate and keep to a minimum the hard copy records you bring on the trip. Consider keeping sensitive information on a floppy disk that you carry on your person.

- Watch how you discard information. Shred or burn paper, and cut floppy disks into small pieces.

- Your notebook computer is a gold mine of information. Protect it carefully.

- Beware of information-gathering by over-friendly foreigners who take a liking to you.

Industrial espionage can even degenerate into industrial warfare. In some areas of Russia, for example, it's hard to tell where the government ends and the mafia begins. Criminal business enterprises control almost everything, and any business traveler there must be careful about whom he deals with and must keep a low profile. One knowledgeable observer applies a new version of the

---

[80] OSAC member companies include such heavy hitters as Avon Products, Coca-Cola, Eastman Kodak, Motorola, Procter & Gamble, and Texas Instuments.

famous von Clausewitz aphorism in this way: "In Russia, crime is the continuation of politics by other means."[81]

Crises

Riots, civil unrest, explosions and other crises can certainly occur at home, but they are especially difficult to deal with during travel. In a foreign country, there's a good chance that language and other problems will loom large, slowing down efforts to obtain help, to find missing persons, to rendezvous with associates, to travel by means other that those that were carefully planned, etc. Even in the United States, a crisis is more difficult to deal with when it strikes the principal in a city away from home. During travel, it is also more likely that the principal will be physically close to important public areas or attending special events (which are likely locations for crises), while at home he is more likely to be at his house or office. The following account describes the author's experiences in Atlanta during and after the bombing incident at the 1996 Summer Olympics:

> In July 1996, at the Summer Olympic Games in Atlanta, my associate Tom Levering and I were responsible for protective operations for the president of NBC, his family, and NBC's guests at the Ritz-Carlton hotel. We were working as subcontractors to International Business Resources, Ltd., headed by Peter Porrello. About 1:30 a.m. on Saturday, July 27, grabbing what little sleep one gets on such assignments, I received a call from our 24-hour command post at the International Broadcasting Center. A bomb had exploded just five minutes earlier. We got an eerie feeling, knowing that the bomb site, Centennial Olympic Park, was just a few blocks from our hotel.
>
> I got up and notified Tom, and the two of us headed out onto the street. NBC had hired scores of facilitators—mostly young people who wanted to be part of

---

[81] Theodore G. Shackley, former CIA associate deputy director for operations and founder of Research Associates International, speaking at the R.L. Oatman & Associates Executive Protection Program, Towson, Maryland, September 19, 1995.

the excitement and had come to Atlanta to perform driving, welcoming, and other tasks in support of NBC's effort. We knew many of them, along with NBC guests, would be among the crowd at the park, which was the site of numerous festivities. After the bomb exploded, the carnival atmosphere at the park had turned into a swirl of confusion. We wanted to make sure those facilitators and guests got out of there safely.

The police were in the process of shutting down the park, setting up barriers to preserve the crime scene. Blaring sirens and racing ambulances added to the chaos. Though the park was a jumble of people, we tried to spot the facilitators by the press credentials they wore. Eyeballing the crowd, we were able to find half a dozen of them as they worked their way out of the park. We gave them instructions on how to reach our hotel—the night's crisis had made travel to *their* hotel difficult—and told them to call and reassure their parents immediately. After we learned what we could at the scene, we returned to the Ritz-Carlton Hotel.

Working in concert with senior personnel at NBC and the International Business Resources security command center, we were able to account for the network's guests and employees. Because we had performed good advance work, were working with qualified personnel, and had a 24-hour communication link through which we passed facts, not hype, we were able to manage the crisis and not become part of the confusion.

We worked through the night and continued our normal protective effort the next day. Our teamwork, preparation, and familiarity with the facts enabled us to articulate to our principals and guests just what had occurred. We also advised senior personnel—both before and after the blast—that Centennial Park was not merely congested but literally mobbed with people, some of whom were the sort who could pose problems.

However, just a few days after the bombing, our principal wanted to visit the site from which MSNBC was broadcasting. That spot was atop the roof of the Chamber of Commerce building, which, like the CNN building nearby, bordered the park. Going there would put him close to the throngs of people crowding around the park. For protection reasons we would rather have kept him away from that site, but when the principal really wants to go, you go. Fortunately, because we had continued to monitor the site since the bombing, we knew that some of the danger posed by the large crowds was offset by a significantly increased police and security presence there. Our familiarity with the site and with current conditions around it enabled us to escort the principal safely to his desired destination.

The Atlanta experience teaches several lessons. It shows the importance of

- understanding the culture and operating philosophy of the client/principal
- having a plan to handle emergencies, so that when one occurs the protection team knows just what to do
- using a 24-hour command center to relay all communications and messages
- possessing the right equipment, such as radios, cellular phones, and pages
- having a close working relationship with senior managers, so that the protection team can better help them make decisions
- continuing to perform the protection team's main job even in the midst of a crisis
- conducting a good advance, so that if an area becomes closed off, the protection team still knows how to get around

One crisis that did not occur in Atlanta was a panicked evacuation of a building that was the site of a private party. The protection team received word that the building next door had received a bomb threat and was being evacuated—and that their building could be next. Without alarming the guests, the team formed an evacuation plan in case their building had to be emptied. As in all executive protection scenarios, the agent must constantly ask,

"What if?" Keeping that question well answered helps the EP specialist prevent some problems and react to others immediately.

During travel, the EP specialist should also keep abreast of local news coverage. If the principal plans a long stay in one place or is in an area where communications are poor or that is experiencing civil unrest or some natural disaster, it can be helpful to register with the nearest U.S. embassy or consulate. The booklet *Key Officers of Foreign Service Posts* is an invaluable listing of U.S. diplomatic contacts around the world. The slim booklet is easy to carry (and *should* be carried) and is available from the Superintendent of Documents at (202) 512-1800.

As was pointed out in Chapter 3, Working the Principal, a catch phrase in executive protection is "use your resources." Applying that idea, the EP specialist stands to gain much help by establishing local contacts for medical, legal, and other assistance. Similarly, it never hurts to have friends in law enforcement at the principal's destination. The agent might wish to develop such contacts by hiring local, off-duty cops as drivers or gun carriers (since it is almost impossible for a U.S. EP specialist to carry a gun legally in another country). The agent might also develop foreign contacts through fraternal organizations and executive protection training classes. Chapter 9, Protection Resources, discusses networking in greater detail. Another resource is the excellent travel security book *The Safe Travel Book*, written by Peter Savage (New York: Lexington Books, 1993), which expands on many of the travel safety tips given here.

The flip side of resources is limitations. Sleep deprivation and ignorance of the local language, customs, and geography can seriously erode the agent's ability to perform his job well. Sometimes it seems the English novelist Samuel Butler was right when he said, "Life is one long process of getting tired." Thus, a final piece of advice for EP specialists is to be aware of—and work to compensate for—their personal limitations during travel.

The art of war teaches us to rely not on the likelihood of the enemy's not coming, but on our own readiness to receive him; not on the chance of his not attacking, but rather on the fact that we have made our position unassailable.

Sun Tzu

Chapter 8
Workplace Violence

Violence has invaded the American workplace. As anyone who reads the newspapers knows, one attack after another has been wiping out workers on the job. Some attacks spring from domestic conflict, others represent the revenge of angry employees, while still others take place in the course of robberies. In general, the high level of violence found in other social venues has followed employees to work.

As the Sun Tzu quote above suggests, safety against workplace violence will not come from expecting incidents not to occur; it does no good to say, "That only happens at the post office." To protect his principal, the EP specialist would do better to assume that attacks will come; he can then try to prevent them and prepare for the few that are not preventable.

Workplace violence looms large in almost every principal's mind after each dramatic news report. Therefore, the EP specialist should be able to explain to the principal what workplace violence consists of, how likely it is, and how the agent is going to protect him from it. Understanding the frequency of workplace violence, the types of victims, the types of perpetrators, typical relationships between victims and perpetrators, motivations and psychology of perpetrators, and styles of attack can help an agent analyze the threat to his principal and erect appropriate defenses.

Because workplace violence, by definition, takes place in an institutional setting, the agent's protective plan is not something he can simply dream up and perform in a vacuum. The effort must be coordinated with appropriate company policies and physical security measures. The environment that must be controlled in order to defend a principal from workplace violence is rarely under the sole control of the EP specialist. In addition, the behavior of other company employees greatly affects the agent's ability to protect the principal. That's why defense against workplace violence has to be a company effort. As was reported in Chapter 1, Threat Assessment, homicide is the leading cause of occupational death for women and the third leading cause of death for all workers. Clearly, workplace violence is a legitimate concern for both the company in general and the principal in particular.

In the EP specialist's early stages of thinking about workplace violence, it helps to dispel a few myths. One is that employee violence is completely unpredictable, resulting from the sudden "flipping out" of a perfectly normal employee. That simply is not true. Not all incidents of violence can be predicted, but in most cases several clues to the employee's intentions can be seen. Employees who exhibit bizarre thinking or obsessions could be on the road to a violent incident. However, the best predictor of future violence by a suspect is a history of violence, and the more prior violent acts he has committed, the more accurate that prediction is. Employees with a history of committing domestic violence, physical or verbal abuse, or antisocial activities are more likely to perform violence in the workplace than employees with more peaceful histories.

Another myth is that employee threats and violence cannot be controlled. That, too, is false. Not only can they be controlled, they *must* be controlled. Threats are often the seeds that grow into violence. In some cases, by quashing threats a company may be able to quash violence. In other cases, the mechanisms used to quash threats (for example, policies stating that threats must be reported to management and that they will be acted upon) may serve the secondary purpose of at least warning the EP specialist where violence might come from. In many instances, hindsight after an episode of workplace violence shows that the incident could have been anticipated and prevented. If a company takes steps to sensitize workers to the warning signs of violence and establishes a convenient way for them to report those signs and other suspicions, the EP specialist will have a much better chance of knowing what may be coming and then being able to protect the principal from it.

The National Institute of Justice, a research arm of the U.S. Department of Justice, has discerned four principles that underlie the assessment of potential workplace violence:[82]

- Violence is a process as well as an act. Violent behavior does not occur in a vacuum. Careful analysis of violent incidents shows that violent acts often are the culmination of long-developing, identifiable trails of problems, conflicts, disputes, and failures.

- Violence is the product of an interaction among three factors: (1) The *individual* who takes violent action; (2) *stimulus or triggering conditions* that lead the subject to see violence as an option, "way out," or solution to problems or a life situation; (3) *a setting that facilitates or permits the violence*, or at least does not stop it from occurring.

- A key to investigation and resolution of threat assessment cases is identification of the subject's "attack-related" behaviors. Perpetrators of targeted acts of violence engage in discrete behaviors that precede and are linked to their attacks. They consider, plan, and prepare before engaging in violent actions.[83]

---

[82] Robert Fein, Ph.D., Bryan Vossekuil, and Gwen A. Holden, "Threat Assessment: An Approach to Prevent Targeted Violence," National Institute of Justice, Research in Action, September 1995, p. 3.

[83] An exception may be the impulsive, individual psychotic homicide, discussed later. However, that sort of person is more likely to select a victim randomly, rather than target him specifically.

- Threatening situations are more likely to be successfully investigated and managed if other agencies and systems—both within and outside law enforcement or security organizations—are recognized and used to help solve problems presented by a given case. Examples of such systems are those employed by prosecutors; courts; probation, corrections, social service, and mental health agencies; employee assistance programs; victim assistance programs; and community groups.

In some ways, workplace violence is just one more danger from which the EP specialist needs to protect the principal. In other ways, workplace violence poses a greater threat than other types of danger because it can affect the protectee regardless of whether he is specifically the target. There are two ways in which an executive can become the victim of a workplace violence incident: by being the target and by being merely a bystander.

The EP specialist's task regarding workplace violence is to educate himself about the phenomenon generally, set up notification systems that will alert him to developing threats, take steps to remove those threats, and establish protective measures that will safeguard the principal in the case of violence that is not anticipated or not prevented. The remainder of this chapter examines the sources and types of workplace violence incidents, discusses the technique of profiling workplace killers psychologically, and suggests a number of prevention and reaction measures. It is important to note, however, that workplace violence is an immensely complex subject requiring comprehensive responses. There is no quick fix.

Sources and Types of Attacks

Workplace violence has many faces. Chapter 1's discussion of threat assessment described the 1993 incident in which Gian Luigi Ferri walked into the offices of a San Francisco law firm heavily armed and began shooting people throughout two floors of the building. He killed eight people, wounded six and then shot himself. That incident, unfortunately, is not isolated; rather, it is representative of a level of violence that is becoming more and more common. It is well known that the U.S. Postal Service has suffered many attacks; typically, in those attacks, a disgruntled current or former postal worker storms into a postal facility and shoots many people. Sometimes he targets those against whom he has a specific grievance; other times, he simply sprays the office with bullets.

In workplaces across the country—blue collar, white collar, large, and small—the shootings continue. The following example typifies both the danger that such an incident can present and the difficulty and importance of preventing such incidents:

Three Shot In Mich. Ford Plant
By B.J. REYES
Associated Press Writer
Thursday, November 14, 1996

WIXOM, Mich. (AP) — A man dressed "like Rambo" and carrying an AK-47 shot his way into a Ford plant Thursday, killing a manager and wounding three other people as he sprayed gunfire through the building and then outside at a highway.

Gerald Michael Atkins, 29, was arrested after hiding in a drain tunnel for several hours. He was not a Ford employee and apparently went to the plant to see a girlfriend who worked there, said company spokesman Bill Carroll.

"He was confronted by security guards at the door and asked to leave," Carroll said. "He then pulled out an assault rifle and started shooting. That resulted in chaos and panic and everyone ran."

Said police Sgt. Richard Howe: "He more or less shot his way into the plant."

About 200 day-shift workers were on their lunch break when the gunman walked into the cafeteria wearing camouflage fatigues. One employee said "he looked like Rambo" and others were struck by his calm as he silently reloaded the assault weapon.

"He was tall, slim, AK-47 in hand. He was loading up as he was coming through the door," said employee Roosevelt Manigo. "When he loaded up, I started running."

The gunman fired round after round as he moved through the 4.2-million-square-foot facility that makes luxury Continental and Town Car models. About half of the plant's 3,200 workers were on duty when the shots rang out.

Manufacturing Planning Mgr. Darrell Izzard, the plant's No. 2 official, was walking down a hallway when he was fatally shot. "We think it was a random thing," Carroll said.

As the gunman moved outside, he began shooting at cars on nearby Interstate 96, which was closed for about five hours and lined with patrol cars.

Two Oakland County sheriff's officers near the interstate were hospitalized in stable condition after being hit by the gunfire. Another man was treated for minor injuries after he was hit by flying glass.

The suspect was able to elude police for several hours by taking cover in a series of storm drain tunnels, Howe said. After officers decided the area was secured, they used a loudspeaker to tell him to come out.

"After a short period of time he exited and gave himself up," Howe said.

Jacques Nasser, president of Ford's worldwide automotive operations, said Ford security has been very tight.

"But when someone basically fires their way—blasts their way—into a facility it's very difficult to prevent," he said.

"It's a big problem in the industry with people sometimes being able to get into the buildings," Carroll added. "There are a lot of entrances and a lot of ways they can do it."

The shooting was at least the fifth at a Michigan auto plant since 1994.

In August, a Ford employee killed a Ford security guard at a plant in western Wayne County over a run-in with the guard's daughter, then shot himself to death, police said. On Jan. 7, 1995, a worker at the same plant wounded his estranged wife, then killed her boyfriend and himself.

On Dec. 9, 1994, a worker authorities said was upset about his job assignment killed his supervisor and wounded a coworker at a Chrysler Corp. plant in Sterling Heights.

On Sept. 10, 1994, a worker opened fire with a handgun as a union meeting was breaking up at a Ford complex in Dearborn. Two workers were killed and two injured.

One key to understanding workplace violence is to realize the various relationships that exist between attackers and victims. In some instances, the attacker knows and specifically targets the victim because of who the victim is personally. In other cases, the attacker chooses the victim (1) randomly or (2) impersonally (because the victim represents something the attacker hates, the victim is easy to attack, or the victim is simply physically in the way). Familiar varieties of workplace violence include stalking, revenge by disgruntled employees, and domestic violence carried out at work. A less familiar variety is revenge by a dissatisfied customer, strange as that may sound. In a recent case, an obstetrician in a Texas town near the Mexican border was shot to death after a patient of his died.[84] The suspicion is that a Mexican drug dealer—the father of a pregnant woman who simply showed up at a hospital in labor and who died four days later of complications—hired an assassin to kill the doctor who delivered the baby. According to witnesses, the drug dealer and the baby's father told the doctor, "You will feel in your flesh what we feel in our hearts for what you have done." A month later, the doctor was shot while walking from his car to his apartment.

People who commit workplace violence are, naturally, driven by psychology.[85] That psychology may be normal or abnormal, the

---

[84] Hugh Aynesworth, "Obstetrician's Slaying Has Border Doctors Up in Arms," *The Washington Times*, December 8, 1996.

[85] This section on psychology draws on the work of James P. McGee, Ph.D., director of psychology for the Sheppard Pratt Health System and chief psychologist for the Baltimore County Police Department. Dr. McGee's training includes completion of the FBI basic and advanced hostage negotiation program and the R. L. Oatman & Associates Executive Protection Training Course. Dr. McGee is a Diplomate in Psychology, a certification awarded by the American Board of Professional Psychology, and a board-certified forensic examiner.

Dr. McGee has assisted R. L. Oatman & Associates extensively, providing psychological profiling and specific recommendations in numerous cases of threats and workplace violence.

difference being based on whether the perpetrator of the violence was mentally ill and the violence was a by-product or result of the mental disorder. Understanding the various motivations that propel people to commit workplace violence is one step in avoiding, preventing, and reacting to such violence. The following discussion of sources and types of workplace violence is general; whether any particular type of violence is a credible threat is something the EP specialist must determine specifically for the principal he protects.

One hesitates to call violence normal, but many types of workplace violence at least flow from normal psychology. *Social violence* is a clash that erupts from conflicts between cultures, gangs, races, and other social groups. The conflict might involve a turf dispute or other power struggle. High-level executives aren't especially likely to resolve their social conflicts with one another through violence; however, social violence can spill into the workplace, victimizing an executive as an innocent bystander. It is also conceivable for a principal to be targeted as a representative of a social group, even if he is not directly involved in any dispute.

Familial or domestic violence erupts from those excruciating circumstances in which love transmogrifies into hate. Spousal, unmarried romantic, and parent-child relationships sometimes flare into violence. If the two parties live together, the violence is more likely to take place at home, but if they are separated, the workplace is as good a setting for violence as any. If such a situation directly involves a protectee, he is likely to know about it in advance—after all, it will be his sweetheart who is gunning for him—so precautions can be taken. Unfortunately, there is a considerable rate of spillover in domestic violence at work; innocent bystanders frequently get caught in the cross-fire. It is not implausible for domestic violence carried out at work against an executive's secretary to affect the executive, too—it is easy enough to walk right into such a situation or to be swept up as a hostage.

Criminal violence consists of violence that is secondary to a criminal act, such as a robber's shooting of a cashier. The robber's primary goal is not to kill people, but he may do so anyway to carry out the robbery; of course, to the person killed, the motive doesn't make much difference. If the principal's work activities place him in situations where criminal violence against the company could also harm him, the agent must take appropriate precautions. *Contract violence*, sad to say, also fits into normal psychology. Such violence occurs when one party hires another to harm a third. There is no particular reason that contract violence should occur at the workplace except that the principal may be perceived as being more vulnerable there because strangers are permitted in the front door, while at the principal's home they are not.

Other types of workplace violence, too, may flow from normal psychology. For example, an employee may attack a coworker, supervisor, or manager over work-related grievances. That scenario usually involves the notorious phrase "disgruntled employee." Alternatively, a non-employee or former employee may attack an employee. The infamous examples here are disgruntled customers and the aforementioned domestic violence carried out at work.

Some types of workplace violence can also result from abnormal psychology or mental illness. Among the risks from persons motivated by abnormal psychology are these:

- individual psychotic homicide (for example, when a person is motivated by hallucinations in which he is commanded to kill someone)
- serial killing (typically of women, children, homosexuals, or prostitutes; there is often a sexual component to the motivation)
- mass murder (family murderers, bombers, poisoners, arsonists)
- workplace revenge (with a scope well beyond those who might have offended the avenger)
- assassination (for irrational reasons, like erotomania)

The preceding lists of motivations, perpetrators, and victims of workplace violence may make the workplace sound dangerous. It *is* dangerous. But that should come as no surprise—contemporary society is violent, and the workplace is a major part of society. As Dr. James McGee, chief psychologist for the Baltimore County

Police Department and director of psychology for the Sheppard Pratt Health System, has observed, if violence in society went from its 1950s level to today's level *overnight*, we would have martial law today. However, since the level of violence rose gradually, most people have become desensitized to it. The EP specialist, by contrast, can never become desensitized to violence. He must be aware that some of the risks his protectee faces out on the mean streets can also spill over into the workplace.

Statistically, executives face a much lower risk of death and injury from workplace violence than do police officers, pizza delivery workers, and clerks in convenience and liquor stores. Still, to some attackers, high-level protectees make the most desirable targets. Remember, a protectee doesn't have to be a highly desirable target in absolute terms, only in relative terms. He might not think of himself as a fat cat, a symbol of power and wealth, but potential perpetrators of workplace violence, from where they stand, might see him that way.

Profiling Workplace Killers

Like most other threats against which an EP specialist protects his client, workplace violence may appear random, but it is not. A trained eye can see it coming—sometimes, at least. To protect his client in the corporate environment, the EP specialist should work with the security and human resources departments to line up resources, such as psychologists, police contacts who can perform criminal record checks, licensed private investigative firms, and others who can help the agent investigate a person who shows signs of being a threat. That way, the corporation can act quickly on any signs that a person may have a tendency to commit workplace violence. Quick action is especially important when the agent or someone else in the corporation spots the early warning signs that are predictors of *imminent* violence.

Psychological profile

There's really no way to say for certain whether a particular person will commit workplace violence. The best an EP specialist can do is to employ the technique of profiling. With that technique, the agent compares characteristics of the suspect with characteristics of known workplace-violence criminals. If there is a high rate of correspondence between the two, the agent may be able to (1) target his defenses more accurately and (2) take steps to remove the attacker before he strikes (through firing, prosecution for stalking or harassment, or other legal means).

Understanding the psychological profiles of different criminal types can help an EP specialist predict who might commit workplace violence. The technique helps the agent move from a large pool of persons to a small one in considering who might pose a risk to the principal. Profiling doesn't give the agent an advantage in all situations, however. When workplace violence is committed by non-employees (angry customers or psychotics off the street), typically the agent will not even have heard of the person before, much less have met or analyzed him.

Different profiles apply to different types of criminals, but in general the profile for a person who is likely to commit street violence is a 15- to 24-year-old male who is a member of a minority group and who has a history of violent behavior, shoplifting, and substance abuse. A different profile applies to a person likely to commit *individual psychotic homicide*. Such a person is actively psychotic, has command hallucinations and persecutory delusions, has a history of violence and psychiatric hospitalization, may be homeless, and has had some past involvement with the police (arrest or other interaction). Attacks by such a person tend to be impulsive and unplanned—he may simply wander in from the street. Attacks by that type of person also tend to be highly violent, with a knife as the weapon of choice.

A person on his way to becoming a *mass murderer* likely suffers from depression and paranoia; blames others for his woes; files many lawsuits; is preoccupied with violent films, television programs, or books; is a police or military "wannabee" who had undistinguished, noncombatant military service; is angry and suicidal; intimidates others by talking about guns; threatens others; has no known history of committing violence; prepares his crime carefully; and has an interest in and sometimes speaks about mass murders. (The last characteristic is the most powerful predictor of all.) The idea that a person who is perfectly normal would ever "snap" and commit mass murder is unfounded; there are always warning signs.

The *workplace avenger* is typically a white male, age 30 to 55, who is single, separated, or divorced. He may be very interested in weapons, be a military veteran, and possess paranoid, narcissistic personality traits. His self-esteem is low, and he is sensitive to rejection and criticism. He fantasizes about homicide or suicide and may be an alcohol abuser. Workplace disciplinary action or termination of employment precipitates a shooting spree motivated by vengeance.[86]

Assassins of public figures also tend to share certain traits. Arthur Bremer, who stalked President Nixon and later shot George Wallace, is a typical example of a public figure assassin. Both contemporary news reports and his diary[87] show him as thinking unrealistically highly of himself, due to what may have been a narcissistic personality disorder. He traveled in pursuit of his first and second targets—Nixon and Wallace—and he gathered information about them from newspapers, television reports, signs posted in buildings they visited, and various people at the scene. Bremer was able to get close to his targets in part because he appeared normal—he looked like an ordinary guy, not an assassin, neither crazed nor well-trained. He bought himself a handgun to perform the assassination (though he was not highly skilled at using it), and he kept a diary of his activities.

Early warning signs

The psychological profiles given above are very general and don't offer the EP specialist much to focus on. However, workplace violence has enough of a track record that criminologists have been able to discern a number of specific, early-warning characteristics and behaviors. They are by no means proof that a person will become violent, but often a person will display one or more of them before becoming

---

[86] Roger L. Depue, *The Avenger Personality* (AGI, 1993).
[87] New York: Harper's Magazine Press, 1972.

violent. Basically, a list of characteristics and behaviors gives the EP specialist and other people who are on the lookout something to look out for. The protective team should prick up their ears if anyone around the workplace does the following:[88]

sends inappropriate written communications (unwanted cards, flowers, pictures, letters)

writes violent notes to coworkers or management

trespasses

stalks

enters surreptitiously

repeatedly refuses to cooperate with others at work

frequently argues with coworkers

displays belligerence toward customers

refuses to obey company rules

sabotages company projects or equipment

speaks of a wish or plan to hurt coworkers or managers

sees himself as victimized by management

threatens suicide

suffers from depression

takes frequent absences

talks in a louder than normal voice

is startled easily

displays increasing irritability and impatience

suffers from problems with concentration and memory

suffers from sleeping problems

routinely blames others for his lack of success

has an unreciprocated romantic obsession

takes up much of a supervisor's time with behavior or performance problems

---

[88] This list is based on ideas from a wide range of sources, including the author's experience; the previously cited work by Fein, Vossekuil, and Holden; S. Anthony Baron's book *Violence in the Workplace: A Prevention and Management Guide for Business* (Bakersfield, California: Pathfinder Publishing of California, 1994); and many other references.

undergoes a drastic change in belief systems

displays unwarranted anger

is unable to take criticism

expresses hopelessness or heightened anxiety

performs violence against inanimate objects

steals equipment

acts with a lack of concern for the safety of others

A slightly different set of characteristics predicts imminent violence (that is, violence that could erupt within two to six weeks). A person in that group would be someone who was recently discharged from a mental hospital and who abuses drugs or alcohol and suffers from active psychotic symptoms, such as delusions, hallucinations, or thought disorders.[89]

When early warning signs are spotted, the EP specialist must follow up on them or see that someone else in the company does so. (In a corporate setting, it would be awkward, at the very least, for the principal's protection specialist to go around investigating everyone in the office.) Although it is important to respect the privacy of a person who shows the early warning signs, especially since the signs alone don't prove he's a prospective murderer, he still needs to be investigated. If the person is an employee, it would make sense to check through his records in the human resources, finance, benefits, security, internal audit, and legal departments. Before doing so, the EP specialist should certainly consult with company lawyers to make sure the research is legal. Ideally, the EP specialist should sort out the legal questions long before he needs to investigate someone, since it may take awhile to obtain the legal opinion.

It also takes time to investigate behavior that seems threatening. Although early warning signs need to be considered, some require only a quick analysis before being safely dismissed, while others call for more extensive investigation. In every endeavor, priorities must be set and the most important matters handled first. Not every act on the list of early warning signs can be investigated. To

---

[89] McGee.

reduce the amount of time spent on investigation, the EP specialist needs to differentiate between *making* a threat and *posing* a threat. Some persons who make threats ultimately pose threats; many persons who make threats do not pose threats; and some persons who pose threats never make threats.[90]

Because the growth of workplace violence is a relatively new phenomenon, the best ways to combat it are still under debate. One matter that experts disagree on is the question of corporate policy prohibiting threats. One school of thought states that the agent must do something to reduce the number of threats issued, many of which represent harmless venting of frustration. If the executive works in an organization where threats from customers, vendors, or employees occur frequently, the company should institute a policy similar to that enforced at airport screening checkpoints: no jokes allowed, and all threats are investigated. The policy should also prohibit the possession of weapons. Once the anti-threat policy has been clearly promulgated, the company should discipline or fire every threat-maker if the complaint is substantiated.

Another school of thought considers every threat meaningful and deems it foolhardy to expect that a policy prohibiting threats will have any deterrent effect. People bent on violence aren't going to be affected by a policy statement—such a policy won't be worth the paper it's printed on. Instead, a company should simply consider every threat meaningful and investigate each one.

Screening and analyzing communications

When a threatening letter or telephone call arrives, there must be a clear means for it to be forwarded to the EP specialist for analysis. Employees won't necessarily think to pass those communications to the EP specialist, the security department, or whoever else should see them. To keep threatening communications from falling through the cracks, the company should establish a requirement that all such communications be reported to a designated office.

---

[90] Fein, Vossekuil, and Holden.

Once a threatening communication arrives in the hands of the EP specialist, he should analyze it promptly. This is one type of correspondence not to leave in a stack to deal with at a later date. Through training and experience, the agent may be able to determine quickly whether the writer or caller is harmful or harmless and whether any further investigation or intervention needs to be done. If more does need to be done, there are two different angles of approach: law enforcement evidentiary analysis and psychological analysis. In most cases, the problem must be approached from both angles at once.

Law enforcement evidentiary analysis. A threatening communication—especially a letter—is not just a message; it is also evidence. Like other evidence, it should be treated and analyzed in certain ways. On receiving a threat letter, the agent should do the following:

- If the letter seems threatening, treat it as police treat physical evidence. Keep extra fingerprints off it; photocopy it for your own follow-up examination; and preserve it in a plastic bag for later forensic analysis or court action.

- Identify the postmark to see where the letter came from.

- Check the envelope's return address, if it has one. Sometimes threatening writers use their real name and address. If so, you know who to investigate for a propensity to violence.

- Check the envelope's destination address. If it was mailed to the principal's home address and that address is not listed in the phone book, the writer might be someone who knows the principal. If the letter was addressed to a specific building and suite at the principal's place of business, that level of detail might suggest that the writer is an insider.

- If the letter is typed, it might be possible to link the document to a specific typewriter. If the letter was produced on a computer, the choice of fonts, the type of printer it was produced on, and other attributes might serve as clues to the writer's identity.

- If the letter is handwritten, compare the handwriting to that used in other letters in the threat file.
- See whether the threat file contains other communications that might look or sound like they came from the same source.
- Consider notifying local or federal law enforcement officials.

With this sort of analysis done, when the psychological analysis is finished, the agent will be all ready for whatever steps are appropriate next.

Psychological analysis. The first level of psychological analysis of a threatening letter can be done by the EP specialist himself. If he feels the letter warrants further analysis, he can refer it to a qualified psychologist.

Some characteristics of threat letters predict later violence by the writer, while others suggest the writer will not be violent or are inconclusive. One telling attribute of a threatening communication is its degree of specificity. If the threat is highly specific—naming the intended victim, listing his home or work address or information about his family, or describing weapons that the writer intends to use—the level of security concern should also be high. By contrast, a letter that threatens not violence but some other action, such as exposure of the recipient's alleged misdeeds, does not typically foreshadow violence.

An agent can educate himself further about workplace violence by attending a training course on the subject. Or, for a better qualified analysis of whether the communicator represents a threat to the principal, the agent can consult outside help. One type of resource is a psychologist with experience in threat assessment, assassin profiling, and other topics related to law enforcement and security. Such a professional can review the communicator's personnel file, look into his employment and criminal history, analyze any hostile letters or other communications the person has directed at the principal or his company, and interview the person's coworkers. The psychologist then would be able to issue a opinion on the likely level of danger posed by the person. Because in most cases the psychologist is asked not to contact the person directly, the psychologist's report typically contains qualifications and reservations. Nevertheless, such a report can give the EP specialist some guidance as to the best way to deal with the problem.

For example, the report might say that a belligerent, hostile, argumentative, and possibly threatening man who was fired from his job probably has certain personality disorders with antisocial features and occasionally binges on alcohol or other drugs but overall presents a low risk for violence.[91] Another report might state that a frightening, irate Vietnam veteran—who is not an employee but who attempts to intimidate company employees with talk of his expertise in weapons use, demolition, martial arts, ambush, and assassination; who talks much about his guns; and who has what he considers to be a major disagreement with the company in question—possesses enough of the characteristics of a workplace avenger or pseudo-commando to pose a threat to company employees. In this instance, the report would advise against confrontational tactics and would recommend that the company (1) pursue a conciliatory strategy and (2) warn its employees not to deal directly with the person but instead leave any future meetings to persons trained to handle potentially violent subjects.

Specifically, what sort of communication merits a closer look? An executive at a major U.S. banking company received, at his house, a strange note from a former employee, along with the former employee's mutilated company ID. The executive passed it to the corporation's security specialist, who referred it to Dr. McGee. The letter read as follows:

> There are voices that say who are you what are you are you real? I will be leaving soon and have no use for this identification card. I will be issued a new one upon my glorious arrival.
>
> Thank you thank you thank you.

---

[91] This and the following scenarios are based on the work of Dr. McGee.

After studying the letter and a limited amount of biographical, legal, and historical information about the subject, Dr. McGee developed the following profile:

B (the alleged letter writer) was recently employed by the bank in a low-level position. Shortly thereafter, a criminal background investigation revealed a history of convictions for burglary and additional arrests for drug possession and burglary. As that legal history had not previously been reported by B, he was fired.

B is a 38-year-old Caucasian male. He is reported to be married, but the marriage is probably unstable, and he may have been married more than once. He is a high school graduate, though school performance was marginal, and his IQ is in the low-average range. B comes from a blue-collar background with divorced parents and turbulent family life and childhood development. Parents and siblings have histories of psychiatric illness and substance abuse. By early adolescence, B began using drugs and alcohol. Drugs of choice initially included marijuana, amphetamines, and alcohol, but it is likely he has tried most other abusable substances.

Currently B meets diagnostic criteria for polysubstance dependence, preferring alcohol and stimulant drugs like cocaine. B has had episodes of unsuccessful treatment for chemical dependence and psychiatric illness. These included inpatient hospitalizations prompted when he reported he was planning to harm himself or others. It is likely that he has actually engaged in some type of suicidal or self-injurious behavior in the past, and he has also been assaultive, particularly while intoxicated.

B's work history is unimpressive. He has a history of problems with coworkers and supervisors, and he has been fired from several jobs. Financial problems are chronic, and he often spends money on drug binges.

At times, particularly during periods of heavy drug and alcohol use, B has experienced psychotic symptoms including auditory hallucinations, delusional thinking with persecutory beliefs, and disorganized and irrational thinking. He has probably received psychiatric diagnoses such as substance-induced mood disorder, substance-induced psychotic disorder, bipolar disorder type II, and mixed personality disorder with narcissistic and antisocial features. Some version of schizophrenia is another diagnostic possibility. B can be thought of as a dual diagnosis patient, which means he simultaneously meets criteria for both mental illness and substance abuse. Dual diagnosis patients display high rates of aggressive and violent behavior toward themselves and others.

Based on that profile, Dr. McGee made the following recommendations:

The content and construction of B's note suggests that he was either intoxicated or experiencing psychotic symptoms such as auditory hallucinations (voices) when he wrote it. The statement about "leaving soon" and "glorious arrival" are thinly veiled allusions to suicide and death. Among perpetrators of violence, B would be classified as a disorganized type. That suggests his violent behavior is likely to be impulsive and unsophisticated rather than well planned and organized. B's risk for violence against bank employees is estimated to be in the moderate range. Any signs of escalation in the form of additional letters or attempts at personal or telephone contact by B should be taken very seriously as an indication of increased risk.

The preceding case fits most people's idea of the threat of workplace violence. The next case shows that obsessive, discomfiting situations can affect a principal even in a workplace at which he is only a guest—the *perpetrator's* workplace. The following is a version of an actual letter sent to a wealthy protectee:

Dear Mr. X,

I hope your staff will not keep you from reading this letter and will let you see it and make up your mind for yourself. I am a 30-year-old fellow with many questions. I don't wish to bother you, but my curiosity is irresistible.

You may not remember me, but I work in the office at the accounting firm you use. For a long time I have been wondering about how you live. What sort of family do you come from? How did you meet your lovely wife? What do you like to do on weekends? What do you like to eat? Have you ever eaten fast food? What do you do all day? You are so successful. How did that happen?

I can only begin to imagine what it is like to be so rich! My life is very different. My wife and I struggle from paycheck to paycheck. But I'm not asking for money, truly.

May I tour your office sometime? It's one of my greatest fantasies. I could see everything and get you to answer all these questions that I can't get out of my mind. I could learn to be successful like you. I think about this all the time.

Please write back. I know that you're busy, and that dreams don't usually come true, but I hope I'll get a response back. This is the first step. This is my fantasy.

Please note that I am not a weirdo. I'm perfectly average. I look forward to hearing from you. If you don't write back, I'll understand.

Sincerely,

Y

The man who received the letter passed it to his protection specialist, who referred it to Dr. McGee for analysis. After examining the letter and collecting background information about the writer, he developed the following profile:

Y is a 30-year-old married Caucasian male employed in a clerical position at the accounting firm used by X. He has held this position for about seven years, and his work performance has been generally satisfactory, though clients and coworkers sometimes perceive him as overly aggressive and intrusive. His wife is a waitress, and they have young children.

Y is a high school graduate with some technical school training. He has average to bright-average intelligence, and his memory, attention, concentration, and other cognitive functions are within normal limits. There is no history of drug or alcohol problems or any criminal activity. He is active in his non-mainstream Protestant church. No signs of major mental illness are evident, although a variant of manic-depressive illness controlled by mood-stabilizing medications cannot be ruled out. There is some evidence that Y has a mixed personality disorder with narcissistic and compulsive features. This causes him episodically to display poor social judgment and grandiosity and act impulsively in ways that are offensive and upsetting to others. Y is extremely defensive and uninsightful about these personality flaws and may become distraught and even enraged when they are brought to his attention. He tends to feel unappreciated and put upon by others and can be quite envious and resentful of those who have more than he does. If he perceives others as not liking or approving of him, he feels their attitudes are grounded in envy of him.

Y's motive for writing to X includes more than idle curiosity. It is an attempt on Y's part to develop a special personal relationship with X that would result in Y's personal gain and achievement of social prominence and economic success. It is likely that Y has well-developed and elaborate fantasies of this special relationship. There is a moderately high probability that without intervention Y will follow up the letter with an attempt at face-to-face contact, possibly using X's accounting work as a pretext. Anything short of a strong rebuke will be perceived by Y as encouragement. However, rejection by X is not likely to be well received and may not even be acknowledged by Y as reflecting X's true wishes.

Dr. McGee's recommendations were these:

1. Y should be confronted about the inappropriateness of his behavior by the management of his accounting firm.

2. Y should be notified that any similar behavior or attempts to have direct contact with X or X's family members is grounds for immediate termination. Supervisors at the accounting firm should be discreetly informed of this as well.
3. Y should receive additional supervision on the job and be monitored periodically by management.
4. Y should undergo a psychological evaluation and, if indicated, counseling.

The risk of violence by Y is low; however, the risk of inappropriate approach behavior by Y toward X and his family members is moderately high. It is suggested that additional information be gathered and the subject be confronted and monitored.

Throughout the entire effort to prevent workplace violence, it is imperative that the EP specialist keep a complete file of all threatening letters and records of threatening phone calls. Such a file is the cornerstone of both psychological analysis and possible legal action.

Investigation

If the agent or his outside consultant decides the communicator should be investigated further—to determine whether he poses a threat to the principal—there are several key items that must be looked into. This level of investigation is separate from and should precede any contact with the subject himself.

The investigation should include the following:

- examination of materials that the subject possesses, collects, or has created, including journals, letters, books, magazines, and other items that may relate to the investigation
- interviews with persons who know or have known the subject, including family, friends, coworkers, supervisors, neighbors, landlords, law enforcement officers, social service or mental health staff, and previous victims of unacceptable behavior (including violence) committed by the subject

- research into records kept by police, courts, probation and parole agencies, mental health and social services, and any persons aware of the subject's interest in a particular target, such as security personnel, managers, victims, or colleagues

Obviously, not all the information above is readily or legally available in every case. However, it is the type of information that the agent may wish to gather to determine whether further work is required.

Throughout the investigation, the EP specialist should focus on gathering information specifically on the subject's attack-related behavior—that is, whether the subject has expressed interest in possible targets; whether he has communicated with or about potential targets; whether he has considered or attempted harm to himself or others; whether he has obtained or practiced with weapons; and whether he has followed or approached potential targets, with or without weapons, at any types of events or occasions.

Specific threat assessment

Once the agent has gathered the relevant information about the threatening communicator, he can properly assess, not the general level of threat faced by the principal, but the specific level of threat posed by the current situation raised by the particular communicator being investigated. To assess the threat, the agent can use the findings of his investigation to answer the following questions:

- Does it appear that the subject has selected a target?
- Does he know the target well?
- Is the subject familiar with the targeted person's work, life style, habits, and schedule?
- Is the target vulnerable to an attack?
- What potential changes in the target's life could make an attack more difficult or less likely, such as moving, spending more time at home, or taking a new job? What changes could increase the risk of violence?

- Does the target fear the subject?
- Do the target's family, friends, or colleagues share that fear?
- Is the target convinced of the need for caution?
- If necessary, could the target plainly communicate to the subject that he wants no further contact with him?
- Does the subject seem to be moving toward or away from attacking?
- If toward, how close?
- What thresholds has the subject crossed? Has he violated court orders, made a will, given away personal items, or expressed a willingness to die or be imprisoned?

Interviewing and intervening

The next step in gathering information to decide whether the subject poses a threat to the principal is to interview the subject himself. However, this is not just another information-gathering step. It is simultaneously an interview and an intervention. In potential workplace violence cases, intervention by the target or his representatives might scare the prospective aggressor away or might spur him to act on his threats. For that reason, it makes sense, first, to consider whether to interview the subject at all.

Should the agent interview the subject? That depends on several factors:[92]

- the agent's need for information (in other words, if the agent is able to gather sufficient information from sources other than the subject himself, there may be no need to risk an interview)
- the facts that led the agent to start the investigation
- the investigator's legal standing in relation to the subject
- the investigator's resources, training, and experience

---

[92] Fein, Vossekuil, and Holden.

- the stage of the investigation
- the investigator's strategy for resolving the case.

In most cases where the subject and target have had face-to-face contact or the subject has spoken or written a clear threat to the target, an interview is a good idea. It helps the agent obtain more information about the subject; it shows the subject that his behavior has been noticed; it gives the agent a chance to tell the subject clearly that his behavior is unwelcome and unacceptable and must cease; and it gives the subject a chance to tell his story, perhaps safely releasing some pent-up steam or relieving the frustration of not being heard or acknowledged.

However, an interview/intervention is not always a good idea. History suggests that it could intensify the communicator's interest in the target or trigger lethal behavior. For example, what if a person has written to a celebrity, expressing his love and formally proposing marriage, but has done nothing else in relation to the celebrity? In such a case, an interview might stimulate his interest, which could otherwise wane. What about a desperate, suicidal ex-wife, who feels abandoned and has been stalking her ex-husband? An interview might make her feel that time is running out and convince her to move ahead with her violent plan before she is jailed.

In general, confronting a subject may help if the subject has something to lose; however, if he has little to lose, then a confrontation may only provoke him. For example, a person with a family and job is likely to back down after being confronted and told to stop bothering the protectee—the threat of exposure means something to him. By contrast, an unemployed, marginally functioning person who is indifferent to public exposure or even welcomes it might be emboldened by a confrontation.

What about arranging for police to pay the subject a visit? Good idea or bad? For various reasons, history shows that in political cases, police visits may improve the situation; in celebrity cases, by contrast, police visits tend to make matters worse.

Throughout the investigative process, it is essential that the agent document his efforts and findings. Not only do written records help the agent analyze the risk and develop possible solutions, but they also facilitate prevention measures and, of course, prosecution, either before or after a violent incident occurs.

Prevention Measures

The first two categories of prevention measures discussed here are geared toward preventing an attack, while the third category is geared toward preventing harm to the principal once an attack is initiated or attempted. The major categories of workplace violence prevention are (1) deflecting or defusing problems before they start, (2) removing the threat—by firing, prosecuting, satisfying, or ignoring the potentially violent person, and (3) physical security—making sure the rings of protection will secure the principal against any newly identified threat. Together, the three categories of prevention measures create a strategy of simultaneous defense and offense.

Deflecting or defusing problems

Several types of situations in the workplace have the potential to lead to violence either at the moment or later on, after the subject has had time to stew over the problem and return to work armed. When the attacker is a non-employee, someone whom the EP specialist has had no notice of or contact with, it's difficult to deflect problems. However, the following suggestions can help deflect or defuse problems involving employees, contractors, vendors, and others who spend a significant amount of time at the principal's workplace.

Background Checks/Preemployment Screening. In many settings, checking the background of prospective employees—and then not hiring people with a history of violent or other difficult behavior—is one way to reduce the number of personnel prone to workplace violence. Typically, an EP specialist is not in a position to implement institutional policies requiring preemployment screening. However, he may be able to suggest such policies to the principal or the director of human resources, who then may be able to institute or at least recommend them. In brief, such policies should require the use of a job application form that includes an appropriate waiver that permits the employer to verify the information reported on the application. Before hiring any applicant, the company should check his references and investigate any violent incidents in his past. Drug screening and psychological testing can also help weed out unsuitable candidates from the applicant pool. However, all screening measures should first be examined by legal counsel.

It might also be appropriate to screen contract personnel who work at the principal's office. Vendors and service organizations whose personnel make frequent visits or spend long periods at the facility should certify that those individuals meet the principal's organization's security requirements.

Safety Valves. Two kinds of safety valves can help reduce the pressures that lead to workplace violence. The first type lets employees, customers, and other relevant parties blow off steam in a safe, socially acceptable way. People who feel strong disapproval or dislike of the principal or the organization he heads need some positive way to communicate their displeasure. Options include employee suggestion boxes, union grievance procedures, and hot lines to the human relations and customer service departments. The idea is to reduce people's frustration and feelings of powerlessness before they decide the only way they can solve their problems is through violence.

A second type of safety valve lets employees report their suspicions of danger. The EP specialist should see to it (through the appropriate corporate channels) that employees are taught to look out for signs of imminent workplace violence. He must also make sure employees have access to convenient, discreet channels for reporting their concerns.[93] Options include periodic internal surveys and violence or threat hot lines. People who suddenly erupt into violent behavior usually have made threats in the past, and

---

[93] One good method is to set up a toll-free 800 telephone number that employees can use to report security concerns, including threatening behavior by coworkers or signs that a coworker could erupt into violence. The advantage of the 800 number is that employees can freely call anonymously from anywhere and not feel that their identify will be disclosed by caller-ID or other call-tracing systems.

employees tend to know about those threats even when management doesn't. Reporting systems can give warnings of those impending dangers.

Keeping the Peace. The workplace is host to many conflicts: personality clashes, pay disputes, policy disagreements, arguments about annual reviews and promotions, etc. When such a conflict escalates to shouting or seething, it could tip out of control and lead to violence. The EP specialist and the principal should both give some thought to techniques that keep such pots from boiling over. That doesn't mean becoming a full-fledged hostage negotiator; rather, it means knowing how to handle a very upset person in a way that keeps the situation from escalating to violence. In fact, success in keeping the peace eliminates the need for a hostage negotiator.

Peacekeeping during a high-energy argument might fall to the principal, who is often in a position of hiring, firing, promoting, and setting policy. It could also fall to the EP specialist, especially if he has a cover position that makes it seem reasonable for him to be talking to an upset employee. Here are a few tips for anyone who wishes to keep a lid on that kind of situation:

- Project calmness and confidence, moving and speaking slowly and quietly.
- Pay attention to the other person so he will know you are interested in what he has to say.
- To avoid giving the impression that the two of you are butting heads, stand or sit at a right angle to the other person rather than directly face to face.
- Tell the person you can see he is upset. Acknowledging a person's feelings helps reduce that person's frustration.
- To give the person time to calm down, use delaying tactics such as offering a drink of water (in a disposable cup that can't become a weapon).
- Place yourself in a spot where the person cannot block your way to an exit.
- In your effort to keep the situation calm, try not to sound cold, condescending, officious, or evasive. But

don't let your interest in the situation tempt you to challenge, threaten, or dare the person.

Careful Firing. Another situation that can raise the likelihood of workplace violence is employment termination. If layoffs or firings are on the horizon, the EP specialist should make sure that whoever handles those activities does so in a way that reduces their violence-producing potential. Even if the layoff or firing is neither conceived nor carried out by the chief executive, a vengeful employee looking for a victim on which to settle his rage may well choose the person who most represents the institution: the executive.

Careful firing uses intelligent logistics and straightforward, calm discussion. On the logistical end, the EP specialist should consider where the employee will be fired and by whom. To avoid both litigation and violence, it is advantageous for two company representatives to perform the firing. That increases the number of witness who could testify as to what was said and may help in defusing uncomfortable situations. It also makes sense, if a man is firing a woman, for a female manager to attend the meeting to discourage false allegations of harassment. The EP specialist is charged with protecting the executive from all threats, including embarrassment, which would be intense if the person being fired accused the boss of offering to cancel the firing in exchange for sexual favors.

Another logistical consideration that can keep the lid on tension has to do with packing. If the executive gives a fired employee 15 minutes to pack up and leave the premises, and no boxes are available, tension will surely rise. It wouldn't be hard to keep a store of boxes and tape on hand to avoid such tension.

The agent may wish to see that company employees who fire others receive basic instruction in how to do so in a way that discourages violence. The agent should offer the following advice to managers who have to fire employees:

- Tell the employee that the decision is final and not negotiable.
- Cite only general reasons for the termination; don't get drawn into an argument over the particular justifica-

tions for firing the employee. Anything that sounds like blame will invite confrontation.

- Help the person focus on the future, reminding him that his experience and education will help him take advantage of the opportunities that are out there.

- Keep a respectful distance from the person. Have no more physical contact than a goodbye handshake, at most.

- The firing is extremely significant to the employee. Especially during a mass layoff, try not to make the person feel he is being discarded cavalierly. Getting fired is one of the most stressful incidents in a person's life, so take care not to do or say anything that the person would interpret as degrading.

- Pay close attention to what the person says. Perhaps without even knowing it, he might give you clues about his likelihood of committing violence or filing a lawsuit.

- To keep the session from dragging on or requiring any follow-up, make sure you can answer any appropriate questions the person is likely to ask.

An additional option is to videotape the termination session surreptitiously. Current technology makes such an option relatively easy. One technique would be to use a super-compact camera, such as a modified pencil sharpener that contains a video lens in the pencil aperture, aimed from a desk directly toward the employee. Of course, it is essential to check with the company attorney before taking any such measure.

Removing the threat

In the preceding section, "Deflecting or defusing problems," the types of security measures mentioned were oriented toward keeping violent people from being hired and keeping normal employees from becoming violent. However, sometimes an organization is stuck with a potentially violent person, either because he is already an employee or because he is a persistent customer. If a person about whom the EP specialist has serious concern is already involved with the organization, what can be done to get rid of him? Basically, the potentially dangerous person can be (1) fired, (2) prosecuted, (3) bought off, or (4) ignored.

Firing for the Purpose of Removal. A prudent EP specialist wouldn't allow a ticking time bomb to remain next to his protectee day after day. But an employee who is known or strongly suspected to be predisposed to violence is much the same as a ticking time bomb. There's no sense keeping that kind of risk around, and sometimes firing the person is the best thing to do. Of course, firing raises some risks in the process of eliminating others. In other words, a smoldering employee might erupt *because* of the firing.

The section on firing above described how to handle an employment termination in a way that would not spark a normal employee to violence. However, if it is necessary to fire an employee who has a much higher probability of reacting violently and if that person fits the profile of a workplace killer, then extreme caution is warranted. If the employee is a loner with little to care about besides his job, then, for him, losing his job is like losing his life, and he may take it very badly.

In many cases, the protectee will be able to excuse himself from such hazardous and unpleasant duty. Sometimes, however, even the chief has to do dirty work. All the tips offered in the earlier section on firing apply, plus several additional ones. First, the termination meeting needs to be planned carefully, in advance, down to the last detail. The EP specialist and the principal should practice what the principal will say. They should also decide whether the EP specialist will be present in the room during the firing. If not, he can stand outside the room, and if he hears a prearranged signal for help, he can enter. The signal for that response can be orchestrated in many different ways—with intercoms, by voice, by knocking on the wall, etc.

If the person being let go is especially frightening, the EP specialist should ask the police, with whom he already should have a good relationship, to be present—if not on the spot, at least in the building.

Prosecution. Another way to remove the threat of violence posed by an employee, customer, vendor, or other party who poses a threat to the principal at the workplace is to arrange for prosecution. Various criminal and civil remedies relating to stalking, threats, and harassment can help EP specialists intervene before a violent attack occurs.

The idea of jailing the threatening person may hold great appeal, but the relief offered by the legal system is usually meager, temporary, and difficult to attain. Also, in practice the prosecution approach also requires the previous measure (firing), so it's a major undertaking.

If the EP specialist and principal are considering arranging for the subject to be prosecuted, they should wait until they are confident it can be done successfully. That means accumulating the necessary evidence to get the person both charged and convicted. The problem with legal intervention, however, is that it only helps if the suspect has something to lose. The threat of fines or a long prison sentence may not deter a person who desperately desires revenge or is prepared to die to achieve his objective. At bottom it is up to the EP specialist to know how to identify, evaluate, and manage persons who present a high risk of committing violent acts.

Capitulation. If someone poses a threat to the principal, the agent's natural reaction is to focus on the principal, removing him from harm. However, sometimes it is effective to focus on the potentially violent person, the threatener. It might offend one's sense of justice even to consider giving in to that person's demands, but in some cases it is simply more practical to give the person what he wants or needs rather than continue to risk a violent episode. For example, if an employee who fits the workplace avenger psychological profile desperately wants an early retirement, it is cheaper and safer to give him what he wants, even if he doesn't strictly deserve it. Similarly, if a manic-depressive, drug-using weapons nut wants a refund on a product he bought from the company, and under normal circumstances he would not be entitled to it, the EP specialist may wish to suggest bending the policy simply to satisfy and get rid of the person. Another scenario is that a non-employee has developed an inappropriate, potentially violent fixation on an employee. In that case, it might help to ask the person's family, friends, neighbors, or associates for ideas on how to change the subject's thinking or behavior; mental health and social service staff may also be able to help.

Extinction. If a ranting non-employee is raising concerns, one strategy to consider is simply ignoring the person. That strategy is also called "extinction." A case in which extinction might be appropriate would be a campaign of inappropriately angry and aggressive letters written by a dissatisfied, mentally unbalanced customer. If his psychological profile suggests that his bark is much worse than his bite, it might pay off to do little more than notify him that his letters and calls are no longer welcome—and then *monitor but not respond to* any future messages from him. Firing is not an option because he is not an employee; prosecution isn't possible because he has not crossed the line into open threats, and taking legal action might agitate more than pacify him; capitulation may not work because he primarily wants to complain, not to be reimbursed or otherwise compensated; so warning him once and then ignoring him may be the only path to take.

Physical security

Physical security at the workplace was discussed in detail in Chapter 6, Home and Office Security. Those same measures would protect the principal from the workplace violence threats described in this chapter. However, the security measures may need to be fine-tuned a little if the EP specialist deems the principal to be under threat of attack. The agent should consider whether any aspects of the building's physical layout or access control would allow an attacker to approach the principal. If the principal likes to have a lot of contact with the public, then the EP specialist may have to be more aggressive in dealing with potential workplace assailants. If the principal spends most of his time safely sequestered from almost everyone, then the EP specialist may not have to expend much time or energy on workplace threats in which the principal is not specifically targeted (such as being caught in the crossfire of a domestic battle). Not that those threats are unimportant, but the EP specialist has to target his protective efforts where they are most needed and will have the greatest effect.

The agent should also reevaluate the normal security measures, such as good lighting, access control, intrusion alarms, panic alarms, safe rooms, easy-to-use phone systems, tight sign-in policies, metal detectors, and video systems. The agent may also wish to distribute floor plans to trusted persons outside the building so that, in a hostage situation, police and SWAT teams could obtain those maps to plan their actions.

Reaction Measures

"Reaction" here means *after* a violent incident has started. Violence in the workplace is a disaster, and like any other disaster, it requires a rapid, coordinated, and trained response to prevent further injury, damage, and death. Once a violent incident is underway, the EP specialist needs to get the principal away from the scene, contact the police, summon medical help, and take other steps to remove, defend, and repair the principal.

After the event, the EP specialist should reevaluate the chain of events that led up to the violent outbreak and allowed the principal to be endangered. The agent should consider the following: Is such an attack likely to happen again? Do many people hold similar grievances against the principal or his organization? Is it likely that someone will want to pick up the torch and continue the violent person's uncompleted mission? Are hiring practices and physical security adequate? Are employees communicating their concerns about imminent workplace violence to company management?

This follow-up analysis is one *post mortem* where the agent must truly hope the term is used figuratively, not literally.

The good general cultivates his resources.
Sun Tzu

Chapter 9
Protection Resources

Accountability and responsibility for executive protection fall to one person alone—the protection specialist. However, given the great variety and complexity of the tasks he has to handle, executive protection could never be a one-person job. James Bond could speak many languages, shoot expertly, and find his way around the most exotic city (and, of course, name any wine in one sip), but even he needed help: M ran the shop, Q supplied him with equipment, and contacts throughout the world supplied him with information. Likewise, a good EP specialist may be an able planner, driver, communicator, and defender, but can he also hope to be a lawyer, a technical surveillance countermeasures (TSCM) expert, a law enforcement officer, and an entire information network?

Even an organization as sophisticated, well-established, and thoroughly equipped as the U.S. Secret Service can't meet its protection obligations without the logistical support of the military and the staffing support of local law enforcement agencies. A small protection operation in the corporate, celebrity, or private sector depends even more on help from others.

This chapter describes three categories of resources that an EP specialist should cultivate: (1) law enforcement contacts, (2) intelligence and other information, and (3) specialized assistance, such as legal advice, technical surveillance countermeasures, and supplemental personnel.

Law Enforcement Contacts

The most obvious and sought-after resource is a good law enforcement contact. An EP specialist cannot expect to manage a personal protection operation without being able to call occasionally on a police insider. Such an ally can help with everything from intelligence and off-duty assistance to crisis support. Depending on the prominence of the principal, behind-the-scenes support is something that most law enforcement agencies are willing and happy to provide. But an agent can't expect to get that kind of assistance by waiting until the need arises and making a cold call. Here, as elsewhere in protection, advance work makes all the difference.

How does one begin? For a protection specialist who started out in law enforcement, the approach is easy—a cop-to-cop dialogue between the EP specialist and line officers can open a lot of doors. When, in addition to sharing that background, the agent represents a prominent local citizen and can potentially offer paid work for off-duty officers, the dialogue will flow even better.

An alternative, especially for those without a law enforcement background, is to begin at the top. The agent should call the chief's office and ask for an appointment to discuss the protective operation's needs, questions, and concerns. The first meeting with the chief or the person he designated may not be warm and encouraging, but over time the relationship can be nurtured. If the protectee is a well-known local figure, a politically astute chief of police will recognize the benefits of cooperation. If the protectee doesn't hold sway locally, the chief may want to cooperate simply to spare his city the embarrassment of having the principal attacked there.

For a protective organization with sufficient resources (including money and a principal with clout), an excellent approach is to host a luncheon, dinner, or other social event for the chief or chiefs of police who are responsible for the areas in which the principal lives, does business, or both. In a large metropolitan area, the EP specialist should invite the city police chief, the chiefs of the surrounding major jurisdictions, and the heads of local federal offices, including the Secret Service and FBI. Such a gathering gives the agent an opportunity to express his concerns, explain the nature and objectives of the protection program, and, on behalf of the principal, thank the guests for their support.

The author held such an event within months of establishing a new corporate protection organization, and the effort produced priceless benefits for years. However, to keep such a relationship alive, one must nourish it with occasional visits, phone calls, or invitations to lunch.

Obviously, the agent's approach to all this has to be sensible and well crafted. He has to present a valid reason for his request for cooperation and assistance. That reason is the carefully assessed level of risk to the principal, not the fact that the principal is a prominent citizen. In discussions with the police chief, the EP specialist can acknowledge that the law enforcement agency is charged with protecting the entire community, but still diplomatically point out that some citizens—by virtue of their standing in the community and in the world—have special needs.

One of the prizes the agent is after is access to the department's intelligence section. The objective is to gain better insight into activity that matches threats identified in the principal's risk assessment. Ideally, the agent would arrange to be contacted whenever the police department's intelligence profile raised a concern that could affect the principal. Depending on the size of the police agency, the EP specialist might want to ask for an operational liaison below the chief's level.

Whether the protective operation is a one-man show just getting off the ground or a large, well-established corporate detail, a relationship with local law enforcement executives is crucial to its success.

Intelligence and Other Information

Intelligence here means information that helps an agent protect his principal. It refers primarily to facts or tips about potential threats. A warning that carjacking has increased along the principal's route to work would be intelligence. Advice about run-flat tires would not—that would be technical information. This section discusses both types of data in its treatment of newsgathering, networking, benchmarking, and countersurveillance. Chapter 1, Threat Assessment, addressed the importance of gathering intelligence and other information when analyzing the types and probabilities of threats to the principal. In this section, the lesson to remember is that information-gathering requires resources, which an agent must cultivate carefully.

Newsgathering

Part of the job is to track information about individuals, organizations, and conditions that might pose a threat to the principal. What resources will help a protection specialist stay informed about such matters? Everyday news sources—newspapers (national and local), newsmagazines, and broadcast and cable television news programs (local, national, and CNN, for example)—set the baseline. The ordinary reading an agent does to keep current with the news is an automatic first step.

More-targeted newsgathering can be done via the Internet. For example, an agent can set up a personalized news service by instructing a computer program to search daily for any references to the principal's name, his company, his industry, and any relevant characteristics that make the principal a potential target, such as his religion, ethnic background, or status as a wealthy or politically important person. The program will then search for keywords in news reports from many sources. The software can also be instructed to search for the names of particular persons, groups, or conditions that could threaten the principal, such as "Tupac Amaru" or "militia." Setting up a personalized news service is simple, common, and cheap—there's no reason not to do it. Also, amazingly, some potentially threatening groups have their own sites on the World Wide Web, complete with pictures of members. Periodic electronic visits to those sites can help an agent anticipate any interest those groups might develop in the protectee.

The Internet approach can result in the automatic production of a personalized, daily, on-screen "newspaper" that includes articles only about subjects likely to affect the principal's well-being. It's even possible to use the Internet to gather up-to-date weather reports for the principal's upcoming travel destinations. Thus, appropriate software and well-informed information-systems personnel (to help choose and set up the software) are important resources.

If the principal is a corporate executive, another resource for the task of newsgathering is the company's public relations office. Part of that group's job is to monitor news sources for information about the corporation and its executives. The PR department can also let the EP specialist know when a news source is preparing a story about the principal. That way, the agent can start planning how he will protect the principal once the story comes out and unwanted, extra attention is focused on him. This is especially important if the story is going to be unfavorable.

Networking

From the news media and the Internet it is only possible to obtain certain types of information: hard facts, numerical trends, and other publicly exchanged information. An EP specialist, however, also needs to develop other types of knowledge—advice and tips that are more subjective or private. Sometimes he may even need to ask for information that is being kept a secret. (That doesn't mean stealing proprietary information. It just means asking the right questions privately. As the old saying goes, a secret is something you tell to only one other person at a time.) That sort of information is not going to turn up on the evening news—it has to be fleshed out from other people directly.

Just what is this subjective, private information that an agent seeks through networking? It is, for example, a tip like these:

- a certain hotel in Paris is no longer a safe place to stay

- a certain U.S. airport has become unbearably difficult to travel through
- a certain company, at home or abroad, is a particularly good supplier of protection support personnel
- a certain type of car is especially useful in protective operations

Basically, networking is a pipeline to a great number of the resources that an EP specialist needs. When it's time to retain a good lawyer, hire extra protective staff for a big event, send a staffer off for training, or select a dependable, user-friendly home security system, the EP specialist has a better chance of finding the right solution if he asks around, gets informal advice from insiders—in short, if he uses his network.

That explains *why* to network; what about *how* and *with whom?* For an agent just getting started in protective work, a natural group to start networking with is classmates from an executive protection training school. Anyone, new or experienced, who attends such a school or any other gathering of potentially good contacts should do the following:

- Be friendly. If it's difficult to think of what to talk about, ask a person about himself. That's the fastest way to get someone started on his favorite topic.
- Collect business cards from people at the gathering. On each card, jot down a few facts about the person to jog the memory later.
- Keep the official class or attendee list. Such a list is a shortcut to the beginning of a network.

After the meeting, it's time to organize the contact information collected. If the school contained 30 people, each of whom would be a good contact for information on a different subject, that is simply too much to remember. It's much better to use a computer contact management program; that way, when the agent needs to know some inside scoop about a certain topic, he can search his contact database for the person who knows about it.

When a network is well developed, information will flow several ways. The agent wants to know whom he can call on for information when he needs it, but he would also like to receive unsolicited tips from contacts who think he would be interested. To bring a network to that level of maturity and usefulness, two other steps may be necessary:

- The EP specialist should angle to get invited to more meetings. He can join organizations that hold conferences or offer to speak at meetings he would like to attend.

- The specialist should think about what he can offer to others, what he can give them to make the networking mutually beneficial. For example, he might be able to send a contact a useful article (maybe even one the agent wrote himself), share some security-related information about a particular travel destination, or describe how he solved a particular challenge in executive protection work.

Several types of meetings provide networking opportunities. Professional associations, such as the American Society for Industrial Security, typically sponsor topic-specific training meetings throughout the year and hold one major convention annually. Trade shows offer an opportunity to talk with equipment vendors to learn of the latest in security technology. Participation in certification programs, like the Certified Protection Professional designation from ASIS[94], presents networking opportunities like those at training schools.

An organization targeted directly at protection specialists is the Protective Service Alliance. PSA provides contacts, information, and publications specifically on the subject of executive protection.[95]

If the agent's protective operation is associated with a large company, it may qualify for membership in the U.S. State Department's Overseas Security Advisory Council. (OSAC is described

---

[94] American Society for Industrial Security, 1655 North Fort Myer Drive, Suite 1200, Arlington, VA 22209. (703) 522-5800.

[95] Protective Service Alliance, c/o Varro Group, Inc., P.O. Box 8413, Shawnee Mission, KS 66208. (913) 432-5856.

in Chapter 7, Domestic and International Travel.) With more than 1,400 organizations as members, OSAC presents another great networking source.

Benchmarking

A popular management technique is benchmarking, or the process of deliberately, carefully comparing how other companies perform their work. In benchmarking, people typically examine other companies' products, services, and especially processes to gain ideas on the best ways to run their own businesses. Something quite different from industrial espionage, benchmarking is an open exchange of information, typically done in a spirit of professional development rather than competition. For example, information systems specialists from several corporations of similar size might meet with each other to discuss the best ways of implementing computer networks. Once a specialist sees how his peers are doing their jobs, he has obtained a benchmark against which to measure himself.

Executive protection specialists can do the same. One agent who protects a wealthy client can meet with agents who have similar clients, and they can tell each other how they do what they do. In the security field, of course, people would take pains not to give away specific details that might compromise their clients' safety, but there are plenty of techniques and processes that can be shared. After all, if the group has been properly checked out (that is, everyone present is a bona fide EP specialist), then information can be exchanged in a spirit of cooperation—one colleague helping another. In most cases, one agent isn't competing to land the job of protecting another agent's client.

Benchmarking isn't a vague, philosophical management gimmick—it's all about being practical. *Fortune* magazine describes the way corporate benchmarkers at Rank Xerox[96] were sent to the company's most successful regions with this mission: "Simply find

---

[96] Rank Xerox is an 80 percent-owned subsidiary of Xerox, operating mostly in Europe.

out how it was done; don't try to figure out why it worked."[97] Will it always feel good to see how well someone else does the job, especially if he excels in an area where the observer is weak? Well, no. *Fortune* quotes Robert Hiebeler, partner in charge of Arthur Andersen's global best-practices group, as saying, "The goal of identifying best practices is to disturb yourself in a positive way."[98]

In sum, benchmarking gives an EP specialist—who typically operates with much discretion and in relative solitude—a standard against which to measure his skills and a source of new ideas for the best ways of doing the job of executive protection.

Countersurveillance

A further form of intelligence-gathering is countersurveillance, which helps one assess the possibility that the principal or the protective operation is being observed. It's a matter of watching for watchers.

In this chapter on resources, the key point to note about countersurveillance is that most times the agent himself is too busy watching the principal to conduct a systematic, comprehensive countersurveillance effort. Therefore, he cultivates resources that *can* do so. Those resources include the following:

- *Staffers in the protective detail.* In a detail of three, it makes sense to have two stand with the principal and one blend in with the crowd and watch for watchers.

- *Other employees of the client's corporation.* The agent can teach them some awareness and observation skills, which they can put to use as they go about their ordinary work.

- *Contractual support personnel.* The EP specialist can hire them to serve as extra eyes and ears during times when the risk increases or for routine and periodic countersurveillance assistance.

---

[97] Thomas A. Stewart and Ed Brown, "Beat the Budget and Astound Your CFO," *Fortune*, October 28, 1996.

[98] Justin Martin and Joyce E. Davis, "Are You As Good As You Think You Are?", *Fortune*, September 30, 1996.

An example of a countersurveillance effort is casual observation of an area that the principal has just visited. Someone not easily identifiable as being with the protective team should stay behind, dressed to blend in, and look for repeat or unusual visitors. Hindsight is always crystal clear, but the repeated presence of Arthur Bremer around the George Wallace campaign could have served as a red flag to someone conducting countersurveillance.

Some protective details videotape gatherings in places that their principal visits, repeating the process two or three times. They then study the tapes to see whether any individual keeps turning up. If so, they must ask themselves whether he seems to have a keen interest in the protectee. All this can be done in a low-key manner. A protection detail doesn't want to bring attention to itself. Also, it must be sure to ask legal counsel what steps it should take to avoid violating any privacy laws.

Another example of countersurveillance takes place before the principal arrives at a site. Despite one's best efforts, it may be difficult or impossible to vary the principal's driving route consistently. In case someone has developed an interest in how and when the principal gets to and from work, it's useful to have a member of the protection team conduct a countersurveillance survey along the route. The purpose is to determine whether the principal is being watched and, if so, by whom. This is not an exotic countermeasure—it's simply a smart defensive tactic. Ideally, it should be done by the same person over time; that way he has a better chance of noticing the repeated presence of the same persons or vehicles.

Specialized Assistance

Experts have long been the subject of scorn. The American educator and Nobel laureate Nicholas Murray Butler called an expert someone "who knows more and more about less and less." Still, no agent can understand the intricacies of every aspect of executive protection—sometimes experts must be called in, and before they can be called in, they have to be found and checked out for capability and reliability. The following sections on legal advice, technical surveillance countermeasures, and supplemental person- nel cover only a few major categories of specialized assistance. Each EP specialist should take the time, early on, to consider what other types of help he might need and then lay out plans for how to get such help.

Legal advice

Executive protection is a legal minefield.[99] The only way to traverse it safely is to develop a source of legal advice. That source might be the in-house counsel at the protectee's corporation, or it could be an outside attorney with experience in advising security operations. Regardless, the time to cultivate that particular resource is *before* an incident occurs.

Step one is to find a suitable lawyer. Here is one matter where networking can be a big help. How does one find a good mechanic, doctor, or building contractor? Certainly, the most familiar way is by asking around. If the agent has developed a network of other protection specialists, he will have a body of people to consult about their experiences with particular lawyers.

Step two requires the protection specialist to meet with the lawyer and describe the particular circumstances he expects to encounter. Those circumstances include the whole range of activities that the protection effort encompasses—threat assessment; personal protection of the principal ("working the principal"); advance work; security in automobiles, at work, at home, and while traveling; hiring and firing staff; carrying weapons; and many other activities. In return, the attorney can describe the major categories of legal considerations the agent should be aware of. Obviously, the agent will want to be able to call on the attorney if something goes wrong (in other words, if the agent or principal is arrested or sued), but the best legal advice is preventive. The attorney can offer advice about how to safeguard the protective operation legally

---

[99] This section does not purport to be, nor should it be construed as, legal advice or opinion. Because the law is complex and varies by jurisdiction and situation, readers should consult a lawyer about specific questions, policies, and procedures.

(through proper training, hiring, legal agreements with contractors, etc.). After initial consultations, the agent will also have the attorney on hand to answer specific questions as they pop up.

Because laws vary from state to state and from country to country, it's impossible to discuss here all the legal considerations an EP specialist might need to know. However, a few categories of legal concern stand out and can be addressed in general.[100]

Weapons. The question of carrying weapons—both guns and other devices—can become complicated because of the great variation of laws by city, state, and country. That complexity puts the EP specialist in the situation of having to maintain a difficult balance. If the agent has too little concern for the legality of carrying weapons, he could unintentionally break the law and end up getting embarrassed, arrested, or both. If he has a disproportionate concern about carrying weapons, he might fail in his duty to protect the principal.

The following are a few details the agent should ask his attorney to answer. A different answer may apply for each jurisdiction in which the agent operates.

- Must I register my handgun?
- Is it possible to get a permit to wear the gun under my jacket (in other words, to carry a concealed weapon)?
- What must I do to transport the gun legally?
- What should I do if I wish to have armed protection while traveling?
- What other items, besides firearms, are considered weapons under various laws? Tasers, kubitons, ASPs, chemical sprays? What are the laws regarding carrying or concealing them?

These considerations can easily become highly complex. If the agent plans to accompany the principal on a trip from Los Angeles to the Washington, D.C., area, using Baltimore-Washington Inter-

---

[100] For much of the information in this section, the author wishes to thank Thomas C. Morrow, J.D., of the Law Offices of Thomas C. Morrow, P.A., 15 East Chesapeake Avenue, Towson, Maryland 21286. (410) 583-0500.

national Airport, he will need to know the weapons laws of California, Maryland, Washington, possibly Virginia, and the various counties and municipalities he will pass through, not to mention FAA regulations. (And, unless he is a law enforcement officer on official business and the pilot says it's ok, he can't carry the firearm on the plane—just in checked baggage.) An agent who is a former law enforcement officer, or even a current one, should not rely on professional courtesy to get him out of trouble if he violates a jurisdiction's weapons laws.

Use of Force. The smartest EP specialist avoids the use of force. By working smart, the agent may never have to use force at all. Force has many undesirable consequences. The adversary's force could overpower the agent's force, resulting in death or injury to the client or agent. The adversary could be injured by what was deemed excessive or illegal force by the agent, resulting in legal problems and bad publicity for the client. Even a slight use of force could cause a minor situation to escalate into a major one.

It helps to know the traditional terms for various levels of force. *Assault* is an attempt or offer to do bodily harm to another. *Battery* is any unlawful physical force inflicted on another person. *Assault with intent to murder* is assault or battery with a weapon pointed toward a vital part of the body; intending to commit grievous bodily harm equals the intent to kill. *Homicide* is any act that results in the death of another. Not all homicides are murders, but all murders are homicides. *Murder* is generally classified as follows:

- *First degree:* intentional killing with willfulness, deliberation, and premeditation but without legal justification or mitigation.
- *Second degree:* killing with the intent to kill or inflict serious bodily harm but without premeditation or deliberation.
- *Voluntary manslaughter:* killing that would be murder except for the presence of a mitigating circumstance.

EP specialists aren't especially likely to be charged with the first two degrees of murder in the course of their work, but a charge of voluntary manslaughter could be sought if an adversary dies in an attack against a principal. Also, protection agents, like anyone else, are vulnerable to charges of vehicular homicide or vehicular manslaughter in cases where their driving was grossly negligent.

"He is wise who tries everything before arms," wrote the Roman dramatist Terence. Truly, knowing when to use force and how much to use is difficult. The agent is likely to have only a second to consider the question—if he has any time to think about it at all. To improve the quality of his snap decisions, the agent should develop a use-of-force plan in advance. Known in criminal justice theory as a force continuum, such a plan would call for using the least level of force that would work in a given situation but would match increasing offensive force with increasing defensive force. Of course, from a protection perspective, the greatest danger lies in underestimating the threat, which could result in an insufficient defense of the principal.

In general, violence and situations that come close to violence are to be avoided. Clients don't want to be associated with rough stuff, and the use of force often leads to trouble. The EP specialist should remember that his job is to protect the principal, not to capture, injure, or kill bad guys. Legal advice regarding the use of force is indispensable, but the best guideline is to follow Sun Tzu's strategy of winning by use of the "sheathed sword."

Defenses. Although it's best to avoid it, sometimes force is necessary and justifiable. In fact, necessity and justification are closely linked in the various legal defenses of the use of force. Traditionally, those defenses have been grouped as follows:

- *Defense of others:* The agent has the same rights to defend the principal as the principal has to defend himself.
- *Perfect self-defense:* This is a complete defense against homicide charges. Self-defense is justified only where a person has reasonable grounds to believe, and in fact does believe, that he or another person is in imminent danger of death or serious bodily harm. Perfect self-defense makes conduct, even homicide, justifiable or excusable when the agent believed, and it was reasonable (even if not correct) to believe, that his actions

233

were necessary for his safety or the safety of the principal. However, in such cases, several conditions apply:

— The agent must not be the aggressor. Any fighting he does should be defensive. For example, he could push an assailant away, then step back, then push him away again if necessary, all the while stepping back and maintaining a defensive posture.

— The agent must not use greater force than reasonably necessary in light of all the circumstances. If the agent uses excessive force, he may legally become the aggressor, giving the original assailant the right to use force in self-defense.

— The agent has a duty to retreat or avoid danger if the means to do so are within his power and consistent with his safety and that of the principal. However, there is generally no duty to retreat if the attack is taking place within one's dwelling, including a hotel room.

- *Imperfect self-defense:* This occurs when the agent believes that force is justified to maintain his safety and that of the principal, but that belief is found to be unreasonable. Imperfect self-defense does not excuse conduct, but it eliminates the element of malice. Thus, a homicide would be reduced to voluntary manslaughter, while assault with intent to murder would be reduced to assault or battery.

- *Prevention of forcible felony:* A person may use force under the guidelines above to prevent the commission of a forcible felony, such as kidnapping or robbery.

Liability. To businesspeople, property owners, and anyone else who has something to lose, liability is the legal nightmare of the late 20th century. Because of its cost in time, money, and reputation, liability is something for a protection team to avoid at any price.

In general, an EP specialist or his organization runs the risk of being held liable for intentional, negligent, or accidental acts. The ins and outs of liability are too complicated to address here. However, a few issues that are particularly relevant to protection operations must be pointed out.

First, an agent has no legal obligation to intercede to save the life of another person (other than the principal). That means if the principal and the agent, while walking down the street, see an old woman getting mugged, they are not legally required to intervene and face no possibility of liability for their inaction. However, if the principal says, "Go help that woman," and the agent does, they open themselves up to potential liability if the agent injures the woman or uses excessive force against the mugger. Of course, there are moral and public relations dimensions to that scenario, too, in addition to the question of the agent's leaving the principal unguarded, so the principal and agent should discuss, in advance, their policy about intervening in such situations.

The scenario can be further complicated if the agent is an off-duty police officer. In that case, he might have an obligation to intercede, and if he commits a tort in the process, the principal might be held liable. The question of liability is often left unclear in work agreements. Even when it's covered in a contract, the private employer may still be pursued as the nearest deep pocket.

Second, there's the question of training. An EP specialist or his employer could be deemed negligent if a member of the protection team committed a wrongful act and was improperly trained at the time. For that reason, the agent must make sure his staffers are trained correctly at the start and then stay up-to-date through regular refresher or qualifying training courses. The training needn't all be formal. It can consist of discussion groups, lectures, seminars, guest speakers at lunch, and other teaching methods, but it must be well documented. To prove the training took place, the EP specialist should hold onto detailed training records (class list, outline or agenda, date and length of course) and personnel files for each staffer, active and retired. The training and record keeping are expensive, but their cost is nothing compared to the sums the protective operation will save on insurance and, of course, liability judgments.

Avoiding situations that lead to liability (unnecessary intervention, excessive force, poor training) is one approach to reducing liability. A concurrent approach is to structure a protection program that maintains such a high quality of leadership, supervision, training, and attention to detail that the risk of liability is minimized. Not only does that approach rather obviously reduce the number of mistakes and accidents that could lead to liability, but it also enables the protective operation to show (in court, if necessary) that it has done everything humanly possible to prevent or avoid the incident.

Technical surveillance countermeasures

On his own, an EP specialist can help his principal practice good information security measures, many of which were discussed in Chapter 7, Domestic and International Travel. However, if the principal wants a high degree of certainty that he isn't being snooped on, the particular task of searching a space for eavesdropping equipment will require a specialist—and that specialist is another resource that the agent needs to acquire.

Technical surveillance countermeasures are the various means by which one looks for surreptitious listening or viewing devices in a room, a building, an automobile, an airplane, any other place, or any object that the principal uses. The specialty known as TSCM is highly sophisticated, and keeping up with it is beyond most EP specialists' normal scope of knowledge.

Long before there's any suspicion that the client is under surveillance, the agent should use his network of contacts to locate a recommended TSCM expert. No matter how enthusiastically the expert is endorsed, the agent will have to check him out first. That means looking into references from other clients, learning about his background, even checking his criminal history if possible. This preparatory work is essential because the TSCM expert, if hired, will be given access to the client's inner sanctum and will have a better opportunity than anyone else to *plant* eavesdropping devices if he is crooked. Ideally, the agent should also meet the TSCM expert (or at least interview him by telephone) to determine whether he will be a suitable resource when the need arises.

When would the need arise? An agent certainly can't call in a TSCM expert every time the client checks into a hotel suite—a good, careful, physical and electronic sweep can easily cost several thousand dollars. In most cases, the agent himself should physically search the principal's office, home, and car for eavesdropping devices, using a technique much like the bomb sweeps described in Chapter 5, Automobile Security, and Chapter 6, Home and Office Security. In routine situations, such searches can be supplemented with other techniques for foiling eavesdroppers, such as switching hotel rooms at the last minute or moving telephones from room to room. But it might be necessary to summon a TSCM expert in the following situations:

- The agent finds an object that looks like it might be an eavesdropping or visual surveillance device. (Such a find should be treated as evidence and reported to the FBI. In most cases, it should also be left in place and operating; that may make it easier to catch the eavesdropper.)

- The principal has an especially sensitive meeting coming up.

- The agent wishes to get a room or car into a clean condition, meaning that, as far as is humanly possible, it is known to be free of surveillance devices. Afterwards, the agent can labor to keep the area clean through access control and other measures.

- The agent or principal *suspects* that electronic surveillance is being performed. Perhaps one of these conditions is present:

  — The actions of a competitor or adversary suggest that confidential information is leaking out.

  — Strange sounds or volume changes have been noticed on phone lines.

  — The phone often rings and nobody, or else only a tone, is there.

  — A radio or television has suddenly developed strange interference.

  — The principal's home or office has been burglarized, but nothing or not much was taken.

— Odd physical signs are present. Electrical wall plates seem to have been tampered with. A small, circular discoloration appears on the wall paint. Drywall dust is present on the floor next to the wall.

— Utility trucks and workers spend a lot of time near the principal's home or office, doing repair work, or show up to do work when no one called them.

— Service or delivery trucks are parked nearby with no passengers in them.

To use a TSCM expert wisely, the agent has to know at least the basic concepts of modern eavesdropping. Here are a few high points:

- A wiretap is a device or procedure that, as the name implies, taps into a communications wire, whether it's part of a telephone line, private branch exchange (PBX), local area network, video system, or alarm system.

- A "bug" is a transmitter that is placed in the area being spied on and that intercepts communications and transmits them out of that area to a listening post. Bugs exist in all shapes and sizes. Some run on batteries; others use local electric supplies; and still other use no electricity at all. Among the varieties of bugs are acoustic, ultrasonic, radio frequency, optical, and hybrid.

- Bugs are readily available and easy to use.

- Bugs can easily be placed in cellular telephones; wired telephones and the wires that lead to them; various other appliances, especially public address systems and intercoms; electric supply lines; computer equipment; furniture; and homes, offices, cars, aircraft, and boats.

- Cellular phone conversations can be snooped on electronically without the need to plant a bug at all. Although such eavesdropping is illegal, it is easy to do with a radio scanner. The principal should be made aware of that risk, and the protection specialist needs to be cautious when discussing his business over that medium. In particular, he should never use the principal's name or other information that could compromise security if overheard.

- In addition to conducting detailed physical searches, TSCM experts use several other techniques to search for eavesdropping devices: radio frequency analysis, telephone system analysis, non-linear junction detectors, and others.

It's important to note that the dangers associated with cellular phones extend beyond eavesdropping. First, because a cellular phone contains a transmitter, an intercept operator can home in on the signal and use the phone as a tracking device to locate the principal—even while the principal travels about by car, and even when the phone is not in use. Second, a cellular phone can easily be modified to serve as a remote-controlled bomb that a principal is likely to carry on his person. Months after altering the phone, the assassin can call from halfway around the world, dial a preprogrammed code, and activate the device.

Supplemental personnel

Sometimes a protective operation needs a few extra bodies. The principal may be traveling to a distant location, and it may be too complicated or expensive to bring additional protective agents along. Or the principal may be traveling to a place to which the agent cannot readily bring a firearm, and the agent may feel armed protection is warranted there and so want to hire local, armed assistance. Or a special event may be coming up, or the threat assessment may suggest that risk has increased. But since so much is at stake and so much will be required of the temporary help, not just any old bodies will do. An EP specialist who needs to hire additional, temporary help has only a few realistic options: off-duty police officers who specialize in executive protection, or protection agents who work for another firm.

Most state police or highway patrol agencies field a unit that provides full-time executive protection to their state's governor and sometimes other elected officials. Although these troopers are officially committed to their particular protectees, some agencies permit them to participate in approved off-duty employment. Depending on the state, this group of experienced professionals can be an excellent protection resource. They are commissioned law enforcement officers who have intimate knowledge of the entire state, know executive protection, and can usually carry a firearm off-duty. Gaining access to this resource can be tough, but an agent with a law enforcement background may be able to get his foot in the door. It's well worth the try.

Even among that group, not every officer can be assumed to be suitable—the agent has to check. Maybe the officer is available for off-duty work because he has been suspended while charges against him are investigated. A face-to-face meeting is in order before any work begins. The agent will have to establish his requirements, ascertain the quality of the law enforcement officer, and explain what is expected of him. It has to be explained that the agent, who is ultimately accountable for the principal's protection, is in charge.

The alternative to off-duty law enforcement officers is an executive protection firm. Because lots of pretenders populate the EP business, several precautions are in order:

- The agent should find a firm that has been used successfully by someone else in his protection network. He shouldn't rely on the Yellow Pages or glossy promotional brochures.

- The qualifications, training, and background of the firm's staff have to be examined. Many companies are managed by people with law enforcement backgrounds and contacts. That can be a huge advantage locally. The agent should check references.

- Some firms are *headed* by top-notch professionals with excellent experience—but not *staffed* with such people. For example, the firm's president might be a Secret

Service alumnus, but the agents it hires out could be in-experienced security guards. There's no use engaging a firm like that; it would be better to work alone than to pay high fees for an "empty suit."

- The agent must ask to see documentation of liability in-surance, the firm's license to do business, and staffers' authority to carry firearms. (Beyond looking at the documents, it may be wise to call the relevant agencies to confirm the facts.) He should also find out what kinds of firearms the firm's agents carry and whether they use step-down weapons, such as ASPs or pepper spray.

- When making arrangements for the first time, the agent should ask for specifics about the person who will be assigned to the principal. The agent will need a photo-graph of the person, both for security purposes and to see whether the person presents a professional ap-pearance. A face-to-face meeting is also required.

- The EP specialist must clarify the firm's role. If the hired agents are to be responsible, on their own, for a principal who flies to them unescorted by his own secu-rity person, the ground rules must be firmly established. Even with precautions, that is not a good arrangement; it leaves too much room for error and dashed expecta-tions. The EP specialist could be made to look like a fool for hiring an incompetent whom he has not met to look after the principal.

- A preferable arrangement is for the support protection personnel to work under the supervision of the protec-tion agent, who accompanies the principal. In that case, very specific instructions should be given to the firm's representative regarding the EP specialist's pro-tection mandate, security procedures, and the princi-pal's likes and dislikes.

- When hiring transportation as part of the deal, the agent has to be very clear about his standards. For example, the vehicle should be spotlessly clean, fully fueled, and equipped with at least minimal emergency equipment and a cellular telephone. The driver is not to play tour guide and should not speak unnecessarily. The agent should also clarify his requirements for driving technique (safe driving observing the speed limit, with doors locked and commercial radio off, eyes on the road, and route of travel well practiced). Any professionally operated company will maintain these standards, but the agent should state them anyway the first time out.

- The costs of working with outside help have to be spelled out in black and white. To avoid being surprised by hidden charges, the agent should see that the contract specifies all the details regarding hours worked, travel time, meals, mileage, etc. One careful approach is to use a form that states when the work day starts and ends (for example, 7 am to 9 pm) and leaves a space for the hired agent and the EP specialist both to sign. Other aspects to work out are how to handle overnight assignments. If the contract agent is to assist, he'll have to stay in his room, avoid drinking, and be instantly accessible to the detail.

A glance at this book's contents page shows the range of expertise that an EP specialist must command. But no one acting alone could master *all* the topics associated with executive protection. Therefore, a prudent agent should take the trouble to develop a set of resources that can help him where he needs help.

[Among the] ways of courting defeat [are] de-
fective training...and failure to use picked men.
Sun Tzu

Chapter 10
Training, Job Opportunities, and
Finding the Right Person

The chapters up to this one have discussed the broad view and the details of executive protection, what it is and what it isn't, how to protect and how not to protect. Now it's time to get moving and make it all happen. This chapter first looks at prospective EP specialists (termed "candidates" here), discussing what they should do to prepare themselves for protection work (or how to improve the skills they already possess) and how to find the right job. Then the chapter takes a look from the other side, the viewpoint of a person who wishes to hire a protective agent. The focus will be on what to look for in an agent, how to find one, and how to arrange the relationship between the principal and the EP specialist.

For the Agent

To embark on a career in executive protection, a candidate needs two things: first training, then a job. That's simple enough, but there are many types of training, many types of jobs. Only the candidate knows which types will fit comfortably with his aspirations, budget, and personal responsibilities.

Before heading far down the path to a career in executive protection, the candidate should educate himself as much as possible about the field. Reading this book is a good first step. Next, it's wise to read more about executive protection (in newspapers, magazines, and books) and about the security profession in general. (See the "Resources" section at the end of this book.) Since most executive protection assignments outside of government involve guarding people who are in business or have profited substantially from business, it also pays to learn that field. An agent who is ignorant about the subject his principal is most motivated by will not be a good match for that principal.

If a candidate has a particular type of EP work in mind, it helps to call someone who is doing that type of work and ask how to follow in his footsteps. As long as the candidate doesn't pose a threat to the experienced agent's job, the latter will probably be happy to offer the former some suggestions about what would be useful training and background. Most people are flattered to be consulted and are enthusiastic enough about their line of work to share their insights freely. They may even be able to advise the candidate on the best way to obtain a position in their organization or one that is similar. Still, even with a tip, the candidate will have to do his homework. Some corporations will say they have EP programs but only provide the service at board meetings, shareholders' meetings, etc.

Training, education, and experience

Unless a person works for a sophisticated government protective organization (Secret Service, State Department, or military protective work, or protecting a mayor, county executive, or governor), he will need formal training in executive protection before he can honestly claim to be qualified to perform EP work. Fortunately, a number of good training opportunities are available.

But how can a candidate find a school and evaluate its career-building potential before investing his time (often a week) and money (typically several thousand dollars)? To develop a list of training providers to evaluate, the best technique is to ask EP practitioners what schools they recommend. The list can be supplemented by an Internet search and ads and listings in relevant trade and professional publications.

Evaluating a Training School. No candidate should hitch up with a training course before checking it out carefully. (He should think of that process as a little free practice in advance work.) How does one pick a good school? Basically, here is a list of important questions to ask:

- Do the instructors possess substantive qualifications and real-world experience? Does the school's owner?

- Can I visit the program to get a close look at the quality of teaching?

- Who is allowed to attend? Are applicants subjected to a background investigation? (That is important. Because the contacts a candidate can develop at such courses may help him get his start and be a useful resource long afterwards, he doesn't want his classmates to be a bunch of oddball James Bond wannabees.)

- Does the course cover the right topics? Does it tackle serious, detailed subject matter, or is it fluffy? (See box below for sample topics.)

- What is the level of instruction? Is the course for novices or experienced EP specialists? (It's important to match the level to the student.)

- Will I receive hands-on experience in some aspects of training (driving, firearms use, physically protecting the principal, etc.), or is it all book learning? Or worse, is it all war stories (amusing but impractical anecdotes)? It's also important to strike the right balance and not over-emphasize guns, bombs, karate, J turns, etc. Those topics are exciting but not highly practical, not the real world of executive protection.

- Does the school have suitable classroom space and training grounds?

- Is the school bonded? (Check its liability insurance.) Is it licensed to conduct such training? (Check for complaints lodged with the state and the Better Business Bureau.)

- What do prior students have to say about the course? Can I talk to them personally to check?
- What is the student-to-teacher ratio?
- Does the school provide high-quality handout materials to which the candidate can refer after the course?
- What is the true cost, including lodging, meals, handouts, materials, and instruction? Are there any hidden costs?
- Does the school provide a certificate or a reference that a prospective employer can check when the candidate applies for an EP position?

A reputable school will work with the candidate to answer those questions satisfactorily. It's important to remember, however, that EP schools are businesses. They aren't perfect, and they can't perform miracles. If they promise the moon (especially in the form of a job), the candidate should be wary.

The executive protection training program offered by the author's firm is one example of a well-regarded school. The box below presents one version of a high-quality, relevant curriculum:[101]

Sample Curriculum for an
Executive Protection Training School

Threat assessment

Introduction to executive protection

One-on-one personal protection techniques and choreography

Advance procedures in protective operations

Choreography of protection

Global terrorism and crime

Firearms: handgun, shotgun, simmunition (simulated ammunition), range safety, ideal protection weaponry and ammunition

---

[101] From the R. L. Oatman & Associates, Inc., Executive Protection Program.

Demonstration of automatic weapons use and ballistic vest performance

Practice with various handgun and shotgun rounds

Practical demonstration of EP scenarios (handgun protective combat, shotgun use in protective operations, and simmunition exercise in close protective movements)

Explosives overview and identification, including building search techniques

Dynamics of protective driving

Practical driving exercises: ocular driving (for turning and braking), slalom and accident avoidance, vehicle bomb search, escape maneuvers

Workplace violence

Legal considerations in executive protection

Emergency medicine

Assassin profiling

Proper dress and decorum in executive protection

Practical exercise in protective operations

Dynamics of tactical thinking

Use of step-down weapons

Hand-to-hand, close-in protection methods

Armored cars and their limitations

Vehicle security systems

The art of networking

Communications equipment and methods

Another well-respected executive protection school is the training division of Heckler & Koch International, Inc. That division, headed by John T. Meyer, Jr., is headquartered in Sterling, Virginia.

Some schools are particularly renowned for teaching specific subtopics in executive protection. An example is the Scotti School of Defensive Driving, which is the acknowledged leader in its specialty. Among its courses are Protective Driving for Chauffeurs or

Security Drivers, Executive Awareness (a course for executives who choose to drive themselves), the Security Driver/Bodyguard Seminar, Firearms Deployment During Vehicle Operations, and Police Driving Instructor Certification Program.

Other specialty topics a candidate may wish to gain training in—in a short, specific course—are cardiopulmonary resuscitation (CPR) and emergency medicine, workplace violence, physical security systems, corporate aircraft security, yacht security, and firearms use. There's also a great value in being able to speak a foreign language (especially Spanish, or whatever language is spoken in the places the principal travels to most often), so a language course should be considered.

The Question of Education. Besides training, a candidate also needs education. There's no established requirement for the level of formal education a candidate must have, but most principals are educated people, so a candidate with a good education may blend into a principal's life style better than a candidate with a poor education. It's important to be proficient in math, in reading comprehension, and especially in speaking and writing proper English.

In addition, the candidate should educate himself by reading extensively about the field of security: not just executive protection, but the full range, as he may end up as part of a larger security operation. That means knowing about report writing, investigations, patrol, physical security systems, power to detain, and many other topics.

A candidate should also educate himself about business if he has any intention of protecting a business executive. It's not necessary to be an expert, but knowing general business concepts and what is happening in various industries is helpful. That knowledge makes it easier for an agent to understand what is important about the principal, what motivates him, and what could motivate others to harm him.

There's another use for a general understanding of business. If the protective operation a candidate works in is the security department of a large corporation, it helps (for many reasons, including budget approval and department prestige) to present the

EP operation as part of the business mission of the company, to position it as something other than a cost center. In other words, it's useful to be able to demonstrate a high return on the investment the company makes in executive protection. To do that, of course, it's necessary to understand the business mission of the company and to be able to communicate well with corporate decision makers up and down the ladder. Once a candidate is on the job, here are a few tips for fitting in—and furthering—the corporate mission:

- Recognize that your idea of a suitable protection budget may not match that of the comptroller. Get to know the corporation's budget process; learn how to work with it and how to compromise. If an emergency or special circumstance arises, and you need extra funds to maintain security, look at all the alternatives first, find the most cost-effective solution, and be prepared to justify your request.

- Tune into the corporate cost-controlling measure known as outsourcing. Minimize the protective operation's permanent personnel costs by hiring outside help as needed.

- To keep a protection program alive, you need to get the key corporate players on your side. That requires presenting yourself—and being perceived—as an effective, well-informed, and articulate executive who can represent the corporation and the principal in their best light. It also means discerning and conforming to the corporate culture. You'll have to get rid of the mindset that because you are "security" and have access to the principal, you are privileged and don't have to conform to the organization's rules and culture.

- Avoid a narrow focus. Add value to your mission. For example, develop a corporate crisis management program and tie it into your 24-hour communications center.

Experience. One way to begin an executive protection career is to begin a career in something else: law enforcement. Very little appeals to protectees as much as police experience. The discipline and challenge of a police academy, coupled with successful performance as a police officer, speaks volumes about dedication, self-discipline, and commitment. (That doesn't mean a candidate should put in just a couple of years in a police department and then hit the road for the corporate world—it takes time to develop a useful level of experience.) Although there is less in common between the two professions than one would think, law enforcement experience serves as an excellent basis on which to build an EP career. Also, in some of the larger police departments, there are opportunities for an officer to be assigned to an executive protection unit or other entity, such as an intelligence unit, that has occasional protection responsibility or liaison with the U.S. Secret Service. Such assignments provide experience that would be relevant to private sector EP work.

The same can be said about certain specialties in the armed services. Overseas duty as a Marine embassy guard or service as an aide to a general or admiral (a task that often involves personal security) is a good entree to the field. Service with a military police branch provides the same kind of foundation as employment with a civilian police department.

Another route for developing good experience is to work one's way up the corporate security ladder. That experience can then be capped off with a test-based examination. The American Society for Industrial Security sponsors a Certified Protection Professional designation that requires knowledge of many of the subjects that are important to an EP specialist.

A wise step to take before embarking on EP preparation is to call companies that employ EP specialists and ask what they look for when hiring. Developing the right credentials—in this case, the combination of training, education, and experience—can really help.

How to find a position

After obtaining the necessary training, education, and experience, the candidate needs to find a job.

Contacts. One of the best resources is classmates and instructors at the EP school the candidate attended. From them he can learn about the best places to look for a position. Some classmates may have been employed in a private-sector EP detail at the time they took the course. If the candidate left a good impression on them, they might be willing to see about getting him a position where they currently work. At the least, they may keep their eyes open and let the candidate know if something comes up.

It's also useful to find a mentor who is already in the business. Such a person can offer career advice, send a candidate in the right direction, and provide a straightforward critique about his prospects for employment and any need for improvement.

Proximity. Another entry method is to take a position with the security department of a corporation that supports an executive protection program. A number of corporations have structured, career-ladder opportunities from entry-level officer to international executive protection specialist. The best companies to look at are those that work in an international environment. Worldwide companies are the most likely to need executive protection and facilitation.

A similar approach, if necessary, is for the candidate to take a job near what he wants to do. For example, he might be able to get a job as a driver in a major corporation. True, it's an entry-level position, but he will be next to the boss and get great exposure. A smart employee who wants to work his way up to EP specialist will do more than expected and increase the importance of his job. It's possible to look back at everything in this book and slowly change oneself from a driver to a protection specialist.

Gaining employment as a legitimate protection officer in a good organization can be a challenge. It takes time and effort to build the kind of resume that will get a prospective employer's attention, and even more work to attract an interview and job offer. The candidate has to be patient, smart, persistent, and willing to commit significant resources to land a good EP position. He shouldn't expect to leave a protection training school and, with no other background, be hired to run an executive protection detail. Rather, he should build his resume by getting as much training and experience as he can. He'll have to stick with it, as careers in executive protection don't happen overnight. Once he gets a job, he should stay there and develop a track record. No one likes an agent who has had 10 jobs in five years.

Other Preparation. Executive protection is a physically demanding occupation that requires strength, stamina, and quick reflexes. Sometimes the physical requirements run high, and most of the time the workday is long (10 hours on average). It doesn't make sense to wait until a job interview to begin thinking about getting in shape. It's far better to make physical fitness a lifelong pursuit. That way, when the candidate walks in the front door, the interviewer gets a good first impression, which is a lasting impression.

Being physically fit doesn't mean looking like a body builder. In fact, the musclebound look is a turnoff for most employers. An appearance to emulate would be that of a U.S. Secret Service agent serving on the presidential protection detail or of a state trooper assigned to a gubernatorial protection unit. Benchmarking against those kinds of standards, one can't go wrong.

On an interview and once at work, even more noticeable than one's musculature is one's clothing. A man can't go wrong with a well-pressed, dark blue suit (or other conservative variation), a crisp, starched white shirt, and a conservative but fashionable tie that is well-knotted, dimpled, and cinched up tight to the top of the collar. The shoes should be highly polished, and socks should rise high enough that the candidate won't flash a hairy calf when he crosses his legs. A clean-shaven face will best match most corporate standards; mustaches, beards, long sideburns, and goatees are generally not acceptable. For women, choosing appropriate clothing may require more research into the styles prevalent in the industry or geographic area where the female protection specialist will be working. Also, women's clothes may require a little tailoring to accommodate radios, firearms, and other gear. In general, however, the idea is to dress conservatively—to fit in and not draw attention to oneself. Attention to detail is important in all phases of this occupation; that level of attention includes the way the agent dresses. For that reason, it may even be wise to visit the corporation before an interview to see how people there dress (but be careful not to take a miscue by visiting on "casual Friday").

A candidate who is unsure how to choose the right clothes should not be embarrassed to ask for help in a high-quality clothing store. If the mannequin in the store looks good, it doesn't hurt to buy the whole ensemble. Alternatively, the candidate can consult one of the many, readily available books on dressing for business. In EP, the right clothing is an important investment.

For many reasons, smoking is absolutely taboo. It's unhealthy, it may annoy the principal or others in the detail, it distracts the agent from his duties, and it may draw unwanted attention. If the candidate gets a ride to an interview, he should be sure not to ride with someone who is smoking. The smell will stick to his clothes, and he may be tagged as a smoker even if he isn't one.

Behavior. Another important part of preparing oneself for EP work is to develop good habits. The candidate's attitude and demeanor should be that of a quiet, dignified, competent professional.

Interpersonal skills are critically important. An ideal candidate is strong, emotionally mature, intelligent, mentally flexible, ethical, and upbeat. A hard, glum expression runs counter to the impression that most corporate executives wish to convey. Honesty and kindness are other good core values. An agent also needs good powers of concentration: he'll need to be able to focus on a task in distracting conditions while still paying attention to his surroundings in case immediate action is necessary. Other crucial assets are problem-solving skills, a willingness to learn, and good listening ability.

A degree of humility is also essential. The agent must get used to the fact that he is seeking a service job and that he will often have to subordinate his desires to those of the principal. If that's unpalatable, executive protection is not the right job. Even if the agent eventually becomes a confidante and begins to feel a part of the principal's inner circle, it's inappropriate to get too familiar or relaxed. The agent is still the service provider, and the principal is still the boss. It's important to stay neutral, avoid gossip, and keep a distance from office politics and the principal's home life.

The benefits of good, clean living will be obvious when a candidate is searching for an EP position. In most cases, the applicant will have to submit to a full background investigation, which would cover criminal, motor vehicle, worker's compensation, and credit records, as well as personal and work references and psychological, drug, and possibly alcohol testing to determine his suitability as an employee.

Resume. In cases where a candidate has had no personal contact with a prospective employer, the resume is his first chance to make an impression. Libraries contain many books on how to write a resume. An EP candidate who has little experience with resumes should consult such a book to see attractive, informative formats. In general, the resume should be kept to no more than two pages and should be read carefully for accuracy, neatness, consistency, correct spelling, etc.

The resume is a door-opener. It shouldn't be cute or too clever but should be able to stand on its own merit. Above all, though it should accentuate the candidate's strong points, it must be honest.

In a quest for an EP position, a key resume component is a list of specialized skills. Items to list include these:

- training or expertise in foreign languages (and whether the candidate can write, speak, or understand those languages)
- diving certification
- emergency medical technician certification and its date of expiration
- possession of a valid U.S. passport
- computer skills (and specific programs known)
- hobbies that contribute to one's EP abilities, such as running, skiing, or horseback riding
- martial arts skills (but don't overdo it; most principals aren't looking for Bruce Lee)
- education
- specialized schools attended (though not necessarily every course the candidate ever took)
- willingness to relocate (if true)

The resume should also direct the reader to a good telephone contact. What's needed is a professional tone when the phone is answered. It's no good to let the caller meet a rude response or to have a four-year-old screen the calls.

Not long ago, people would often pay to have their resumes professionally typeset before embarking on a job hunt. The result looked good, but one couldn't change anything once the resume was printed. In the word-processing era, a candidate can actually create a separate resume for each job applied for, emphasizing the strengths he possesses that would most appeal to that employer. Resumes for EP specialists are even turning up on the Internet now—people networking electronically rather than face to face. Also, it never hurts to keep the resume current, as opportunities sometimes pop up fast.

A word to the wise job-seeker: Although you want to demonstrate your experience, you also want to show that you can be discreet, so don't give out private information about others—especially anyone you have protected—in the resume or during interviews.

What to look for in a position

While the candidate's primary goal is employment as a protection specialist, his secondary goal should be a level of comfort with the principal and his company or organization. The candidate's ethical standards and values—high, one hopes—should match the ethical standards and values of the principal. A candidate should never associate himself with an organization or principal that gives even the appearance of engaging in illegal or unethical behavior.

Also to be avoided is any situation with a potential for abusive behavior by a protectee, his family, or others with whom he is associated. By "abusive" is meant someone who blows up for no reason or who belittles people publicly and takes pleasure in it. Who needs that?

This is the time for a candidate to do his homework. He should research the prospective employer, searching for the employer's name on the Internet and finding out about his reputation, business activities, and interests. This is not to snoop unnecessarily on the principal but merely to gather information that would help the candidate decide whether he and the principal would be a good match.

Even something as seemingly insignificant as the principal's hobbies can make a big difference in whether an agent would want to work for him. For example, it wouldn't make sense to take a job protecting someone who is an avid golfer if the agent finds the sport completely boring or, if the agent is prone to seasickness, to protect a principal who loves to travel about on his yacht. Likewise, if the principal travels a lot and the candidate hates to be away from home, the two might not be a perfect match.

Other, more obvious aspects of a job that need examining are the salary, benefits, working conditions, training opportunities, advancement opportunities, and likely job security. The candidate may also want to meet with the protective detail and find out about specific working conditions. Still, if this is a candidate's first EP job, he mustn't get too picky. He'll have to get out there and earn his stripes.

The right job can last a long time. As an agent builds a relationship with the principal, trust forms. Over time, the principal, his family members, and his associates all feel more and more comfortable having him as part of the team. The agent will become more valuable the longer he stays.

For the Principal

Once the decision is made to seek out an executive protection specialist, the protectee may or may not be the person performing the talent search, interviews, and background checks. In a corporate setting, the head of security may play the leading role; in other settings, an assistant to the principal may do most of the preliminary work. In any case, the principal will certainly have to be involved in the latter stages of the process, such as meeting the agent, getting a feel for whether the principal and the agent would get along well, and approving the final selection.

What to look for, what to avoid

The section above called "Training, education, and experience" lists most of the qualities and qualifications a principal should look for in a protection specialist. However, a few points specific to the principal's point of view need to be emphasized here. The first is a thorough background investigation of any candidate who is being considered seriously. To stay on the right side of the law, the client should get the applicant to sign a statement granting permission to check credit, criminal, motor vehicle, worker's compensation, educational, training, insurance, and citizenship status records. It's also vital to look into why the candidate left his last employer or wants to leave his current one. If the client hires a private investigative firm to conduct the background check, he should do his own due diligence first and make sure the firm is reputable, licensed, and bonded.

Hiring right is a big effort, but it's worthwhile. Any agent hired will become an insider in the principal's business life and, to a lesser extent, personal life. Bringing in the wrong person could have very awkward results. In addition, an unsuitable person is easy to hire but hard to fire.

Specifically, the client should check, through background investigation and personal interviews, whether the candidate is appropriately qualified in both personal and professional terms.

Personal. The principal should look for someone who

- is in good physical shape (and will take a physical to prove it)
- is not a substance abuser (and will take a drug test to prove it)
- is willing to work long hours (as can be demonstrated by his work history)
- is discreet (meaning, among other things, that he won't blab everything about the principal in a book)
- has a pleasant personality (as he and the principal will spend much time together)
- is emotionally mature
- doesn't come across at all like the Hollywood stereotype of a bodyguard

Professional. The challenge is that most people who hire EP specialists are not themselves EP specialists. Therefore, they may not know what constitutes applicable experience or training. The person doing the hiring is hamstrung in three ways: he doesn't know what to ask, he doesn't know what constitutes a good answer, and he legally cannot ask (or may be hesitant to ask) many of the things he *should* ask.

Many EP specialists have some background in police or military work. Such experience weeds out people who are unsuited to some of the physical demands of protection work. However, an overreliance on that experience could lead a client into a poor decision. The reason is that there are big differences between EP and police or military service: EP is much less force-oriented; EP specialists have no special legal status that allows them to carry or use weapons or arrest people (they're just ordinary citizens); EP specialists have no authority to order people around; protection work is much more prevention-oriented than police or military service; and EP specialists have to fit into a business setting and understand all that that entails. Also, private protection work requires a different type of judgment and decision-making ability— there's no written code of conduct, no body of law to uphold, no written enforcement policies. It's a lot more freeform. The person responsible for hiring is simply going to have to rely on a combination of ordinary good judgment and advice from more knowledgeable parties. (See "Where to look for agents," below, for suggestions.)

Once several applicants have been checked out and seem to be suitable candidates, it's time for a chemistry experiment—that is, a meeting to test the chemistry between the candidate on one hand and the principal and his family on the other. They have to be able to get along with each other, so the attributes that don't turn up on a resume, like personality and manners, will make a big difference and have to be judged in person.

One approach, when possible, is for the protectee and his spouse to meet the candidate and his spouse over dinner. The protectee's spouse can bring a fresh perspective to judging the candidate, and can do so with the protectee's interests at heart. If the client doesn't want to participate in a dinner meeting, the client's chief of staff could do so. (His perspective is likely to be closer to the principal's than the corporate security director's is.)

If nothing else, at least such a meeting will show whether the candidate has good table manners, what his drinking habits are, etc.

Executive protection is a job that requires a very special type of person. The EP specialist will be exposed to confidential business information, the personal quirks of the client, and other private matters. When hiring to fill such a position, it's best to get it right the first time. For an executive who genuinely needs protection, the hiring decision can actually be a life-or-death question.

Where to look for agents

The best way to develop a list of candidates is to ask around. That means talking to some of the following:

- an investigation firm with which the principal's corporation has connections (perhaps from due-diligence work or preemployment screening assignments)
- other executives or corporations that have personal protection staff
- faculty of reputable EP training schools
- a local office of the Secret Service or State Department (perhaps one of their agents would like to come on board; however, it's important not to be overwhelmed by credentials and a list of famous persons the candidate has protected—the vast majority of Secret Service agents do not perform protective work unless it's a campaign year)
- state and local law enforcement agencies
- the principal's corporate in-house security expert (if he possesses the right understanding of EP work)

The person doing the hiring may also wish to advertise for candidates. For best results, he should advertise only in publications targeted to security or law enforcement professionals. Newspaper ads reach too wide an audience and are overwhelmingly likely to attract unsuitable applicants. Also, an ad should use a post office box for its return address. It's best not to identify the company, and it's mandatory not to identify the principal.

Once a suitable candidate has been found, the principal may wish to hire him on a temporary basis to see if the arrangement works out. (Of course, the agent must sign a confidentiality agreement before coming on board.) If all goes well, the arrangement can be made permanent. If it doesn't, the parties can each go on their way. No matter how the personnel search and selection process is conducted, it's vital not to take any shortcuts.

If the protection operation is large enough or the client's personal budget is sufficient, an excellent way to end up with ideal EP specialists is to think long-term, hire intelligent, trustworthy people, and invest in the professional development of the ones with whom the principal is most comfortable. By putting them through training courses and teaching them what the principal wants and needs, the protection operation or principal can groom them to give peak performance in the future. In that scenario, a good agent is not hired but made.

Final Note

EP work can be exciting and rewarding, but it's not for people who crave glory. A protection agent should never be the center of attention. His satisfaction has to be quiet, internal, deriving from the knowledge that he has done his job well. For as Sun Tzu wrote:

> What the ancients called a clever fighter is one who not only wins, but excels at winning with ease. But his victories bring him neither reputation for wisdom nor credit for courage. For inasmuch as they are gained over circumstances that have not come to light, the world at large knows nothing of them, and he therefore wins no reputation for wisdom; and inasmuch as the hostile state submits before there has been any bloodshed, he receives no credit for courage.

The wise client looks not for brassy bravado but for results, for security, safety, and facilitation. The agent who is humble, intelligent, strong, and able can provide those results by practicing and mastering the *art* of executive protection.

Recommended Reading

Air Traveler's Handbook: The Complete Guide to Air Travel, Airplanes and Airports. New York: St. Martin's Press, 1989.

Baron, S. Anthony. *Violence in the Workplace: A Prevention and Management Guide for Business.* Bakersfield, California: Pathfinder Publishing of California, 1994.

Bottom, Norman R., Jr., and John I. Kostanoski. *Introduction to Security and Loss Control.* Englewood Cliffs, New Jersey: Prentice-Hall, 1990.

Bremer, Arthur H. *An Assassin's Diary.* New York: Harper's Magazine Press, 1972.

Broder, James F. *Risk Analysis and the Security Survey.* Stoneham, Massachusetts: Butterworth-Heinemann, 1984.

Brown, George Albert. *The Airline Passenger's Guerilla Handbook.* Tucson: Fisher Books, 1989.

Chapman, Robert D. *The Crimson Web of Terror.* Boulder, Colorado: Paladin Press, 1980.

Clark, Dr. James W. *American Assassins.* Princeton: Princeton University Press, 1982.

Clausewitz, Karl von. *On War.* Princeton: Princeton University Press, 1976.

Cooper, H. H. A. *On Assassination.* Boulder, Colorado: Paladin Press, 1984.

Cunningham, William C., John J. Strauchs, and Clifford W. Van Meter. *Private Security Trends 1970-2000: The Hallcrest Report II.* Stoneham, Massachusetts: Butterworth-Heinemann, 1990.

Duet, Karen Freeman, and George Duet. *The Business Security K-9: Selection and Training.* New York: Howell Book House, 1995.

Duet, Karen Freeman, and George Duet. *The Home and Family Protection Dog: Selection and Training.* New York: Howell Book House, 1993.

Glazebrook, Jerry, and Larry Nicholson. *Executive Protection Specialist Handbook*. Shawnee Mission, Kansas: Varro Press, 1994.

Hacker, Frederick J. *Crusaders, Criminals, Crazies: Terror and Terrorism in Our Time*. New York: W. W. Norton, 1977.

Jenkins, Brian, ed. *Terrorism and Personal Protection*. Stoneham, Massachusetts: Butterworth-Heinemann, 1984.

Kobetz, Dr. Richard W., ed. *Providing Executive Protection*. Berryville, Virginia: Executive Protection Institute, 1991.

Kobetz, Dr. Richard W., ed. *Providing Executive Protection, Volume II*. Berryville, Virginia: Executive Protection Institute, 1994.

Mantell, Michael, and Steve Albrecht. *Ticking Bombs: Defusing Violence in the Workplace*. New York: Irwin Professional Publishing, Inc., 1994.

Molloy, John T. *John T. Molloy's New Dress for Success*. New York: Warner Books, 1995.

Nudell, Mayer, and Norman Antokol. *The Handbook for Effective Emergency and Crisis Management*. Lexington, Massachusetts: Lexington Books, 1988.

Oatman, Robert L. *Executive Protection Resource Manual*. Towson, Maryland: R. L. Oatman & Associates, Inc., 1995.

Savage, Peter. *The Safe Travel Book*. New York: Lexington Books, 1993.

Scotti, Anthony J. *Driving Techniques for the Professional and Non-Professional*. Ridgefield, New Jersey: PhotoGraphics Publishing, 1995.

Scotti, Anthony J. *Executive Safety and International Terrorism: A Guide for Travellers*. Englewood Cliffs, New Jersey: Prentice-Hall, 1986.

Security Management, monthly magazine of the American Society for Industrial Security, 1655 N. Fort Myer Drive, Suite 1200, Arlington, VA 22209.

Shackley, Theodore G., Robert L. Oatman, and Richard A. Finney. *You're the Target: Coping with Terror and Crime*. New World Publishing, 1989.

Sulk, Lawrence B. *Law Enforcement Counter Intelligence*. Shawnee Mission, Kansas: Varro Press, 1996.

Traveler's Handbook. Baltimore: Johns Hopkins University International Travel Clinic, 1989.

Tzu, Sun. *The Art of War*, ed. James Clavell. New York: Delacorte Press, 1983.

U.S. Department of State. *Key Officers of Foreign Service Posts.* Washington: U.S. Government Printing Office, October 1996.

U.S. Public Health Service. *Health Information for International Travel.* Washington: U.S Government Printing Office.

Index